D0597184

Winning Score

How to Design and Implement Organizational Scorecards

Mark Graham Brown

PORTLAND, OREGON

Productivity, Inc.
P.O. Box 13390
Portland, Oregon 97213-0390
United States of America
Telephone: 503-235-0600
Telefax: 503-235-0909
Email: info@productivityinc.com

Production Editor: Michael Ryder, Productivity Press
Design and Composition: William H. Brunson Typography Services
Cover Design: Stephen Scates, Productivity Press
Proofreader: Susan Swanson, inpages
Indexer: Robert Saigh, Razorsharp Productions

Printed in the United States of America

Library of Congress Cataloging-in-Publication Data

Brown, Mark Graham.
　　Winning score : how to design and implement winning scorecards / Mark Graham Brown.
　　　　p.　cm.
　　Includes bibliographical references and index.
　　ISBN 1-56327-223-7
　　1. Organizational effectiveness—Evaluation.　I. Title.
HD58.9 .B763　2000
658.4—dc21
00-34159

05　04　03　02　01　　　　　　6　5　4　3　2

Contents

Introduction

It's been almost 10 years since Robert Kaplan and David Norton introduced the concept of the balanced scorecard in their pioneering article in the *Harvard Business Review* (January/February 1992). Since that time, there have been many books, articles, workshops, and conferences on the balanced scorecard approach to measurement. This wide interest in measurement of performance is not limited to industry, but also has spread to government, health care, and education. The Quality Alert Institute, operating out of New York, hosts at least 10 conferences a year on implementing the balanced scorecard in government organizations. David Norton's consulting business, Renaissance, has become a huge international firm with several divisions. Many business executives state that they currently have balanced scorecards in their organizations. In addition, they have strategic plans that are well integrated with their scorecards.

Yet, I've been to many balanced scorecard conferences, and consulted with many different organizations in government and industry, and I have not seen many scorecards that I would advise you to benchmark.

WHAT HAVE WE LEARNED SINCE 1992?

When my earlier book *Keeping Score* was first published, in 1996, many organizations were just beginning the balanced scorecard approach to measurement and thus had to add nonfinancial metrics, reduce their overall number of measures, and link some of their measures to their plans. Most of this has now been done. If you look at the current measures in place in many organizations, you will find that:

- Executives focus on 15 to 20 metrics versus 50 or more.
- Measures focus on customers, employees, and financial results.
- Less emphasis is placed on financial measures.
- Some leading or predictive indicators appear on the scorecard.
- Scorecards have been developed for operator levels in the organization.
- More graphics and easy-to-read formats are used to communicate performance data.
- Some organizations communicate data using intranet sites or balanced scorecard software that includes colorful graphs.

In short, I think there has been much improvement since Kaplan and Norton published their first article in 1992. The concepts behind the balanced scorecard are fairly simple to understand, but very difficult to implement. It's true that many organizations have made solid progress, but most still feel like they are only just beginning to understand performance measurement.

How World Class Companies Measure Performance

At a meeting hosted by the Conference Board a couple of years ago, a group of outstanding companies got together to share ideas on performance measurement and present their scorecards to their peers. The companies represented in this meeting were some of the most respected names in the world: Ford, GE Capital, Boeing, Ritz Carlton, IBM, Miliken, Xerox, First Chicago Bank, and Motorola. Many of these companies had won Baldrige Awards, and all of them were regarded as outstanding organizations. I was hoping to get some ideas for this book, but it didn't work out that way. Just about every presenter began his or her presentation with a near apology that went something like this:

> We have recently begun implementing the balanced score-card approach to measurement in our company and do not feel like we have this down yet. We have begun tracking some good nonfinancial metrics, but are a long way from having a scorecard that includes all the right metrics that drive the right behavior from our people.

Keep in mind that these are some of the best companies in the world, and most of them were still struggling to design and implement good scorecards. I saw many creative metrics in the presentations that day, but did not see any overall approach that would meet all of my criteria for an effective, balanced scorecard. The meeting was worthwhile because each company had something unique that they were doing that would be of interest to others.

Ford had some interesting approaches for measuring and predicting customer loyalty. IBM showed some compelling data linking customer satisfaction to profits. Boeing had an interesting way of reporting performance data using color-coded charts. Yet, in spite of such great ideas, everyone admitted that their scorecards still needed much work.

Why Is Measurement So Difficult?

An important lesson from this book is that, though learning the principles behind the balanced scorecard approach to measurement is simple, applying them is exceedingly difficult. Most clients I encounter in both government and industry have experienced the same challenges as the companies that attended the Conference Board meeting.

Measurement is so difficult in organizations because it is not an exact science with hard rules and predictable interrelationships between variables. People run organizations, and their actions are inherently unpredictable. Hence, a measure that made perfect sense at one time might now seem laughable when one sees the behavior it drove in the organization. Measurement is also difficult because important factors are often hard to measure objectively and consistently. Ten different people can go to the same meeting, view the same film, or review the same piece of software, and come up with very different opinions on the quality of what they've seen. The trick is to apply measurements in a reliable, consistent fashion.

In addition, because so many variables impact an organization's performance and so many interactions exist between these different variables, accurate measurement is difficult to attain. When you focus on improving a specific metric, two other metrics might decline. In the 1980s, most executives focused on increased productivity because U.S. industry had arguably become lazy and too content, and productivity of labor and capital had declined. The focus on productivity generated many measures, and productivity did improve. Other areas, however, worsened. Quality became the mantra of the 1990s. The focus shifted to sophisticated methods of measuring product and service quality. Again, quality went up by huge margins. Currently, U.S. cars are as good or better than European or Asian cars, California wines are being exported to Europe in record quantities, U.S. hotels boast service as good as most European establishments, and even U.S. airlines are improving. Quality and customer satisfaction are not differentiating factors in most industries today because the expectations and standards are much higher than they were even five years ago. The price of quality, however, often was lower financial results. Some companies with the best quality in their industries went out of business.

As we enter the 21st century, the new mantra for organizational performance seems to be *balance*. What we have learned in the last 20 years is that it is foolish to focus on any singular aspect of performance: making money, increasing productivity, and improving customer satisfaction are all important and necessary. Trading off quality for financial results, or trading employee satisfaction for productivity, are not answers. Today's business leader is like the circus entertainer who must keep all the plates spinning at the same time: some of the plates need to spin faster than others, and some become more important than others, but they all need attention.

Measuring What Matters

One of the most common objections I hear during the performance measurement workshops I teach is that collecting and analyzing data is so time consuming, and that this time could be better spent doing "real" work. A question I often hear is: "Why would we need a scorecard when we seem to be doing a great job as an organization already without one?" These are both valid points that should be addressed. The approach outlined in this book (and in *Keeping Score*) posits that organizations must measure *only those areas* that will help them better manage and make more accurate decisions. Much of an organization's business can be done consistently well without collecting and analyzing performance data. Hiring a group of astute employees who fully understand their jobs will ensure effective performance most of the time. The real value in performance data is that it allows you to get slightly better at key aspects of performance than your competition. For example, the right metrics might help an organization build stronger relationships with key customers. In addition, performance data give you feedback on whether your strategies and action plans are working.

If you find that the chart of performance data you have been examining every month for the past year is merely confirming what you already knew, you should consider dropping that metric from your scorecard. Performance measures should provide you with information that you would not have discovered without the hard data. For example, some people live their entire lives without ever getting a physical. However, to maximize your life span, gathering data on vital statistics such as your cholesterol level and other blood chemistry factors is crucial. These data indicate where you are at risk, and a doctor can provide advice on lifestyle changes and perhaps prescribe drugs that can be used to improve key measures of your health. Having accurate and timely data on your physical health can greatly enhance the detection of possible ailments at a time when they are treatable. Wait until outward symptoms such as pain appear, and you may be too late. Organizations, too, need metrics that provide warning signals before severely damaging problems arise.

Tip: *Many things in life are done well without requiring formal data. Measure only those factors that will provide you with information you didn't know already and help you improve performance or make better decisions.*

The Top 10 Measurement Mistakes

When I started preparing my list of the top measurement mistakes, I had a hard time limiting it to 10 items. What follows is a discussion of the most common measurement mistakes I've seen, as well as those that are the most damaging to your overall approach to scorecard development and implementation. The list is in no particular order, and some of the measurement mistakes may not apply to every type of organization. I'm sure you will find a few, however, that are practiced by your employer.

Mistake #1: *Tracking Output/Outcome Metrics That Cannot Be Influenced or Controlled*

A good scorecard for any organization should include metrics that focus on meaningful outputs for customers, taxpayers, or other stakeholders. It is important for an organization to measure how it is producing valuable accomplishments or products. However, these good intentions can go awry if the scorecard also includes outcome measures that are important but difficult to influence.

An example might be the overall air quality of Los Angeles as one of the key metrics for the Environmental Protection Agency (EPA) after a specific action has been taken. The problem with this metric is that air quality in every city is affected by factors that the EPA cannot influence, such as population growth, number of cars on the road, geographical factors, and other factors that the EPA *can* affect, such as car and factory emissions. It would be frustrating and inaccurate for the EPA to study a metric that measures overall air quality—a specific measure is necessary, such as the level of certain pollutants from car or factory emissions that exists in the air.

The Coast Guard is responsible for Marine safety and inspects boats to ensure that they have the appropriate safety equipment. The Coast Guard sometimes uses a measure of overall boating accidents when examining the effectiveness of these inspections. The problem with this approach in regard to safety inspections is that it is inaccurate: boating accidents overall can be attributed to other factors, such as alcohol consumption, excessive speeding, and recklessness by boaters. Because the Coast Guard's safety inspections do not have much influence over any of these three factors, overall measurement of boating accidents is not the most reliable metric.

Mistake #2: *Gathering Data That Tells You What You Already Know*

Collecting formal data on established facts is actually quite common. For example, a government executive I know of sends surveys twice a year to his customers (that is, his superiors) at a headquarters in Washington asking for feedback on his performance and effectiveness. Yet he actually spends three to four days a month in Washington, and often is on the phone with his superiors several times a day. The point is that Dan gets plenty of detailed feedback from his Washington customers without the survey, which most of his customers don't bother filling out anyway. When Dan does get surveys back, he has the data summarized and consistently finds that it has already been expressed to him through more effective methods.

Collecting data to verify the obvious, however, is not the same as collecting data to verify an assumption. For example, a manager might suspect that severe morale problems exist in his or her organization. No hard data exists to support this, but the manager *can* identify some symptoms of a possible problem. Conducting a formal survey or using another method to collect data would be useful in this case to determine if, in fact, a problem really does exist, and how bad or widespread it is.

Mistake #3: *Gathering Data for Its Own Sake*

This is by far the most common mistake of the 10. The rule in many organizations is to select a measure that can be objectively tallied, no matter how meaningless it might be. For example, training directors use the attendance in their classrooms as a measure of training success: software developers get measured on how many lines of code they write per day, regardless of how inefficient or creative that code is; engineers get measured on how many change orders they complete; and financial professionals measure the amount of reports they issue on time.

Most meaningful measures of performance in today's organizations involve more than just quantification. Counting attendance rate in a class reveals nothing about the main objective of training—knowledge/skill gain and improved job performance—and such situations will most likely encourage incorrect behavior in an organization.

Mistake #4: *Relying Heavily on Customer Satisfaction Surveys*

All type of organizations—car companies, restaurants, airlines, the health care industry, the IRS, and even the Department of Motor Vehicles—perform customer satisfaction surveys. However, several major problems plague these surveys. First, most people don't have the time or inclination to fill them out and return them. From personal experience, I've concluded that two types of people fill out surveys—really angry people and really bored people. Hence the sample of customers who send back surveys is anything but representative of the entire population of customers. The second problem with customer surveys is that the data often reveal little useful information. Many organizations spend a lot of money to find out that they are a 3.8 on a 5-point scale. What does that mean? What should they be? What if an organization gets a low score on surveys? Usually there is little or no data to find out why the low score was given or how to improve it. Most survey respondents do not bother writing comments to supplement their scores.

Surveys can provide some good basic information if they are administered properly. Airlines get a good return rate on surveys because they hand them out at the start of a long flight, so it gives people something to do, and customers' experiences are fresh in their minds. A major hotel chain sends a survey out about five weeks after a guest stays in the hotel. I can't remember which hotel I slept in last night . . . let alone five weeks ago! Most surveys provide an expensive and seemingly scientific report of meaningless data that are hard to interpret and difficult to act upon with any certainty.

Mistake #5: *Executives Focusing on Detailed Metrics*

Many executives regularly analyze detailed metrics that should be reviewed and controlled by lower-level staff. Because these executives spend so much time with their heads under the hoods, they rarely look out the windshield, and often fail to steer their organizations in the right direction.

Executives need summaries of performance on factors such as financial performance, employee morale, and customer satisfaction. It is appropriate to delve into greater detail when performance is below standards or targets, or if an improving trend has reversed or flattened out. The mistake many executives make is regularly reviewing too many detailed reports and charts of performance measures.

The best cure for this dilemma is to use one of the scorecard software packages I review in Chapter 12. These online dashboards allow executives to scan their organization's overall performance, zero in on potential problem areas, and delve deeper into key metrics when necessary. If all the gauges show green and no "idiot lights" are flashing, the executive can spend time looking out the windshield.

Mistake #6: *Measures Are Not Linked to the Strategic Plan*

Part of the problem with traditional performance measures is that they focus on the past. Measures of past performance are not of much help to managers making decisions about future direction. While it is important to learn from our mistakes, historical data are not enough by themselves to help achieve future success. A good balanced scorecard contains several strategic or future-focused metrics that tell the organization how it is doing on its path toward its vision. For example, a strategic measure for one firm looked at the company's image with customers and in its industry. The company was trying to change its image, and this metric allowed them to gauge the success of their advertising, marketing, and operational functions in changing public perception. In Part 2 of this book, I will go into detail on how to develop a strong vision and define strategic metrics that tell an organization how it is doing in achieving that vision.

Mistake #7: *Failing to Define Practical Correlations between Key Metrics*

Including leading indicators on your scorecard is only helpful if you can predict how they will impact the lagging indicators. The companies and organizations I've encountered rarely define correlations between leading and lagging measures and between soft and hard measures. They spend time, money, and other resources to get leading measures like customer or employee satisfaction to improve, without knowing what these improvements will do to lagging indicators like productivity, sales, or profits.

Statistical correlations might exist and be so slight as to not warrant investing effort in improving a leading index. For example, a 4 percent improvement in employee morale might lead to a 1 percent reduction in absenteeism and a .5 percent improvement in productivity. The resources required to produce a 4 percent improvement in employee morale might be significant, and the resulting improvements in absenteeism and productivity, might not come close to recovering the investment.

In Chapter 13 we will examine how to find links between measures on your scorecard and how to use this information to set better goals/targets and make more scientific decisions about running your organization.

Mistake #8: *Reporting Data That Is Difficult to Read and Analyze*

Most performance reports in organizations get documented in a spreadsheet format that includes 15 to 20 columns of figures in 8-point type. I sit next to executives and managers on airplanes every week who pull binders of these spreadsheets out of their briefcases and squint at them trying to find a number or two that might be important. Apparently, most of the numbers are not important, because I watch as these executives quickly scan the pages, highlight one or two on each page, then flip to other sections of the binder, looking for more detailed data to help detect a trend or diagnose a problem. This approach to communicating performance data makes it highly unlikely that all important data will be recognized—the spreadsheet binder is a complicated and time-consuming way for any manager to review performance.

Other organizations supplement their spreadsheet performance reports with graphs that depict trends over time or show levels of performance compared to targets. While these graphs are usually better than the spreadsheets, most are extremely hard to read and often contain six to eight lines of data on a single chart, so it is next to impossible to identify a single trend line in the overlapping lines of data.

There is a better way. A handful of forward-thinking software companies have developed packages that report performance data in colorful, easy-to-read graphics that can be communicated via a companywide intranet. These packages pull data from existing databases (finance, sales, etc.) and display it in a consistent graphic format so that a manager can glance at the scorecard and detect possible problem areas. In Chapter 12, I'll review some major balanced scorecard software packages on the market that enable you to communicate data better.

Mistake #9: *"Superstitious" Process Metrics*

Most large organizations are always in the midst of implementing a series of programs or initiatives designed to improve performance. During the early 1980s, many organizations had productivity improvement programs. In the late 1980s and early 1990s, it was rare to find an organization that was not implementing a Total Quality Management (TQM) initiative. Today we find initiatives such as Lean Manufacturing, Activity-Based Costing, Strategic Planning, and even Balanced Scorecard. To measure progress in implementing these programs, most organizations develop a series of process measures, such as:

- Percent of employees participating on teams
- Number of key processes flowcharted
- Number of processes improved
- Percent of workforce trained in lean manufacturing techniques
- Percent of processes/functions for which ABC analyses has been completed

Once you start measuring these activities or process metrics, you can bet that scores will improve. I call these "superstitious" process measures because management has faith that they will make their organizations healthier. The problem is, there is often little or no data to suggest this.

For example, a Federal Government organization measures the percentage of its contractors that have implemented a new, complicated, and expensive safety program. Contractors are complying and implementing the program, but most have seen no improvement in key measures of safety outcomes like reductions in accidents. Another organization that measured percent of employees on teams got to 100 percent over a four-year period, and came close to going bankrupt because important work was not getting done while employees were in team meetings writing mission statements.

Don't get me wrong; process measures are important and necessary. However, they must be correlated with outcome measures or you will create an organization of busy people who are adding little value to the organization.

Mistake #10: *Measures That Drive the Wrong Performance*

No one intentionally comes up with damaging measures. They only become damaging when we later see the behavior that was driven by them. If you have read my previous book on metrics, *Keeping Score*, you may recall the story of the chain of fast-food restaurants that measured managers on how much chicken they had to throw into the garbage at the end of a shift—that is, the amount of chicken that was cooked and prepared but not sold and thus ended up as "waste." Restaurant managers learned to get a good score on this measure by not cooking any chicken until someone ordered it. Most customers, however, because they had to wait up to 15 minutes for their order, left and went elsewhere. The company had no data on the number of customers who left angry; thus, managers continued cooking only to order so their "chicken efficiency" numbers looked good.

A manufacturing company measured one of its business units on sales revenue and inventory turns. Toward the end of the year, they had a surplus of inventory and it was looking like they were not going to make their sales goal, either. A general manager decided to mark down the inventory about 25 percent and managed to clear it all out before the year-end. This decision allowed the manager to exceed his goal for both sales and inventory turns. The problem was, the business made no profit that year because of the deep discounts offered to move the inventory.

Both of these companies are managed by smart people who didn't realize the behavior that their performance measures would drive. Finding these "chicken efficiencies" on your scorecard takes hard work and often requires some trial and error before problems are uncovered.

TWO TYPES OF METRICS

While it is important to have a balanced scorecard and a mix of measures that focus on customers, shareholders, employees, and other stakeholders, I have found that it is important to separate *mission-related measures* from *vision-related metrics.* Most of the measures on your scorecard will tell you how the organization is doing at achieving its mission. Mission-related metrics might focus on sales, profits, satisfying customers, safety, and producing high-quality products and services. These measures are important to keep the company in business, and they tend not to change much over the years. Mission-related metrics focus on the basics and are often similar to the measures of other organizations in the same field. For example, all car dealerships measure service comebacks (customers who come back because their car was not repaired right the first time); all hotels measure revenue per available room; and so on.

Vision-related measures are not generic, and they tend to vary by company or organization. Three to five of the metrics on your overall scorecard should focus on the key success factors needed to achieve your vision. I call these "strategic" measures because they link directly to the organization's strategy for achieving the vision. Strategic or vision-related metrics do tend to change quite a bit over the years.

For example, a company that was looking to expand internationally developed an international growth index that tracked their progress at selling outside of the United States. They watched this measure for several years, until they became a major player in the international market. This strategic metric was then dropped as a separate gauge on their corporate scorecard. Strategic measures focus on problems that need solving, opportunities that need exploiting, or the success of new ventures.

HOW THIS BOOK IS ORGANIZED

Parts 1 and 2 of this book both focus on different aspects of how to link performance measures to your mission (Part 1) and to your vision and strategic plan (Part 2). The majority of organizations I've worked with have struggled with linking their scorecard to operational and strategic plans. My hope is that this book will clarify the difference between mission or business fundamental metrics and strategic metrics that link to an organization's future vision. Part 2 includes some chapters on defining vision and key success factors.

Even though this is not a book about planning, I find that many organizations lack a clear vision and confuse key success factors with business fundamentals, so the topics warrant discussion here.

Part 3 shows you how to actually implement the scorecard to improve performance. I've seen a number of scorecard projects fail because of poor implementation rather than poorly designed metrics. A large part of the success of a scorecard initiative is using the right techniques for communicating performance data. A number of good software packages now on the market not only help you communicate data in easy-to-read charts, but also allow you to perform an infinite variety of analyses of the data to aid in planning and decision making. Some of the better software programs for scorecards are reviewed in Chapter 12.

Simply having good data on the right factors is not enough to improve performance. The key to success is making the metrics matter. What this means is linking performance data to other organizational systems such as performance appraisal, recognition, and compensation. How to link metrics to appropriate consequences will be discussed in Chapter 13. The final chapter of the book presents a step by-step plan for designing and implementing a balanced scorecard project in your own organization.

Throughout the book you will find a series of highlighted tips. These are good guidelines or rules to follow when designing and implementing your own performance metrics.

The appendices to the book include case studies of real scorecards from real organizations, which have been slightly disguised. Reviewing these case studies and their corresponding answer keys can go a long way toward increasing your understanding of the concepts in this book. I think you will find that it is fairly easy to critique another organization's scorecard—what you may find more challenging is coming up with recommendations for improving it. Trying your hand at these case studies, individually or as part of a team, will help you avoid some of the same mistakes made by others, and possibly give you some ideas you could apply successfully in your company.

PART 1

DEVELOPING OPERATIONAL METRICS AND PLANS

Mission: Figuring Out Who You Are

A crucial point to understand about performance metrics is that most of them have little to do with an organization's strategic plan. An effective scorecard or set of metrics includes a few strategic measures that link back to the plan, but most of them tell the executives and managers how the organization is performing on a daily or monthly basis. Not having a clearly defined mission can lead to the formation of a flawed set of performance measures. In this chapter, I'll review the process for defining your organization's mission. Even if you think you've already accomplished this, I suggest reading this chapter anyway. Many organizations have mission statements that require improvement.

What is a Mission Statement?

A mission statement defines an organization's purpose. It is not the same as a vision statement, which focuses on the future and defines what the company wants to become. A mission statement focuses on the present day and describes the organization's products, services, customers, and key work processes. Scott Adams, creator of the cartoon strip Dilbert, has a better definition of a mission statement:

> "A mission statement is a long awkward sentence that demonstrates management's inability to think clearly."

A mission statement should make it clear what the organization does not do, as well as what it does. A good mission statement should answer the following questions:

- What are our products and/or services?
- What are our key processes (e.g., manufacturing, designing, installing, transporting)?
- Who are our customers and stakeholders?
- What makes us unique and distinguishes us from competitors?

The test of a good mission statement is that it should not fit any organization other than your own. If it would fit most companies in your industry, or even one other competitor, then it is not a good mission statement.

Who Needs a Mission Statement?

It may seem odd that a company with a long history of success would bother to try and create a mission statement. If one were designing a new company, a mission statement might be necessary to define the scope of the organization and differentiate it from existing businesses. However, organizations and businesses that have been around for awhile create most of today's mission statements. For example, I recently worked with a large group in the Army, the Industrial Operations Command (IOC), which manufactures weapons and ensures that Army personnel have the right equipment to do their jobs. This particular group has existed for a long time—why would they need a mission statement when, apparently, they know what they're doing after all these years?

A mission statement was important for this group because their mission changed. In the past, the IOC managed a number of manufacturing plants and distribution centers operated by Army personnel. In the mid-1990s, it began contracting out more of its work to outside companies. In their terminology, they were transitioning from facilities that were government operated to those that were contractor operated. The IOC has had its financial and human resources cut, and has outsourced much of the work that used to be done by Army personnel. So, even though the IOC has been operating for many years, a mission statement was important for them in defining their new role as managers rather than suppliers.

Organizations need not bother with a mission statement if they do not expect to change their products/services, customers/markets, size, or scope. This may be true of a number of small to medium-sized companies. For example, your favorite neighborhood bar or restaurant might not need a mission statement if they have no intentions of changing the business. Even a large company, such as a taxi service with 200 cabs or a wholesale produce distributor, may not need a mission statement. Mission statements are important for companies that tend to forget the business they are in and what they're good at. Publicly owned companies are always looking to grow, which means that they must sometimes expand outside of their existing business. These diversions often wreak havoc with the company's core business.

J. Peterman's Rise and Fall

The J. Peterman Company started with a $500 investment, a $20,000 loan, and a single product: a cowboy duster coat that was advertised in *The New Yorker*. In just over 10 years, J. Peterman became $50-million-plus enterprise, with its own stores and catalogs that had become collectors' items. The J. Peterman Catalog stood out from other mail-order catalogs because of its eloquently written descriptions of the merchandise,and watercolor paintings of the clothing and accessories. The company became even more well known when Elaine Benis, a character on the *Seinfeld* television program, started working for J. Peterman as a copywriter for the catalog. (Actor John O'Hurley, who did a fabulous job playing Peterman, has gone on to host his own travel/adventure show and can be seen in a variety of commercials.) The J. Peterman Company made a few moves to capitalize on their increased notoriety resulting from the Seinfeld show, such as offering the "Elaine Benis Suit" in one of their catalogs.

The company also decided to expand beyond strictly mail order, and opened a number of stores during the last few years. Their store near Grand Central Station in Manhattan was beautifully designed, and did over $800 per square foot in sales.

In January 1999, the J. Peterman Company filed for Chapter 11, and has since been purchased by Paul Harris Stores. Peterman blames much of the failure on the lack of a clear mission that kept everyone focused on the factors that made the company successful in the first place. Although they did not have a formal mission statement, Peterman thought that he had communicated the mission through an overall business philosophy upon which the company was founded:

> We did always have one thing in writing, a general philosophy in our catalog. It was: "People want to live life the way they wish they were." The problem was that such a philosophy, so broadly stated, didn't give our employees nearly enough guidance. We should have developed a precise mission statement or something along those lines. It's easy for me to do that now. In fact, I can sum up the concept of the business in six words: "unique, authentic, romantic, journey, wondrous, and quality." The items we sold—the ones that were most successful—were all of those things.[1]

Peterman goes on to explain how losing focus on those six words caused the company to stray far from what it was known for. Their catalog became crowded with commonplace items such as T-shirts and khaki shorts, which could be found at 20 other places and often for less money. If the company had used Peterman's six words to select merchandise; things might not have ended the way they did.

John Peterman has gone on to new ventures, but his company will live on in our memories for many years as long as *Seinfeld* reruns continue to air.

Sears—A Broad Mission Can Lead You Astray

In 1992, Sears lost $40 billion on $540 billion in sales—the worst year in their history. In their desire for annual growth, they lost their roots, and some major surgery was needed to restore the company to health. In the 70s and 80s, Sears began to expand into many new

---

[1] Peterman, John. "The Rise and Fall of the J. Peterman Company," *Harvard Business Review*, September–October 1999, p. 62.

businesses: Allstate Insurance, Budget Rental Cars, Dean Witter Financial Services, and Caldwell Banker Real Estate, among others. While many of these companies were quite successful, Sears stores continued to decline in service, revenue, and merchandise quality. The Sears name was still well known and respected, but the company was losing retail business to Target, Wal-Mart, and Penney's. Analysts were saying that trying to do too many different things had distracted Sears and was hurting their retail business.

A new CEO was appointed in 1992 to turn the company around. One of his first actions was to sell all Sears' business units that were not part of their core competency: retailing. So, off went Caldwell Banker, Discover Card, Allstate, and the rest. CEO Martinez even closed Sears' legendary catalog business due to many years of poor performance. The company established a new vision and mission and communicated them to all employees. The new mission focused on Sears stores and related services, such as appliance and home repair. The mission differentiated them from other retailers because of their size, target markets, variety of services, and merchandise selection. The mission also fostered change by establishing Sears as a place where women would like to shop—Sears had always been thought of as a man's store, featuring Craftsman tools, DieHard batteries, Kenmore appliances, and other hardware products. Sears created a new advertising campaign emphasizing the "softer side of Sears." They focused on women's clothing, cosmetics, and other products to draw in consumers who had never thought of coming to Sears to buy such products. To avoid losing their core customers, their ad campaign also promoted the "many sides of Sears."

The vision is to make Sears a "Compelling place to shop, compelling place to work, and compelling place to invest." Although they have yet to achieve this vision, they have made some serious progress in restoring the company's position.

Sears is a perfect example of a company that may have made some bad decisions because they lacked a clear mission. If they had a mission that kept them focused on the retail business, they might not have become so diversified and paid more attention to Sears stores. A mission statement should help you evaluate potential acquisitions and other avenues of growth to make sure that these new endeavors really fit your mission and core competencies. Companies with a long history of success tend to become arrogant, thinking that they can excel in any business; they often stretch too far, and need a failure to teach them the importance of a clear mission that states what they are and, more importantly, what they are not. This is why the mission needs to be somewhat narrow and focused—but not excessively so!

Avoid Mission Statements That Are Too Narrow

We've seen how a mission statement that is too broad and vague can lead an organization into business endeavors that are destined to fail. In such cases, most organizations return to focusing on their primary business. This can often cause huge losses and damage image, stock performance, and employee morale. It is rarely a death sentence, however. Most companies learn from their failures and go on to new successes. If its core business has not been compromised, a company can usually go back to excelling at it. General Electric, for instance, had branched into many businesses before Jack Welch was appointed as CEO. He narrowed the company's focus, keeping ownership of the parts of the business that were number one and two in market share and selling off all the rest.

Having a mission that is too narrow can be even more danger-ous. A narrowly defined vision may keep you focused, but you may be focusing on products or services that no longer meet customer needs. Those of you who grew up in the 1960s probably remember Zenith as the best television on the market: "Quality goes in before the name goes on." Zenith had a mission to make the best TVs in the world, and for a while, they did. Yet it's hard to find a Zenith television set today. I drove past a Zenith facility in suburban Chicago last month that looked like it was still open, but all the television sets I've seen in the last 10 years seem to be made by Japanese or Korean companies. Zenith is still in business, but they are much smaller than they were, and their narrow mission of building the best television sets prevented them from branching out into other markets, tech-nologies, and products as their TV sales declined.

Motorola is one of Zenith's neighbors in suburban Chicago. Motorola also made television sets, and radios. However, they no longer do; they have branched into many new businesses and continue to develop new markets and products. Motorola's mission did not focus on building only "the best" televisions or radios. Their mission, of "applying technology to the benefit of the public," has allowed them to branch into new fields where they became market leaders over the years: cellular phones, pagers, police radios, and a number of products sold to industry.

Of course, there is still a large market for televisions and radios; however, other companies now make them better and cheaper than most U.S. companies. Motorola recognized early on that the market for these products was going to belong to foreign companies, so Motorola exited these markets and focused on others. One of Motorola's key competencies was research and development focusing on new technologies—television and radio were mature technologies when Motorola exited these markets. It is important that mission statements do not focus on *specific* products or services; doing so can blind you to new opportunities and changes in technology that may be required for future success.

Dilbert's Approach to Developing a Mission Statement

Scott Adams, creator of the popular Dilbert cartoon strip, must have the greatest job satisfaction. After eight years in middle management jobs at Pacific Bell, Scott is now independently successful satirizing corporate life in general. After being gone from the corporate world for many years, Scott decided it would be fun to go back to the business world as a consultant. He wanted to see if he could disguise himself, and go into a company to help them create a mission statement that was pure nonsense, and have the executives in the company buy into it. Scott explained:

> My goal is to see if a group of executives will allow somebody who has very few credentials, except for good hair, to come into their meeting and get them to write a mission statement which is so impossibly complicated that it has no real content.[2]

---

[2]"Mission Impertinent," *San Jose Mercury News West Magazine*, 11/16/97.

Scott selected a company where he had a connection: Logitech, a 3,000-employee Silicon Valley manufacturer of computer mice and related devices. Adams' friend, Logitech co-founder Pierluigi Zappacosta, agreed to the ruse, and thought it would teach his executives a powerful lesson. He had recently formed a New Ventures Group that needed to develop a clear mission and vision.

After donning a wig of thick brown hair and a false mustache, Adams was introduced to the Logitech executives as Ray Me'bert, strategic planning consultant. After explaining that he had managed a number of colossal business failures, and had an MBA from Harvard, Adams began leading the group in developing their mission statement. His approach is typical of how companies approach this task:

1. Brainstorm a series of words and phrases that describe the organization.
2. Prioritize the words and narrow them down to the most important ones.
3. Combine the list into a sentence or brief paragraph that describes the company mission.
4. Edit the words until they sound right, or until everyone gets too tired to argue for their favorite word or phrase.

This is pretty much the exact same process I have seen followed many times in large corporations and government organizations.

Logitech began the meeting by putting up their existing mission statement: The New Ventures mission is to provide Logitech with profitable growth and related new business areas.

Consultant Me'bert suggests that this is much too vague, and they need to start over. He explains the importance of the "Mission Triad," a nonsense conceptual model typical of consultant double-talk (see Figure 1-1).

The mission statement that the Logitech finally agrees to is as follows:

The New Ventures mission is to scout profitable growth opportunities in relationships, both internally and externally, in emerging, mission-inclusive markets, and explore new paradigms and then filter and communicate and evangelize the findings.

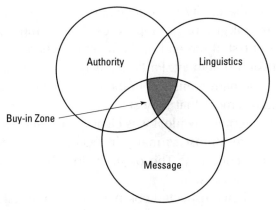

Figure 1-1.

This is exactly the type of jargon-filled mission statement that is quite often the result of a consultant-led meeting. The Logitech groups begins to smell a rat when consultant Me'bert suggests that they write a song to communicate the mission to employees. He removes his wig and mustache as he draws the Dilbert character on the flip chart. After a few seconds of deadly silence, the team begins laughing, realizing that they have been had. They reluctantly admit that none of them suspected the farce.

ENSURE THAT YOUR MISSION IS EFFECTIVE

At this point, you might be questioning whether or not you even need a mission statement. As I mentioned earlier, a mission statement is important for guidance in decision making. Paul Kalkbrenner, a client from Shea Homes in Phoenix, explains that: "A mission statement is like a compass—it helps you find your direction and points you the right way when you get lost in the forest of today's business world." To ensure that your mission statement is a good one, it should be:

- Broad enough to still apply many years from today
- Specific enough to communicate direction
- Focused on your key competencies or capabilities
- Free of jargon and buzz words.

In evaluating the clarity of your mission statement, it is a good idea to quiz several groups of employees. One company I worked with gave a brief test at the end of the meeting where they communicated the mission statement. Participants had to write a paragraph explaining the company's mission in their own words. This exercise revealed to management that they still had some major work to do on the mission statement: while it was clear to the executives, among the staff there were almost as many interpretations as there were employees in the company. The organization returned to the flip chart to rewrite their mission.

Even among highly respected companies, mission statements are not all perfect (see list on facing page). The Mary Kay Cosmetics statement is the most unusual because it focuses on providing opportunities only to women. Wal-Mart's mission is noble, but they don't carry the same merchandise as higher-end retailers such as Neiman Marcus. Nike's is probably the most honest. I think the statements from Disney, 3M, and Marriott are clear, inspirational, and pertain to the overall purpose of their respective organizations.

Lutheran Brotherhood, A Company with a Clear Mission

If you are not Lutheran, you probably never heard of this successful organization that started out as a life insurance company for Lutherans. LB currently has 1.1 million customers, or "members," manages $26 billion in assets, and distributes about $70 million a year in charitable outreach to Lutheran organizations such as schools, churches, and charities. As a not-for-profit organization, LB gives back all of its profits to Lutheran causes.

Lutheran Brotherhood recently went through a planning exercise to define their mission and vision for the future. They had been through a number of similar exercises in the past, but the company was changing direction, so the strategic plan was extremely important during the late 1990s. They were attempting to expand beyond just being an insurance company to being a full-service financial firm, offering Lutherans auto insurance, liability insurance, annuities, mutual funds, credit cards, and a whole array of financial products. In essence, they were looking to grow the company both by adding new members and by diversifying their offerings to existing members.

A DOZEN COMPANY MISSION STATEMENTS

Boeing: To push the leading edge of aviation, taking on huge challenges innovatively and doing what others cannot do

3M: To solve unsolved problems

Walt Disney: To make people happy

Hewlett-Packard: To make technical contributions

Wal-Mart: To give ordinary folk the chance to buy the same things as rich people

Sony: To experience the sheer joy of advancing technology and applying it for the public's benefit

Merck: To preserve and improve human life

Mary Kay: To give unlimited opportunity to women

Teaching Co.: To ignite in all people the passion for learning

Marriott: To make people away from home feel that they're among friends and really wanted

Patagonia: To use business to inspire and implement solutions to the environmental crisis

Nike: To experience the emotion of competition, winning, and crushing competitors

---

Their mission statement is short, to the point, and meets all of my criteria for being a good one:

> *Our mission is to work together to provide financial security to members and to serve Lutherans, their congregations, institutions, and communities.*

This is a great mission statement because it will probably still work 50 years from now. It is clear that the company focuses on what it is good at: providing financial services and charitable outreach; and the fact that they focus on Lutherans only differentiates them from hundreds of other financial services firms. It is also written in plain English, without buzzwords like "paradigm," "synergy," or "world class." Their statement might apply to only one other company in the world—Aid Association for Lutherans (AAL). AAL is a very similar, slightly larger company, with a mission much like that of LB. The two companies used to focus on different branches of the Lutheran Church, but today that is no longer true—both now have members from all branches of Lutheranism.

U.S. Army Industrial Operations Command

The Industrial Operations Command (IOC—previously mentioned), part of the U.S. Army Material Command, is headquartered in Rock Island, Illinois and has 37 facilities located throughout the United States. It has a budget of over $4 billion and employs 400 military personnel, 23,000 civilians, and 10,000 contractors. The IOC provides the Army with materials, equipment, weapons, ammunition, and many other supplies it needs to do its job during both war and peacetime. The IOC runs very much like a profit-making company, with customers that actually pay for the goods and services they receive. In fact, in 1996, 82 percent of the organization's revenue came from customers. Because their mission and scope were changing during the 1990s, the IOC developed a strategic plan in 1996, which included a very well-written mission statement:

> *Provide the maintenance, manufacturing, munitions, and war reserve support to execute our Army's global power projection strategies.*

This may sound confusing to the average reader, but it is very clear to Army and civilian IOC personnel. The mission statement meets all of criteria I've outlined: it is short, clear, defines products/services and customers, and could not be confused with any other group in the Army or the rest of the U.S. government.

A Better Approach to Developing a Mission Statement

Although teams are very effective when used correctly, they might work as a deterrent to writing a clear mission statement. I believe a mission statement is better written by one person. Some of the best

I've seen were initially drafted by the CEO or some other executive, sent out for comments/revisions, and finalized without committees or meetings. A first draft should be written by a single, strategic individual; then revisions should be incorporated based on feedback from others in the organization.

The following checklist will help you decide if your mission statement is on the right track.

CHECKLIST FOR EVALUATING MISSION STATEMENTS

A mission statement should...

☐ Clearly distinguish your organization from any competitors.

☐ Define what the organization does, and more importantly, what it does not do.

☐ Identify key abilities or competencies.

☐ Allow the organization to make better decisions about future opportunities.

☐ Define products and services without being too narrow.

☐ Be no more than a paragraph in length.

☐ Be clearly understood by all employees.

☐ Be written in plain English without buzzwords.

☐ Focus on the present, and not be combined with a future-focused vision statement.

☐ Be examined and rewritten as necessary when the company scope changes.

Values:
Defining What
You Stand For

Identifying values is a relatively new phenomenon in organizations. The idea of defining values for a company may have come from the Total Quality Management movement. Early versions of the Malcolm Baldrige Award criteria asked a company to define its "quality values" and explain how they are communicated to employees. This caused many organizations that follow the Baldrige criteria to create a series of values and post them in the lobby and on internal communications.

WHAT ARE VALUES?

Values are like a code of morals or ethics that define what a company stands for, believes in, and considers acceptable and unacceptable in its quest to achieve its vision. Values should generally not be business focused, but be focused on employees, the community, customers, or other stakeholders such as the people who live near company facilities. All companies and organizations have a set of values. New employees in any organization must often spend a couple of months learning the culture of the company by watching the behavior of others, and perhaps learning by a little trial and error. The value statements that appear on a plaque in the company lobby are rarely those the organization lives by, however. Often, behavior is inconsistent with the words on the wall, and this makes it tough for new employees to figure out what the real values are.

As a consultant to business and government, I work with a wide variety of organizations each year. Most do post values somewhere, and some have even do a good job of communicating their values; however, rarely do I find an organization that lives by even a couple of its stated values. The following is a list of some of the real values I've seen in today's organizations.

- You need to work at least 55 to 70 hours a week to pull your weight.
- Risk taking is only rewarded when you succeed.
- Failure is unacceptable, even if you do learn from it.
- Safety is only important because it costs us money when we have accidents.
- We hire bright people that know how to cheat regulators (IRS, EPA, etc.) in order to save the company money.
- Our competitors are generally stupid and are rarely better than us at anything.
- People that quit our firm are generally ones we don't mind losing.
- We don't believe in communicating much to employees about the company's future—they won't understand it and hearing bad news may hurt their productivity.
- Whenever we have to reduce our staff, we keep it quiet until the last minute.
- We never want to be dependent on a few suppliers/ contractors because they will have the upper hand and exploit us.

I imagine that at least some of these value statements ring true to you and apply to your employer. I would applaud an organization honest enough to display its true values on the wall. Employees would have much more respect for such an employer. Nike appears to be a company that is a little more honest than most about what they stand for. Even their mission statement smacks of honesty: "To experience the emotion of competition, winning, and crushing competitors." Crushing the competition and focusing on winning may sound a bit aggressive to some people, but that is partly what business is all about.

Typical Company Values

It's funny that most organizational values are defined by the same series of vague words. It's almost as if a list exists with 50 choices, and each of the Fortune 500, along with every major military and government organization, has picked 6 to 12 words from it to define their values. Those I see most often are shown in Figure 2-1.

Buzzwords like these are a cop-out—they indicate that the company has not put any thought into what it really stands for. Companies select their words from the list, put them on plaques, hand them out on wallet cards to each employee, and get back to their main business. Such "statements" are vague, making it very difficult for employees to tell if their behavior is consistent with the values. Furthermore, they insult employees' intelligence because they are often obviously far from the real values by which the organization operates.

TYPICAL VALUES BUZZWORDS		
• Quality	• Integrity	• Honesty
• Empowerment	• Trust	• Innovation
• Customer Delight	• Leadership	• Excellence
• Partnering	• Accountability	• Performance
• Competence	• Risk Taking	• Diversity
• Communication	• Teamwork	• Sharing
• Cooperation	• Family Life	• Safety
• Employee Development	• Perseverance	• People
• Results	• Productivity	• Passion
• Loyalty	• Devotion	• Stewardship
• Recognition	• Rewards	• Opportunity
• Support	• Respect	• Listening
• Growth	• Pioneer	

Figure 2-1. Frequently Used Values Buzzwords

VALUE STATEMENTS DEFINED

Value statements are not buzzwords or inspirational mottoes. They are carefully composed declarations of an organization's beliefs, ethics, and code of desirable behavior, intended to guide employee decision making and activity.

The value statement should describe the type of behaviors, attitudes, and thinking that the company wants to reward.

One of the better statements I've read comes from clothing manufacturer Patagonia: "We believe in a soft landing—if we promote you into a job and you fail to perform well, it is looked at as the company's fault, you are allowed to go back to your previous job, and the company works at developing your skills before you are given another chance for promotion." Now, there's a real statement of a value. Everyone understands what it means, and it's easy to make sure that the company lives by it. Many of the top managers in this company learned from their failures before they became successful. In some organizations, if you fail in a job assignment, your career is over, and you're better off looking for a new employer, because everyone will always see you as a failure. They probably won't fire you, but rarely do you get a second chance at the same sort of position.

Cargill—A Company That Lives by Its Values

Cargill, Inc. is an international marketer, processor, and distributor of agricultural, food, financial, and industrial products and services with some 82,000 employees in 59 countries. I have never seen an organization with a stronger corporate culture or set of values so well deployed. I didn't learn about Cargill's values by reading the list they print in their company communications; I learned about them by examining their business operations and getting to know their people.

I have been lucky enough to experience Cargill's quality commitment and culture while training their personnel on various locations in the United States, Asia, Europe, and South America. Their consistent set of values, work ethic, and genuine friendliness is amazing. They hire people from the countries in which they do business, with very different cultures and backgrounds. Yet, every employee has the same values regarding business ethics and interpersonal relationships.

One of Cargill's values is that they are extremely loyal to their employees, and their employees are extremely loyal to them. When someone begins a career at Cargill, he or she generally stays until retirement. The company is very careful about who they hire, but once an employee is on the payroll, the company remains loyal to that person. All companies have made hiring and job placement mistakes, and Cargill has not been immune to this; the difference is that Cargill feels like they have failed as a company if an employee fails in a job assignment. Loyalty is a rare commodity in today's world, particularly among big corporations. Cargill stands out as one of the few companies I've worked with that truly treats its employees like family members.

Another value of this company is that it will not adapt its ethics to the culture of the countries in which it does business. With most international companies, the rule is: "When in Rome, do as the Romans do." Cargill has a firm sense of ethics and forbids practices such as greasing the palms of politicians or officials. Even though this is common practice in many countries, Cargill refuses to bend their ethics.

THE ROLE OF THE CEO

The values that an organization lives by seem more driven by the personal values of the CEO or leader than any other factor. This is particularly true when the CEO is the founder of the organization.

Southwest Airlines was named best company to work for in America by *Fortune* Magazine in 1997. Herb Keleher, founder and CEO, has a strong set of values about how to run an organization that have been translated into the culture of this company. Having a sense of humor and having fun at your job are two values that Herb personally embraces and that permeate his company. Southwest has grown and continued to maintain these values partly through careful selection of employees and managers. Values are difficult to teach—an employee comes in the door with a mindset that may be very difficult to change or transform through training. An unethical individual is not likely to become the model of ethical behavior after a two-day ethics course, for example. Southwest evaluates about 1,500 resumes for each employee that it hires, considering values and personality traits (like sense of humor) more so than technical skills. Technical knowledge and skills can be taught; personality cannot.

What makes Southwest unique is that they have managed to create a large management team with the same values and personality traits as their founder and CEO. They do this through very careful selection and training to help hone leadership skills. They have not figured out how to clone Herb yet, but they have come close, with a strong leadership team that demonstrates his same values. A strong, charismatic leader is common in many successful organizations. The problem is, when that leader leaves, the values and culture often fall apart. Many successful companies lose their edge when a strong leader retires or moves on. These organizations often feel like they've lost their soul. Those that don't miss a beat when their leader moves on are the organizations that have a team of senior executives that are homogenous in their style and values.

Another company that has done a good job deploying the values of the CEO though all levels of management is Appleton Papers of Wisconsin. Appleton Papers is a manufacturer of specialty coated papers and is known for inventing carbonless paper, under their brand name "NCR." CEO Dale Schumaker is the type of boss everyone wishes they had. Dale comes across as humble, a good listener, and someone who is passionate about his company and its employees. He plays basketball several times a month at the Appleton YMCA with his hourly workers at lunchtime, and his office door is almost always open. One of Dale's values is that your personal and family life are just as important as your job. This value is communicated down to all employees, and Dale has done a remarkable job of building an executive team that demonstrates these values.

This value of balancing personal life and work has paid off handsomely for Appleton Papers. Turnover in their seven plants/mills is almost nonexistent. When people come to work at Appleton Papers, they stay. Turnover in many paper mills is 40 percent or more per year.) As part of a project, I talked to more than 75 people at Appleton over a couple of weeks, to find out why it's such a great company to work for. The reasons turned out to be quite simple:

- **No losers:** Appleton is very careful about hiring people with the right skills, work ethic, and personality to fit in with other team members.
- **Listening:** Appleton recognizes that even workers hired to do physical labor have ideas worth hearing. Appleton has a benchmarked suggestion program, many types of teams, and numerous opportunities for employees at all levels to help the company improve.
- **Family vs. job:** Workers are treated like members of the Appleton family, and the company strongly encourages balance in employees' lives outside of the company.

Both Southwest and Appleton Papers have remarkable leaders who have defined the companies' values and ensured that they are a strong part of the entire corporate culture. When these two CEOs step down, both companies will continue on with the same set of values.

CREATING A SET OF VALUES

Defining your organization's values is different from writing a mission or vision statement. Figuring out who you are and what you want to become in the future is much easier than defining the values by which you want to run your organization and implementing them day by day.

Most organizations already have a set of values—the problem is, they are usually the wrong ones.

One company I worked with defined their current values on the left side of a flipchart and their desired values on the right side. Some examples are shown in Figure 2-2.

Honestly assessing your existing attitudes and ethics is the first step in creating a set of operative values. You may want to keep some the same; others may need to be radically adjusted. Doing this requires a group that is not afraid to be honest about how the company really operates.

How We Are Today	How We'd Like to Be
Fiercely competitive	Cooperative and sharing
Tolerating poor performance	Accountable for poor performance
Reward workaholics	Encourage balance in employees' lives
Guarded communications	Open communication at all levels
Punish failures	Accept failures and learn from them
Distrust suppliers	Partner with proven suppliers
Stingy with training dollars	Continuing investment in developing employee skills/competencies

Figure 2-2. Example of One Company's Current vs. Desired Values

One way of collecting the data on your existing values is through anonymous surveys or focus groups with employees. I've seen surveys constructed that consist of a variety of statements about corporate culture and values, and employees assess the degree to which each is true of the company. Collecting data on your existing values this way is quite helpful, because the results are not subject to debate if the survey is done well. Perception is reality in this case.

DEPLOYING YOUR VALUES

Implementing a company's values requires an incredible effort, and not many organizations do it well without a crisis and the appointment of a new leader. Changing your corporate culture is quite possible, however, if adequate resources are applied and you have the time to wait for the change. The first step in changing the culture is clearly communicating the need for change and the new set of values. This must be done using many different media and often involves training. Some creative companies manage to make the values training both effective and enjoyable. For example, Sandia Laboratories hired Dilbert creator Scott Adams to help them create a game to teach employees their values and set of ethics. This approach made what would have been another dry, boring workshop one that the staff enjoyed and remembered.

It is important to coach executives in deploying the new values and eliminating behavior that is inconsistent with them. Getting them to agree to such coaching may be a struggle in and of itself, but getting them to break habits embedded over many years is the true challenge. Sometimes these coaches are outside consultants who work one-on-one with executives. Other times, executives agree to coach each other. Some organizations have found that a few of their managers just couldn't or wouldn't change; the only solution was for them to leave the company.

Integrating Values in the Recruiting and Selection Processes

Changing the values of an established organization with many seasoned employees is extremely difficult, particularly when senior executives flaunt the new values in their behavior and decisions. The easiest and most effective way of changing corporate culture or values is through careful selection of the right people. One value of Southwest Airlines is that employees, especially their frontline employees, need to have a good sense of humor. One way the company determines this is by having job applicants tell a few jokes in front of the selection committee as part of the selection process. If applicants fall flat, they are often referred to one of the bigger airlines, which tend to be quite serious. The point is that a sense of humor is something people bring with them; it is not really trainable. Southwest realizes that they need people with a good sense of humor to maintain their culture, which values having fun at work.

Integrating values into your recruiting and selection process is not all that difficult. One company I know of has applicants respond to a series of statements about values and work ethic to see if they agree or disagree with them. The questionnaire is carefully worded so that the "right" answer is not obvious. A questionnaire like this can be the beginnings of a screening process, but obviously more is needed to evaluate a person's real values. Interviews can help. A skilled interviewer can ask about the person's life and experiences, and draw out specific examples that form a profile of the values by which the individual lives his or her life. Checking references can also help, if you ask specific questions. By hiring people who have the same values as your organization's, you will eventually get to the point where the desired culture becomes reality.

In a firm with low turnover and growth, however, this approach takes too long. Still, I have seen a number of large firms of this type actually change their values and culture in a significant fashion. Often a crisis initiates such a change, but real work is needed to facilitate the change. One such organization is Ford Motor Company. I worked as a consultant to Ford back in the early 1980s, and again in the mid-1990s, and saw a huge change in the values and culture of the company. Ford has managed to maintain some of the positive aspects of their culture—which date back to the company's beginnings—and create a new culture that focuses on quality, ethics, and providing a positive work environment for employees. The company's products and overall business success in recent years make them worth emulating.

Rosenbluth Travel's Family Farm Values

Rosenbluth Travel is a $4-billion travel agency headquartered in Philadelphia. The firm has tripled in size in five years, expanded to 45 countries, and was recently listed in *Fortune* magazine as one of the 100 best companies to work for in the United States. The company has an interesting approach to defining and communicating its values. You'd more expect this approach in a company like Cargill (agricultural business) than Rosenbluth (travel agency), but it works for them. They formulated their values around those of a family farm:

On the family farm, team members are able to fill in for each other on a moment's notice—it's a necessity.

- Most family farmers elect to do as much as possible themselves because resources are often distant and costly. Therefore, the emphasis is on self-sufficiency in the field and on the front lines, as opposed to headquarters and functional domains.
- When it comes to farming, there are no vacations, holidays, or sick days. The work must be done 365 days a

year, so it is critical for neighbors to help each other: business units and departments take note.

Notice how these values both clearly articulate Rosenbluth's expectations of their employees and present the rationale behind those expectations. Some might see the farming analogy as corny, but the business model upon which the family farm is built is a sound one. The major difference between these values and the list of generic values discussed earlier is that Rosenbluth's statements make explicitly clear which behaviors are acceptable and which are not. For example, employees will understand that sick days are not gratuitous and should be used responsibly. The theme of teamwork and helping each other is also very apparent.

VALUES AND METRICS

Rarely do I see a scorecard that includes a metric on the extent to which the organization actually lives by the values it professes to support. If values are so important, shouldn't an organization regularly measure the extent to which it adheres to them? Not necessarily. I doubt that Southwest Airlines has a formal metric that measures the extent to which they exhibit a culture based on having fun at work. Yet, I'm sure that managers and executives gather all sorts of anecdotal data each day that tells them that their culture and values are still in place. Southwest has built such a strong culture based upon its values that it doesn't need a formal measure on the corporate scorecard confirming they are being continually practiced.

When it comes to measuring culture change or the extent to which values are communicated and followed, it is difficult to come up with meaningful metrics. One company measures the percentage of employees who can recite its eight values without looking at their wallet cards. Another company measures the percentage of employees who believe that it lives by the values it professes, determined via an anonymous employee survey and series of focus groups. A chemical company I'm familiar with actually measures the extent to which employee behavior is consistent with its values. They have defined a list of desired behaviors associated with each of their "core values" and use observation and surveys to evaluate the extent to which employees and managers exhibit the behaviors.

Many organizations evaluate the degree to which employees exhibit their values as part of the annual performance appraisal process. This could be used as a metric, but it probably would not be an effective one. For one thing, the ratings an employee receives are often based largely on the most recent events in the appraiser's memory. In addition, there is usually a great degree of variability in how managers expect employees to demonstrate the values in their behavior.

For organizations that are not where they want to be when it comes to practicing their values, and for those trying to change their old values and ways of doing business or trying to create a new culture, it makes sense to measure the extent to which the new values are being practiced—until the culture change has occurred. Once the new values are clearly part of the organization's culture, the values gauge might be dropped from the dashboard completely. When your company reaches this mode (like Southwest, 3M, Cargill, and other companies that have firmly instilled their values in their culture), anecdotal data is probably sufficient.

A checklist to aid you in evaluating values follows.

CHECKLIST FOR EVALUATING VALUES

An organization's values should:

☐ Specify a code of acceptable and unacceptable beliefs and behavior.

☐ Be unique to the organization, not based on generic buzzwords used by hundreds of other companies.

☐ Be consistent with the organization's real business practices.

☐ Be linked to hiring, promotions, and performance appraisal.

☐ Flow from the ethics and behavior of senior leaders.

☐ Be clearly understood by all employees.

☐ Not be subject to change as years pass or as strategy changes.

Metrics: Selecting the Right Operational Performance Measures

In Chapter 1, you learned the importance of having a clear mission statement that clarifies the major reasons for your organization's existence. Most of the performance metrics that appear on your scorecard will relate back to this mission and let you know how you are doing on fulfilling it. The purpose of this chapter is to provide you with information on designing the overall structure of your scorecard and selecting metrics that link back to your mission and goals (see Figure 3-1.)

An organization scorecard is a collection of performance measures that provide information on performance. There is no one right way of doing this; I have seen a number of good scorecards that were organized differently. What is important is that the structure fits the nature of your organization's work, that it is understandable to your people, and that a few basic design principles are followed.

Step 1: Framing—Designing the Overall Scorecard Structure

Step 2: Identify Broad Operational Goals by Scorecard Category

Step 3: Select Metrics That Link Back to Mission and Goals

Figure 3-1. Steps in Designing the Scorecard and Selecting Metrics

Step 1: Framing—Designing the Overall Scorecard Structure

There are several different models on which to base the structure of your scorecard. The one you select does not matter nearly as much as the metrics you end up including on your scorecard. Figure 3-2 shows the architecture for the Stanislaus County, California dashboard.

Kaplan and Norton's Balanced Scorecard Model

One option for designing your scorecard is to adopt the approach recommended by Robert Kaplan and David Norton, authors of *The Balanced Scorecard—Translating Strategy into Action* (Harvard Business School Press, 1996).

Kaplan and Norton suggest a scorecard that consists of four categories of data:

- **Customer measures**—might include survey data, buying behavior, loyalty measures, and measures of internal quality or other dimensions that are important to customers.
- **Financial measures**—traditional accounting or finance measures such as sales, operating expenses, P/E ration, profits, growth, etc.

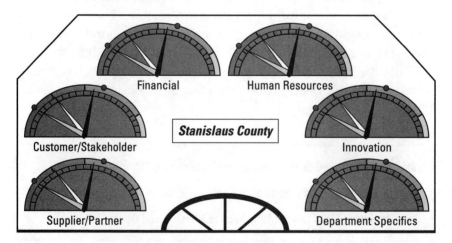

Figure 3-2. Example Scorecard "Architecture" or Categories

- **Internal measures**—measures of productivity, efficiency, safety, environmental performance, internal quality, industry-specific metrics, process metrics, supplier/partner performance, etc.
- **Innovation/growth measures**—metrics that focus on new product/service development, research, innovations, employee competencies, morale, process improvements, growth into new markets, etc. Kaplan and Norton's model provides a widely accepted approach that is easy to understand and fits most business organizations.

The Baldrige Award Model

Another approach to scorecard design is to follow the Baldrige Award criteria. Many business and nonprofit organizations use the Baldrige model for self-assessment and to sort processes and results into a logical and widely accepted framework that is provided by the criteria. The Baldrige Award criteria separate results into five categories of data:

- **Customer-focused results**—could include customer satisfaction surveys, loyalty measures, customer dissatisfaction metrics like complaints or returns, as well as internal measures of variables that impact customer satisfaction.
- **Financial and market results**—all traditional financial measures would go in this section, along with measures of market share and any financial metrics that might be unique to the organization.
- **Human resource results**—measures of employee safety, health, morale, turnover, training, intellectual capital, recruiting, and other metrics that study the performance of the organization's human resources.
- **Supplier and partner results**—this section of the scorecard includes measures that assess the performance of key suppliers, contractors, distributors, or business partners. Metrics might include number of suppliers, supplier "report card" scores, cost of supplier goods/services, certified suppliers, etc.

- **Organizational effectiveness results**—this last category of results includes measures of productivity, efficiency, unit costs, cycle time, project-management measures, new products/services, process measures, and industry-specific metrics.

The major difference between the Baldrige and Kaplan and Norton models is that the Baldrige approach has separate sections for human resource and supplier performance data. Measures of supplier performance would probably go in the "Internal" box of the Kaplan and Norton model. Metrics relating to employee satisfaction, learning, and development would go in the "Learning and Growth" box of the Kaplan and Norton scorecard design. The five categories in the Baldrige model work well in organizations that are labor-intensive and spend a lot of money on outside suppliers or contractors. What I like about the Kaplan and Norton model is that it asks for measures of innovation, learning, and growth; company scorecards often neglect measures in these areas. Furthermore, all of their measures focus on past and present time periods.

Discover Financial Services Scorecard

Discover Financial Services is part of the financial giant Morgan Stanley, Dean Witter Discover. Discover Financial Services provides the Discover credit card and other related financial products to merchants and consumers. The company also provides merchants with the Novus Network for transaction processing. The company uses the Baldrige criteria to assess its business units and develop strategic plans, so it made sense to adopt the five Baldrige results categories for their scorecard design. However, they also liked the Kaplan and Norton model because the company was looking to be more innovative and grow in size and market share. Therefore, their model ended up being a hybrid of the two approaches.

Discover Enterprises has six boxes on their scorecard:

- Customer Satisfaction/Dissatisfaction Results
- Financial and Market Results
- Human Resource Results

- Supplier/Partner Results
- Operational Results
- Innovation and Growth Results

Discover Financial Services started at the business unit level. One business unit, Network Services, was selected as the pioneer for the scorecard initiative because its leader was excited about the approach and viewed the scorecard as the means to address the need for meaningful, actionable performance measures. This approach allowed him to eliminate some of the less meaningful metrics from his scorecard that were leftover from the company's effort. Once the project for Network Services was underway, another major (and even larger) unit in Discover Financial Services began its own balanced scorecard project.

The Scorecard Structure of a Leading Securities Firm

One of America's most successful securities firms is leading the industry by redefining the concept of a full-service stockbroker. Always well known for its research and exceptional customer service, it has now expanded its menu of services to clients to encompass online trading, online research, and a variety of advice packages to tailor their services to individual investor preferences. In creating this new, full-service firm, the company needed a new set of metrics to measure their progress toward their vision.

The company embarked on a scorecard initiative, beginning with marketing, then gradually moving to the branches and other aspects of the business. It reviewed generic models for scorecard design, but decided to create its own. The four categories of data on its scorecard are:

- **Business Impact and Growth**—these metrics examine how each sector of the organization is contributing to its image, growth, and financial success.
- **Customer/Partner Satisfaction**—how the company builds loyalty from internal and external customers through their own efforts and by partnering with suppliers and vendors.
- **Organizational Excellence**—what the organization must excel at internally to meet overall goals and objectives.

- **Innovation and Learning**—these metrics look at the organization's ability to expand and improve products, services, and processes to meet or exceed client needs.

Military Scorecard Designs

While the Kaplan and Norton or Baldrige models for scorecard design fit most businesses, they do not fit as well in government, military, or nonprofit institutions. The basic principles still apply, but the scorecard categories need to be adapted. District Fourteen in the U.S. Coast Guard, headquartered in Honolulu, first designed their scorecard in 1995. Rather than adapt an existing model, the team selected four categories of measures:

- **Mission Performance**—includes performance measures that look at how the Coast Guard performed on actual missions, as well preventive measures that look at readiness of equipment and people.
- **Customer Satisfaction**—measures of internal and external customers and stakeholder satisfaction.
- **Leadership and Human Resource Management**—includes safety metrics, employee satisfaction, training/development measures, and a metric that looks at leadership and teamwork.
- **Internal Process Efficiency**—these metrics included savings from process improvements and efficiency measures.

Another group in the Coast Guard, District Seven in Miami, designed their scorecard slightly differently. They had sections that looked at Mission Performance and Mission Readiness. District Seven is the busiest Coast Guard District in the United States, so they always had plenty of data in the Mission Performance box of their scorecard. They also wanted to have a scorecard category that looked at innovation and new product/service development. Their vision was to originate most of the innovations and new services in the Coast Guard. Hence, it made sense to include an entire category of measures that examined this aspect of their performance.

Neither Coast Guard organization had a section on their scorecards for Financial Results. I had also helped Hickum Air Force Base develop a scorecard that did not have a Financial Results box. According to Col. Bruce Brown at Hickum, he did not want to convey the idea to military and civilian personnel that their mission was to worry about money and budgets. Staying within budget and reducing expenses is certainly important and was measured on their scorecard, but they did not need an entire category of financial measures. It was important that the scorecard categories selected for the Air Force base linked back to their basic mission.

Strategic versus Operational Measures

Another point to consider is that the scorecard must accommodate all operational measures that link back to your mission, as well as a few strategic metrics that are derived from your future vision and key success factors. The scorecard does not need a separate section for strategic metrics, but you need to make sure that the strategic metrics fit into the categories you have selected. An easy way to communicate the difference to people is to draw a picture of an actual dashboard (see Figure 3-3) that shows three large gauges that signify the strategic metrics, a series of smaller gauges that represent the operational measures, and a band of "idiot lights" or alarms along the bottom of the dashboard, indicating measures that don't need to be watched each month as gauges, but that are critical if performance exceeds or goes below certain levels.

For example, many organizations have stopped tracking system downtime because their systems are almost never down anymore. Rather than have a gauge that almost consistently shows zero downtime, this metric becomes an idiot light that only comes on if downtime occurs or if a certain level of poor performance exists. I'll talk more about the use of software and graphics for communicating performance data in Chapter 12. You will also learn about "Dashboard Software," which allows you to display performance data that looks like the dashboard on a car.

The Importance of Consistency

A few organizations allow each business unit and/or facility to design its own scorecard categories. This approach helps create ownership of the scorecard design and allows separate units and

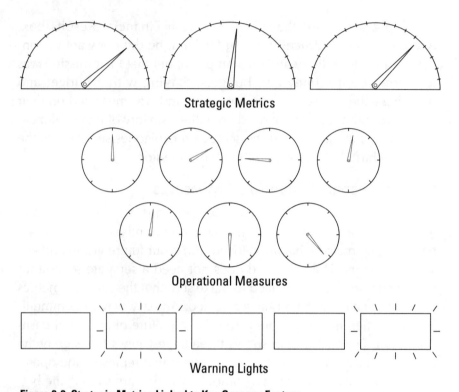

Figure 3-3. Strategic Metrics Linked to Key Success Factors

departments to tailor scorecard categories to their own situations. For example, a support department like Finance or Human Resources might have a different way of sorting and categorizing their performance metrics than a profit-making business unit. In most cases, I think it is a mistake to let each unit or department determine its own scorecard categories. This leads to confusion and often allows for poorly designed scorecards. For example, one support department I worked with created four boxes on its scorecard that corresponded to their four major work processes. All of the measures were operational in nature, and they completely neglected to include metrics that focused on customers, employees, or the future.

Tip: Develop an overall scorecard design that can be used consistently by all levels and functions in the organization.

The overall design of the scorecard is not as important as picking one design and sticking to it throughout the organization. The individual metrics may differ quite a bit throughout the organization, but the scorecard categories should be consistent.

STEP 2: IDENTIFY BROAD OPERATIONAL GOALS BY SCORECARD CATEGORY

Identifying the categories or overall design of your scorecard is one of the easiest steps in the process and should not be agonized over or debated because the categories are simply a way to sort your metrics. The next step is to write some broad goals in each of the scorecard categories that outline what you are trying to accomplish. Many of these goals tend to be quite broad, but that's OK, as long as they are important for your organization. Examples of such goals for each scorecard category appear in Figure 3-4.

Tip: The goals you write at this stage relate to your mission, not your vision, and should address all the fundamentals of keeping your organization in business.

Setting Your Own Goals

The broad goals listed in the chart are intended to get you thinking of ideas—you really need to develop your own. You might find that some generic goals fit the needs of your organization, and can be used as is; however, this should not be the case with most of your goals. It is important to think through exactly what you are trying to accomplish before settling on specific goals. Many organizations select high-level goals without giving them much thought. Keep in mind that these goals will result in measures, targets, strategies, as well as time and money spent to achieve them. Think about whether or not you really want or need to accomplish this goal. Following are some examples of commonly specified goals that are usually unrealistic.

Be the Employer of Choice

A typical goal that I see in the human resource section is to become "employer of choice." In other words, the company wants to be able

---

EXAMPLE GENERIC GOAL STATEMENTS

CUSTOMER

☐ Improve overall levels of customer satisfaction

☐ Improve loyalty from targeted customers

☐ Percent increase in repeat business

☐ Reduce complaints/problems

EMPLOYEE

☐ Become the employer of choice in our industry

☐ Improve overall levels of employee safety

☐ Continually increase core competencies

☐ Reduce turnover of desirable employees

☐ Increase employee involvement and productivity

FINANCIAL

☐ Increase sales

☐ Reduce operating expenses

☐ Increase profit per customer or per product/service

☐ Improve return on capital/asset utilization

OPERATIONAL

☐ Reengineer key work processes to reduce costs and improve efficiency

☐ Improve product/service quality

☐ Increased partnering with suppliers

☐ Decrease rework and errors

☐ Improve timeliness and empowerment

INNOVATION/GROWTH

☐ Improve the new product/service development process

☐ Achieve growth in targeted new markets

☐ Continually introduce new products/service ahead of competitors

☐ Use the latest technology to ensure high performance and productivity

☐ Focus on continual learning and improvement in all areas

Figure 3-4. Example Generic Goal Statements

to hire the best and the brightest and to keep them by being a great place to work. The problem is, most organizations that claim to want to be "employer of choice" have lousy pay and benefits, provide lit-

tle training for employees, expect 60+ hours a week from everyone, and are always the last to purchase any new technology. In other
words, they are so far from currently being the employer of choice
that this is not a reasonable goal. Further, the company would probably never spend the money or commit other resources to become the
employer of choice anyway, so why bother setting the goal?

Improve Customer Satisfaction

What organization wouldn't want to improve customer satisfaction?
This usually goes on the list of goals without anyone questioning it.
The problem with automatically selecting this as a goal is that customer satisfaction is often fine and does not need improvement; or,
improvements in customer satisfaction may not lead to improvements in sales, growth, profits, or other outcome measures. I am not
suggesting that customer satisfaction improvement might not be
important. I am saying you better look at current levels and consider
how improving satisfaction will help your organization before setting
this as a goal.

A number of organizations have spent millions of dollars and
labor hours over the last 10 years in the name of quality and customer
satisfaction. Yet, many have found that more satisfied customers do
not necessarily spend more money and are not even more loyal to an
organization or its products/services. Thus, while customer satisfaction levels have risen, this has not led to concurrent improvements in
profits, sales, or even retention of valuable accounts/customers

Continually Improve All Key Work Processes

Continuous improvement and learning were the mantras of the early
1990s when most organizations were trying to implement Total Quality Management and Reengineering initiatives. After many years of
flowcharting and attempting to improve hundreds of processes, many
organizations found out that continuous improvement is time consuming, expensive, and simply unnecessary. Most work processes
were designed with sound logic, and actually work quite well without being "reengineered." Continuous improvement of everything is
a ridiculous goal. If any organization really needed to improve all its
processes, it would have been out of business long ago. As with

improving customer satisfaction and becoming employer of choice, continuous improvement is one of those generic goals that winds up in a strategic plan because everyone is afraid to challenge it.

How to Define Your High-Level Goals

Once you have agreed on the scorecard categories, it is a good idea to have the senior management team brainstorm a list of possible goals in each category. The goals should all include a verb, but need not be measurable or quantifiable. For example, it would be all right to have a goal that states, "Improve the product development process." After brainstorming 30 to 40 possible goals for each of the scorecard categories, you need to get the group to narrow them down to two to four per scorecard section. In doing so, remind the group that the goals must relate back to the mission and should include different aspects of performance. For example, you would not want to have all of the goals in the Financial box pertain to improving profitability. Also, it is a good idea to keep the goals brief, like the examples in the chart.

Tip: Challenge all proposed goals by asking,
"Is this really something we need to do to stay successful,
or are we OK in this area?

Once you have succeeded in getting the group to agree on the two to four goals for the first section of the scorecard, proceed in the same manner with the remaining sections. Goals in the Financial box seem to always be the easiest to write; and those in the Innovation and Growth section are usually the most challenging. This entire process of writing goals for each major section of the scorecard should take four or five hours, assuming a group of 10 to 15 people.

STEP 3: SELECT METRICS THAT LINK BACK TO OVERALL GOALS

The next step in the process is to define metrics that relate back to each of the high-level goals. Some of these will be obvious and easy. For example, the metric for a goal that says "Increase sales from targeted customers" might be dollars in sales from target customers compared to last year, or percent of sales from targeted customers, or percent increase in sales from targeted customers. The metrics identified in this section should be specific enough to appear on a graph of performance. So, for example, you could not get away with saying that a metric is "overall employee satisfaction." You need to get more specific, stating instead something like "percent of employees rating a 4 or 5 on overall job satisfaction question in annual employee survey."

Tip: Beware of metrics that rely on tallying items of questionable value—some of the most important aspects of performance cannot be measured simply by counting.

Using a Team to Identify Metrics

The brainstorming and prioritizing process described for goal setting also works well if you use a group or team to identify metrics. Prepare a flipchart with one goal at the top and get the team to spend 15 to 30 minutes brainstorming all the possible ways to measure achievement of that goal. Make sure to include any existing metrics that might be valuable on the scorecard. It should be easy for the team to think of at least 10 to 20 possible metrics for most goals. Measures can be ratios, comparisons, or indices made up of several individual measures; expressed as a percent, actual amount, rating, etc. The problem is selecting those vital few that best represent the organization's overall performance. Do not allow the team to select all or most of the metrics and combine them into an index, as this defeats the purpose of prioritizing.

Types of Metrics: Counting and Judgment

All measurement is based upon one of two types of metrics: counting or judgment. Most of the statistics kept in baseball are based on counting—hits, runs, balls, strikes, bases stolen, and so on. There is some judgment involved when calling errors or balls and strikes, but baseball is a game based mostly on counting the accomplishments or failures of the players. Diving, on the other hand, is a sport that is measured using a judgment system. Judges have a definition of what a "perfect 10" dive looks like, and they evaluate each dive on a 1-to-10 scale based on how close it comes to the perfect score.

Metrics Based on Counting

Counting metrics are almost always preferable to judgment metrics because they are more objective and usually less time consuming. Many good organizational measures are based on counting; for instance:

- number of new accounts
- number of complaints from customers
- number of units produced
- number of days with no accidents
- dollars in sales
- return on investment
- number of services performed
- number of seconds of downtime
- turnover
- dollars in sales from new products.

Counting important items, like money and products or services, is necessary to evaluate organizational performance. Counting metrics can get out of hand, though, when organizations start counting things that are senseless or don't really add value. For example, some needless counting-based metrics are:

- number of attendees at training courses (i.e., butts in chairs)
- number of meetings attended
- number of reports completed
- number of publications by scientists or academics
- number of processes improved
- number of suggestions from employees

Tip: Avoid counting irrelevant items that may
appear legitimate at first.

Metrics Based on Judgment

Many aspects of organizational performance cannot be adequately judged by using counting-based metrics—judgment is required.

There are four basic types of judgment-based metrics, as shown in Figure 3-5.

	Specific Criteria	Opinion
Rating	1 (Best)	2
Ranking	3	4 (Worst)

Figure 3-5. Matrix of Judgement-Based Metrics

The best approach is number 1, because performance is based upon a rating system with specific criteria. The best known example of this type of measurement system is that used for the Malcolm Baldrige Award. Companies are given a score out of possible 1,000 points based upon how well they meet very specific and detailed criteria. Examiners judge the organization's systems and results and then, after discussing them, reach agreement on the score. This system has proven quite reliable when used to test an organization examined by different teams.

Safety and financial audits or inspections are also good measurement approaches that are based upon judgment with specific criteria. A measurement system based on opinions is usually bad because of the subjectivity involved. Judges for the Academy Awards use a rating system that is based on their subjective opinions of each film that has been nominated. There are no specific criteria that I know of for winning an Academy Award, but actors with English accents seem to be favored, and comedies in general are looked down upon.

The worst type of judgment-based metric is one where individual or corporate performance is ranked according to subjective opinions. I've seen a number of performance appraisal systems like this. A manager first rates each employee based on his or her subjective opinion of the employee's performance, and then ranks employees from best to worst based on more subjective opinions. It's no wonder most employees and managers alike hate performance appraisal systems. Rank ordering tends to occur when no specific criteria or scale for establishing a rating exists. Even when ranking is based on hard facts—such as ranking the sales figures of individual salespeople—measurement systems of this type tend to be negative because someone always ends up at the bottom of the list.

Tip: If you must use judgment to gather performance data, try to use a system that establishes ratings using specific criteria

---

Ratios and Comparisons

Often, singular metrics are meaningless unless they are presented as a function of some other measure, or at least compared to some other measure. Some common ratios are the P-E ratio used by brokers to evaluate companies, or the ratio of assets to liabilities. Most ratios are better than singular metrics because they compare some aspect of performance on a unit basis. For example, simply looking at sales or investments is not very meaningful unless one has a corresponding metric for comparison.

Percent of goal achieved is a common ratio or comparison metric found on the scorecard of many companies. This metric tends to be misleading, because those goals are often set improperly to begin with. An organization might be at 90 percent of goal achievement and still be doing a poor job compared to competitors or industry averages. Using competitor and industry data for part of a ratio is always preferable to your own goal or target.

Past, Present, and Future Metrics

One important aspect of a balanced scorecard is that it has a roughly equal number of metrics that focus on past, present, and future perspectives. Past measures provide data on outcomes or outputs that have already occurred. Such metrics are also called lagging indicators because they show performance that has already occurred. Present-focused metrics tend to look at a shorter time span (i.e., how are we doing today) and at things that can be addressed to correct poor performance. Future-focused metrics are not predictions or forecasts; rather, they are leading indicators that should serve to predict the performance of the *present* and *past* (or lagging) indicators. These leading indicators are the most critical of all because they help an organization manage better. They are also the types of metrics that I least often find on a scorecard.

Figure 3-6 provides some examples of past, present, and future metrics I've seen in organizations.

EXAMPLE PAST, PRESENT, AND FUTURE METRICS

Past Metrics	Present Metrics	Future Metrics
Financial		
Profit	Cash flow	Booked order $
Return on investment	Stock price	$ in R&D
Total expenses	Budget remaining	$ in capital vs. budget investments
Customer		
New business	Customer survey	Referrals from customers
Lost customers	Complaints	Loyalty
Length of relationship	Returns	Exit barriers
Employee		
Turnover	Morale survey	Recruiting success
Accidents	Safe behaviors	Safety Audit Scores
Absenteeism	Stress level	Referrals by existing employees
Operations		
Units per hour	Work in process	Scheduled production
Defects/scrap	Related process metrics	Product/process design reviews
$ saved in process	Use of team process	Identification of opportunities
On-time delivery	Cycle time for key processes	Scheduling completed
Learning and Innovation		
Training completed	Development planning	Human capital index
ROI —new products	New products in design	Number of ideas in review
Products/services	Industry firsts	Number of patents copied by competitors

Figure 3-6. Examples of Past, Present, and Future Metrics

> *Tip: Include a metric that looks at the past, present, and future in each box of your scorecard, except the box that focuses on innovation, learning, and growth. It's OK if all the measures in this box are future-focused.*

As you can see from the examples in the table, the future metrics are the most difficult to define. Most organizations have plenty of good metrics that focus on the past, and a few that look at the present. These are the metrics that often end up being included on the scorecard, with little or no modification. The leading indicators, or future-focused metrics, are the most challenging to identify.

Identifying Measures That Predict the Future

The real test of a good leading indicator or future-focused metric is that it strongly correlates with lagging indicators or past-focused metrics. For example, one company found that its customer loyalty index (leading) was highly correlated with actual customer buying behavior (lagging). Hence, this was a good measure because it allowed them to predict future success. As the customer loyalty measure rose, future income could be projected accurately. Rarely do I see good leading indicators like this in organizations, however. Most companies that do have leading indicators or future-focused metrics on their scorecard have not proven the links to lagging indicators. For example, employee morale surveys are supposed to predict turnover and other past-focused measures of employee dissatisfaction. I have yet to see a company that can show this kind of correlation. Similarly, many organizations measure customer satisfaction, but few can show that increased customer satisfaction correlates to increased sales or profits from those satisfied customers.

> *Tip: Conduct research on potential leading indicators to make sure they correlate with lagging indicators before including them on the scorecard.*

It is dangerous to select leading indicators that don't correlate to lagging indicators. You may spend valuable resources to make the needle move in a positive direction on the leading indicator gauges, but if improvement in a leading indicator score does not lead to concurrent improvements in outcome measures, your time and money will have been wasted. Another problem with poorly defined leading indicators is that positive performance provides a false sense of security. Executives scan the charts of leading metrics and feel good because they all show good levels and trends, so no changes are made. By the time the organization figures out it is in trouble (lagging indicators), it is often too late to correct the situation.

One simple way of challenging potential leading indicators of future measures is to use logic to try and explain how improvements in the leading indicator will translate to improvements in outcome measures. Assuming it passes the logic test, ask if any research has been done to show a correlation between the leading and lagging indicators. If both the logic and literature review tests are positive, a study should be done in a small sector of the organization to determine if, in fact, the leading indicator actually helps predict future performance levels on the lagging measures.

The Issue of Control

Control is another issue to consider when defining metrics that relate back to your mission. That is, can your organization take actions to make the needle on a particular gauge move in a noticeable fashion? No one has total control over any metric. If I told you that I was going to measure your overall level of health by recording your weight and cholesterol, these would be good metrics. Both are proven to be correlated with serious health problems (e.g., heart disease), so they are important, and they are both measures that we can affect by our lifestyles. Even though perhaps 50 percent of your cholesterol and weight might be determined by heredity, diet and lifestyle determine the other 50 percent. You can do many things to lower your weight and cholesterol; hence, these are good measures.

Tip: *When evaluating possible metrics, ask "Can we influence performance on this measure and make the needle move?," not "Can we control performance on this measure?"*

In a business, the CEO is held accountable for profits, growth, stock price, and a number of key metrics. Yet the CEO does not have complete control over any of these measures—all three of them are influenced by many other individuals in the company and by factors outside of the company. Nevertheless, profits, growth, and stock price are good performance measures for any CEO because his or her actions in running the company can make the needles move on these gauges.

Using the checklist below, evaluate the metrics that address the mission portion of your scorecard.

EVALUATING MISSION-RELATED METRICS

☐ There are no more than 20 metrics, tops (12 to15 is better).

☐ Metrics are important and link back to overall goals and mission statement.

☐ Metrics are a roughly equal mix of those that focus on the past, present, and future.

☐ Counting measures are based upon meaningful things, where possible.

☐ Judgement metrics are based upon ratings established using specific criteria.

☐ Metrics are as objective as possible.

☐ Metrics will drive the right behavior from employees and partners.

☐ Collecting data on the metrics is feasible and cost effective.

☐ Leading or future metrics can be linked to lagging outcome measures such as income or growth, where possible.

☐ Employees cannot easily cheat on measures.

☐ Measures will be understood by most employees.

☐ Measures lend themselves to being tracked on a regular basis so that changes can be detected in performance when there is still time to do something about it.

☐ Measures depict aspects of performance over which we have quite a bit of influence.

Targets:
Setting Goals
and Objectives
to Track Progress

The good metrics or gauges on your corporate dashboard provide only half of the information you need to better manage performance. Goals and targets allow you to use the gauges to tell whether or not you are doing a good job. Targets or objectives must be set for each metric on a company scorecard in order to make the measures meaningful. The process of setting targets or objectives is rarely done well, however. In this chapter, I'll discuss some of the pitfalls in setting targets and provide guidance on the proper methods to use.

THE IMPORTANCE OF SETTING TARGETS

Targets provide us with inspiration; they give us something to shoot for. Targets are a major part of any strategic or operational plan. A target is not a budget or standard, but a quantifiable level of desired performance. For example, your target for your weight might be 180 pounds, or your target for making good time while driving to Palm Springs might be two-and-a-half hours from Los Angeles. Plans usually include shorter-term or annual targets as well as longer-term targets that might look three to five years out. Targets might be ranges or absolute numbers, but they are never vague and unmeasurable. A measure without a target provides no information. It is only by combining performance data with a target that this feedback becomes helpful to a manager. Looking at performance data without knowing the desired level of performance provides no useful information. Finding out that your cholesterol is 300 is not too meaningful until the doctor tells you that 200 or less is normal, and that 300 is a heart attack waiting to happen.

It is important that an organization set its targets scientifically because managers will evaluate their performance against those targets and expend valuable resources striving to achieve them. Simply looking at last year's numbers and bumping them up by 20 percent might be a disastrous process. The guy with cholesterol of 300 could subtract 20 percent, or 30 points, from his level, setting his objective at 270. When he reaches 270, he stops the diet and exercise program and relaxes—he has reached his goal. Two months later he has a heart attack and wonders how this could happen after he had reached his cholesterol goal. The same sort of thing happens to organizations that set arbitrary goals.

In reviewing the plans of many business and government organizations, I have seen more bad targets than good. Following is a discussion of some of the more common mistakes I have seen organizations make when setting targets or objectives.

Incremental Improvement Targets

Back in the 1970s and 1980s, when management by objectives (MBO) was the favored approach to planning, organizations would look at past performance and set their target at 5 to10 percent higher than the previous year's. This approach was sensible, and it focused on the need for continuous improvement. The MBO game was one that many learned to play well—though often to the detriment of their companies. They set their target high enough so the boss would think they really had to stretch to achieve it, and low enough so that they could achieve it with a minimal amount of effort and coast most of the year. In this way, some companies targeted themselves right out of business. While they were getting 5 percent better each year, a competitor blew them out of the water by getting 50 or 100 percent better.

Another problem with setting incremental improvement targets is that the level of current performance must be considered. The effort required to improve customer satisfaction from 85 to 90 percent might be significant and not really be necessary or worth the investment.

Tip: Incremental improvement targets make sense when you are at a low level, or when it is impossible to get comparative data to use in setting better targets.

Arbitrary Stretch Targets

A fad that started in the 1990s and is still active today is the setting of arbitrary stretch targets. If a company is experiencing healthy 5 percent growth each year, a stretch target might be to push that to 30 percent annual growth. Stretch targets are thought to force employees to think differently about approaches to getting goals achieved, fostering innovation, and process re-engineering. This sounds great in theory, but does not work well in practice. The problem with most stretch targets is that they are set arbitrarily by pulling numbers out of the air—like "100 percent improvement" or "six sigma." An obvious problem with such arbitrary stretch targets is that employees *know* the numbers were pulled out of the air, and hence are unreasonable. Rather than being inspired to pursue higher levels of performance, employees lose their faith in senior management for being so out of touch with reality as to think that such targets are achievable.

A second, more serious problem with stretch goals is the money and time spent trying to achieve them. Often, the resources required to even come close to achieving a stretch target are not aligned with the value provided to the firm. For example, say your target was to achieve 95 percent customer satisfaction in your customer service department. In order to achieve this, you need to add 25 percent more people to your staff and purchase a $5-million telecommunications system to increase capacity and reduce hold time. Would this be worth the investment if customer satisfaction were already at 89 percent? It's doubtful.

Setting arbitrary stretch targets is one of the most common and dangerous planning practices I've seen in business and government. For example, a military organization sets a stretch target of cutting costs by 30 percent in three years, and a $200- million manufacturing company sets a stretch target of $1 billion in sales in three years— with no idea how it will get there, as its biggest competitor has 90 percent market share. In both cases, employees would realize that these stretch goals, set ridiculously higher than current performance, were ludicrous; and far from being motivated, they'd be discouraged from even trying.

Tip: Challenge outrageous stretch goals by investigating
the resources needed to achieve them

"Big Hairy Audacious Goals"

Jim Collins, author of the book *Built to Last,* suggests that good companies tend to set "big hairy audacious goals" for 10 to 30 years in the future. BHAGs are not to be confused with stretch goals, which tend to focus on shorter time frames such as three to five years. BHAGs, according to Collins, are more like long-term vision statements that specify a desired outcome or market position. In an article in the July/August 1999 issue of *Harvard Business Review,* Collins mentions Baldrige winner Granite Rock as a company with a good BHAG. Granite Rock, a 100-year-old company that sells gravel sand and concrete, has a goal of having a level of customer service that rivals Nordstrom, the upscale department store that is famous for its personalized service. This is quite an audacious goal for a company that sells rocks. However, Granite Rock has come a long way toward achieving this BHAG, set 12 years ago. One mile-marker of their progress was winning the coveted Malcolm Baldrige Award in 1992. Another indicator of their progress is continued growth in both profitability and market share, even though the company charges about 6 percent more than its larger competitors for a commodity product.

BHAGs versus Vision Statements versus Stretch Goals

After a while, all these terms start sounding like different names for the same concepts. Vision statements typically address the future of the entire organization and tend to be quite broad. Big Hairy Audacious Goals usually address a longer time frame than a vision statement. The best vision statements look three years out; this keeps employees focused on something they can envision actually happening while they're still with the company. BHAGs tend to focus on an accomplishment that may require 10 to 30 years to achieve. BHAGs also tend to focus on a singular aspect of performance. For example, Granite Rock's BHAG focuses on customer service. Hewlett Packard has a BHAG to create a culture of innovative, risk-taking employees who love coming to work. Kimberly-Clark set a BHAG in 1971 of going from a mediocre paper and forest products company to becoming a world-class consumer product company. Stretch goals tend to focus on an extremely aggressive improvement for a particular metric—for example, reducing employee turnover from 40 percent to 5 percent, or tripling volume sales in five years.

USING BENCHMARKING TO SET TARGETS

Another practice that sounded like a good idea at the time but has not panned out so well is benchmarking. Benchmarking is the process of finding another organization that performs a particular process better than just about anyone, and studying that organization to learn how it's done. Untold numbers of trips to Disney World and stays in Ritz Carlton Hotels have been charged to company expense accounts in the name of benchmarking. While both Disney and Ritz Carlton are outstanding companies with many practices to benchmark, the concept has gotten out of hand. Benchmarking is a recommended approach to analyzing the best performers in a specific industry, but it is just one factor among many that should be used to set your own targets.

Studying a world-class or benchmark organization to find out its levels of performance on key metrics, and looking at the processes it uses to achieve those levels, can actually be quite useful. A target based on a benchmark company is much better, of course, than simply making up a target by pulling numbers out of the air. At least with a benchmark you know that some company in the world has performed this well. Yet setting targets based on those of a high-performance company in another industry may be inappropriate. Your work processes, customers, and resources may be so different that the targets do not make sense. Furthermore, you may not have the resources necessary to achieve the levels of performance found in a benchmarked company.

For example, your local Department of Motor Vehicles (DMV) office might decide to benchmark the call centers in Discover Financial Services because they are known to have one of the best call centers in the country. The company regularly achieves 20-second answer time, with almost no blocked or abandoned calls. The last time I called my local DMV office, I spent 10 minutes listening to the various menu choices on the automated call system and pressing various buttons before I got in the cue to wait another 15 or 20 minutes to talk to the "next available customer service representative." And this was after calling six or seven times earlier that day and getting a busy signal.

Wouldn't it be great if the DMV had the same level of prompt service I receive when I call 1-800-DISCOVER? Sure it would, but for the DMV to set its performance targets by copying those at Discover is not feasible. Discover Financial Services has recently built several new, state-of-the-art call centers in Phoenix, Salt Lake, and Columbus that are not only beautiful and functional, but also include the best computers and telecommunications systems on the market. Realizing that working in a call center is a tough, stressful job, the company has bent over backward to be a pleasant and enjoyable place to work. Discover always has a dozen different contests and recognition programs going on, allows employees to dress casually, has cafeterias with great food (and a lake view in one of their facilities), and offers opportunities to earn incentive pay. In short, it's little wonder that Discover's performance is so outstanding—they pay for it.

While it may be possible for other credit card companies to approximate the levels of performance achieved by the Discover call center, the DMV will probably never get there. When we call the DMV we don't expect to get through right away, and we don't expect DMV offices to be state-of-the-art facilities. The DMV could never afford the levels of performance attained by Discover—but neither does it have strong competitors. Its customers are a captive audience. The DMV, however, *has* improved the efficiency of some of its processes—transactions such as annual registration renewals can now be done through the mail. This has saves time for both residents and DMV employees.

Then again, perhaps people would pay more for more efficient service from government organizations. Consider the state of California, which has pioneered a new concept for toll roads. Many states now have an automated toll system whereby drivers are sent a monthly bill depending upon how often they drive the toll roads. This speeds up traffic, because there are fewer tollbooths and drivers needn't always worry about having the right change. The interesting approach in California is to charge drivers different amounts based on the level of traffic in the nontoll lanes. The state has found that people will pay to ease the aggravation of driving in bumper-to-bumper traffic, so it charges according to traffic conditions. One day you leave work at, say, 2:00 P.M. and you might pay 90 cents to drive in the toll lanes (assuming traffic is light). The next day you leave at 5:00 P.M. and might pay $3.50 for using the same toll lanes. This great concept illustrates that people will pay for better service from government organizations.

I encourage you to go out and study benchmark companies and organizations to get a sense of what is possible, but I caution you about adopting benchmarked levels of performance as your own targets. This rarely works well.

Tip: Benchmarking tells you what is possible, but don't use the performance levels of benchmark organizations as the sole source of data for setting your own targets.

COMPETITOR PERFORMANCE

The best source of information for setting targets is competitor performance. This is also the most difficult type of data to obtain. Competitors won't send you their performance reports or invite you in for a tour. (In Chapter 7, on Situation Analysis, I discuss some techniques used to gather data on competitors.) Aside from being difficult to obtain, a second problem with using competitor data to set targets is that your competitors probably don't use the same metrics or measurement methods you do. Perhaps you measure quality or system downtime differently. Even financial measures might differ— such as the formulas you use to calculate gross margin—so they are difficult to compare.

Competitor data is usually most available on business fundamental metrics. For example, one hotel can find out about the prices, restaurant service, and revenue per available room of other competing hotels fairly simply. As long as the two properties are similar and in similar cities, this data can be very helpful in setting targets or objectives. Using data provided by third-party research firms also can be a great way of accessing a broad competitor database. For example, car companies have benefited from using J.D. Power to measure customer satisfaction. Airlines, hotels, and other industries are also using J.D. Powers' customer satisfaction data because everyone is graded on the same scale.

Target Ranges

With some types of metrics, it is more effective to establish a range of acceptable performance as opposed to a single, absolute target. These target ranges, often referred to as control limits, apply especially well to process metrics, which usually allow for some upper and lower deviation from a standard. For example, the correct temperature for an oven during the baking process might be 350 degrees, but variations of plus or minus 10 degrees would probably be acceptable. Target ranges sometimes apply to output metrics, such as on-time delivery of a package or a risk-assessment score for a potential mortgage customer. As with any type of target, these ranges should be set based upon research. Factors outside of your control, such as weather or business cycles, must be taken into consideration, along with resource constraints.

However, establishing target ranges based on the best and worst performance over the last year is not the answer either. This ensures that you will almost always be on target, but staying within the desired range may not produce acceptable outputs. For example, perhaps you have an old oven with a faulty thermostat and the temperature varies as much as 50 degrees from the setting from time to time. This level of variation is unlikely to produce consistent baked goods.

LINKING TARGETS TO METRICS

Almost everything on an organization's scorecard is dependent upon other measures of performance. Employee morale relates to safety and productivity. Turnover relates to payroll and training costs, which impact overall expenses, which impact profits. A well-designed scorecard that cascades down several levels in the organization is a prerequisite to having a meaningful set of targets or objectives. It helps to diagram interrelationships when setting targets, so that you realize how much more improvement will be needed in a leading indicator to reach a target for a lagging indicator. An example of such a diagram is shown below.

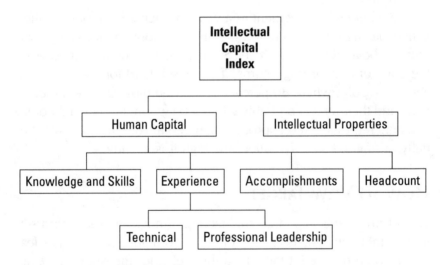

Figure 4-1. Intellectual Capital Index

Such a diagram could encompass several more levels, but this example is adequate to emphasize the importance of linking targets to metrics. For technical aspects of performance, setting these targets or standards is mostly science. For something vague like human capital, much more guesswork is involved.

PURSUING CONTINUOUS IMPROVEMENT

Some things can always be increased or improved. Investors look to stock prices to continue increasing; companies always strive to improve profits; and publicly held companies are almost always looking to expand. Beyond such obvious conclusions, though, you need to challenge the idea that performance on *all* measures needs to improve. Clearly, you do not want to see any declining trends in results. However, maintaining, rather than attempting to improve upon, a high level of performance might at times be appropriate. Improvement generally costs money and other valuable resources. Many management programs have all failed to deliver as much as they promised in improved performance without concurrently increasing costs. Doing it right the first time may be cheaper than fixing it, but doing it right sometimes takes more time and hence costs more.

Continuous improvement as a value or theme in an organization is fine. Taking this concept too literally and applying it to target setting can be a problem, however. Some aspects of performance reach the point of diminishing returns. If you work hard for many years to get to the point where 80 percent of your employees love the company and their jobs, it probably will not be worth it to reach 85 or 90 percent. Yet, that is the approach many organizations take—continually raising the bar, no matter how high it is already.

HOW TO VIEW TARGETS

One of my clients in a large engineering firm is dead set against setting quantifiable targets for any of his performance metrics. His fear is that when people hit the target, they relax for the rest of the year. This does occur when people look at target as a destination rather than a mile-marker along the route. A target is a short-term level of accomplishment that tells you that you are making progress toward your mission and vision. It's OK to take a breather and congratulate yourself after hitting a target, but you also need to realize that, in most cases, the bar will now be raised. Setting annual targets as stepping stones towards a five-year goal is much better than just setting the five-year goal. Five years is a long way off, and people don't respond well to long-term targets or goals. Break targets down into smaller increments so that progress is obvious, and then people and organizations tend to perform well.

A metric without a target provides no useful information for managing performance. Targets allow us to evaluate levels and trends in performance data and make decisions about actions to improve performance when necessary.

The checklist below will help you to properly evaluate your corporate targets and objectives.

CHECKLIST FOR EVALUATING TARGETS AND OBJECTIVES

Make sure you consider the following information when setting targets:

☐ Your overall mission and vision.

☐ How competitors perform.

☐ Your own past performance.

☐ Resource constraints, including technology.

☐ Customer and other stakeholder requirements.

☐ Impact on other targets and metrics that are related/linked.

☐ The time frame for achieving the target.

☐ How benchmark or best-in-class companies perform.

☐ Your own best performance.

☐ High-level goals or targets dictated by headquarters or the corporate office.

PART 2

DEVELOPING
STRATEGIC
METRICS AND PLANS

Gauges: Developing a Performance Index

One of the biggest challenges in designing an organizational score-card is convincing senior management to narrow it down to less than 20 metrics. Most managers are unconvinced that they can get a good feel for organizational performance by looking at a dozen or so metrics. Conceptually, they buy the idea of the vital few, but still have trouble letting go of the trivial many that they are accustomed to monitoring. A good way of satisfying some managers' need for detail while not having 50 gauges on the scorecard is to combine several separate metrics into an index. Indices are quite common on score-cards for senior managers and executives, because they need not see all the detailed metrics that make up the scorecards of their direct reports. In this chapter, you will learn when to construct such an index and how to go about creating it.

WHAT IS AN INDEX?

An index is a combination of several separate measures added together or averaged to result in a single, overall indicator of perfor-mance. We use indices in everyday life. Perhaps the best known is the Dow Jones Index, a fairly reliable indicator of the overall U.S. stock market based on the performance of 12 companies. A big change in the Dow will likely prompt you to look more closely at the stocks and/or mutual funds that you own personally. Thus, the Dow

Jones Index serves its purpose well as an overall indicator that cues investors to review the performance of their own investments. If the Dow doesn't change much, we might not bother checking our investments as assiduously.

What's Included in an Index?

Organizations need indices on their scorecards to provide a good picture of performance based on a few major gauges.

One company I worked with combines all of its major measures into one metric that reflects the overall performance of the company. Included in this index are financial performance, customer satisfaction, market share/growth, employee morale, and safety. While it would be nice if one could judge the health of an organization by looking at one number, I think this is taking the concept of an index too far. There are so many different variables included in this one index that it is probably not a good indicator of overall company performance. Furthermore, I don't know of any executive who would be content with looking at just one number each month to monitor business.

A better approach is to keep each index focused on a single aspect of performance. For example, you might have a financial performance index that combines sales with profits with growth; or a customer satisfaction index that combines customer survey data with repeat/lost customers with complaint data.

Tip: Make sure each index focuses on a single dimension of performance, such as customer satisfaction, employee morale, or financial performance.

What Does an Index Do?

A performance index allows you to combine several different metrics that are measured in different ways, and where an increase in the metric may be positive or negative, depending upon the measure. Figure 5-1 is an example of how one company combines the following metrics into an index.

As you can see from this example, four different metrics are combined into the Employee Satisfaction Index. For the first metric, the

EMPLOYEE SATISFACTION INDEX		
Metric	**Unit of Measurement**	**Good Performance**
Survey	avg. score (5-point scale)	up is good
Absenteeism	avg. percent per month	down is good
Complaints	number and severity (1–5)	down is good
Turnover index	number people quitting × level	down is good

Figure 5-1. Employee Satisfaction Index

unit of measurement is a rating on a 5-point scale, and the higher the score the better. The second metric measures absenteeism in percent, and down is better. The third and four metrics both involve counting the actual number of complaints or employees quitting and multiplying those numbers by a weighting factor, depending on the severity of the complaint or the level of the employee leaving. With both of these last two measures, a lower number is better. The magic of an index is that these four very different metrics can be combined into one overall indicator that tells us about employee satisfaction. Turnover is a lagging indicator, and perhaps the strongest indicator that employees are unhappy. The other three metrics are more minor, so they might be weighted less because they are a less serious indicator of a problem.

Constructing an Index

A step-by-step description of how to construct an index for your own scorecard follows. Examples will be provided for each step, and some models are provided for your own use.

Step 1: *Select a dimension of performance and the individual metrics to be combined.*

The first step in constructing an index is to select an area or dimension of performance on which to concentrate. Your first task in doing this is to pick one of the boxes or categories on your scorecard.

If your scorecard includes the four Kaplan and Norton boxes (i.e., Customer, Financial, Internal, and Learning and Growth), you might pick the Customer box, for example.

Once you have selected the measurement category, select the individual measures that you want combined into an index. It's OK to have both leading and lagging indicators together in one index, and it's fine to have both hard (objective) and soft measures together. It's important that the individual measures reflect the dimension of performance used to designate the index. For example, you might develop a human capital index that includes the following:

- Experience level in years
- Skill level (1–10) × importance of skill (1–10)
- Job performance rating (1–5)
- Job level (1–8)

For each step in this section, we will refer to the customer box of the scorecard, and look at a "Customer Loyalty Index" (see Figure 5-2).

The first measure is a "hard," objective measure of customer buying behavior that compares how much money customers spend with the firm compared with averages from previous years. The theory is that if customers like a company, they will spend more money with it than in the past. The second measure is a soft measure of customer opinions and perceptions gathered via a quarterly survey. The score is an overall rating out of a possible 7.0, which is the highest. The third metric looks at the relative differences in prices compared to the top three competitors. This is also a hard measure, gathered via weekly price surveys, and is expressed as a percent difference.

CUSTOMER LOYALTY INDEX

- Increases/decreases in business—existing accounts

- Customer survey score

- Competitive price differential

- Relationship level

Figure 5-2. Customer Loyalty Index

This financial measure is included in the Customer Loyalty Index because—given products that are of pretty much the same quality—price is one of the major determinants of customer purchases and overall satisfaction. The final metric in the index looks at the existing relationship level with each account. This is on a scale of 1 to 7, with a 7 indicating a long-term partnership, and a 1 indicating that the customer is trying the company out on a small order.

Step 2: *Assign weight to individual measures.*

A simplistic way of assigning a weight to each of the submeasures in an index is to make them all equal. In other words, if there are 4, they are each worth 25 percent. This is appropriate if each metric is equal in importance and equal in its ability to measure overall performance. Most of the time this is not the case—usually, some measures are much more important than others. The total of all the submeasures must equal 100 percent. Each individual metric is then assigned a weight by starting with the most important one first. Once a weight has been assigned to the most important metric, the remaining numbers are distributed across the remaining metrics. In Figure 5-3, weights are assigned to our Customer Loyalty Index.

The amount of money customers spend with us compared to previous years was given the highest rating because buying behavior is the best overall indicator of customer satisfaction. The next most important metric is the level of our relationship with each account. Relationship level is based upon a number of objective measures, such as the amount of time you have been working together and the

CUSTOMER LOYALTY INDEX	
• Increases/decreases in business—existing accounts	40%
• Customer survey score	20%
• Competitive price differential	10%
• Relationship Level	30%
	100%

Figure 5-3. Customer Loyalty Index

percentage of purchases that go to you versus your competitors. Together, these two metrics make up 70 percent of the Customer Loyalty Index. The remaining 30 percent is divided among a leading indicator of customer opinions gathered via a quarterly survey (20 percent) and the Competitive Price Differential (10 percent). The latter was given the lowest weight because many things determine customer loyalty besides price alone, and the strategy in this example is to not always offer the lowest price.

Step 3: *Establish baseline levels of performance for each metric.*

The third step in the process is to gather some actual data on current or baseline performance for each of the four metrics that will go into our index. If historical data exists, this will be an easy step. If not, you could spend several weeks or months designing the data-collection instruments and then collecting the data. For simplicity's sake, we'll assume that historical data exists on the four measures that make up our Customer Loyalty Index.

At this point, you'll want to begin using the Performance Index Worksheet. A model of this worksheet appears in Figure 5-4. Once you establish your baseline performance, you fill it in for each of the four metrics in the "0" column on the worksheet, as shown in Figure 5-5.

As you can see in Figure 5-5, writing in the current performance in the "0" column allows room for performance to get slightly worse, and quite a bit better, in the future.

Step 4: *Establish targets for each measure.*

Your next task is to set targets, for each of the four measures, for where you want performance to be in a year or so. You learned about setting targets in the previous chapter, so make sure your performance targets are not arbitrary; consider current performance, resource constraints, and other factual aspects for each measure. Using the worksheet, write the target level of performance in the 80 percent column, as in Figure 5-6.

In Figure 5-6, we have also filled in another column on the form with the weights for each of the four metrics. (If you'll recall, the weights were decided in step 2.) We are filling in the baseline and targets on the worksheet because this will allow us to convert everything

Index Title _____

Frequency: _____

MEASURES	SCALE													WT	SCORE
	−20	−10	0	10	20	30	40	50	60	70	80	90	100		
			Baseline								Target				TOTAL:

Figure 5-4. Performance Index Worksheet

EXAMPLE

MEASURES	SCALE													WT	SCORE
	−20	−10	0	10	20	30	40	50	60	70	80	90	100		
Increase/ Decrease Business			5%											40%	
Customer Survey			78											25%	
Comp. Pricing			−1											15%	
Relationship Level			3.5/ 6											30%	

Figure 5-5. Developing a Performance Index

EXAMPLE

MEASURES	SCALE													WT	SCORE
	−20	−10	0	10	20	30	40	50	60	70	80	90	100		
Increase/ Decrease Business			5%								25%			40%	
Customer Survey			78								86/ 100			25%	
Comp. Pricing			−1								−5			15%	
Relationship Level			3.5/ 6								4.3/ 6			30%	

Figure 5-6. Developing a Performance Index

to a multiple of 10; we can thus combines different units of measure into a single index.

Step 5: *Complete the scale on the worksheet.*

The next step is easy compared to the previous two. All that is required is to put a value in each box on the worksheet, so performance on each of the measures can be converted to a multiple of 10. To do this, take the difference between the target level (written in the 80 column) and the baseline level (written in the 0 column) and divide that number by seven, so a relatively equal interval appears in each box from 10 to 70. For example:

Target		Current	Difference
Increase/decrease in business	25%	5%	20 20/7 = 3
Customer survey	86	78	8 8/7 = 1

If you don't come up with a round number when dividing the difference by the number of intervals to be filled in, make them come as close to even as possible. Figure 5-7 illustrates this step.

Step 5: Complete the scale

EXAMPLE

MEASURES	SCALE													WT	SCORE
	-20	-10	0	10	20	30	40	50	60	70	80	90	100		
Increase/ Decrease Business	0	3%	5%	8%	11%	14%	17%	20%	22%	24%	25%	27%	30%	40%	
Customer Survey	76	77	78	79	81	81	82	83	84	85	86/ 100	87	88	25%	
Comp. Pricing	0	.5	-1	-1.5	-2	-2.5	-3	-3.5	-4	-4.5	-5	-6	-7	15%	
Relationship Level	3.3	3.4	3.5/ 6	3.6	3.7	3.8	3.9	4.0	4.1	4.2	4.3/ 6	4.5	4.7	30%	
		Baseline					Target						Total		

Figure 5-7. Developing a Performance Index

Step 6: *Calculate the index score based on current performance.*

The sixth and final step in the process is to measure performance again, a month or more after the initial baseline measurement was done, and calculate where you fall on the index. Follow these five steps:

1. Calculate current performance
2. Convert to multiple of 10 using worksheet
3. Multiply by weight to get subtotal
4. Repeat the process with the remaining metrics
5. Add up the total (some number less than 100)

In our example, we waited three months to collect data again on each of the four metrics in our Customer Loyalty Index. At the end of the quarter, performance looked like this:

Increase/decrease in business $13\% = 30 \times 40\% = 12$
Customer survey $84 = 60 \times 20\% = 12$
Competitive pricing $-6\% = 90 \times 10 = 9$
Relationship level $4 = 50 \times 30\% = 15$
   Total   **= 48/100**

The example worksheet in Figure 5-8 gives you a better idea of how this was done.

Step 6: Complete index score based on current performance

Increase/Decrease Business: $13\% = 30 \times 40\% = 12$
Customer Survey: $84 = 60 \times 25\% = 15$
Comp. Pricing: $-6\% = 90 \times 15\% = 13.5$
Relationship Level: $4 = 50 \times 30\% = 15$
Total: $= 55.5/100$

Figure 5-8. Developing a Performance Index

CUSTOMER SATISFACTION INDICES

Designing a performance index is a great opportunity to use creative metrics. Some of the best metrics I've seen in organizations are performance indices. Back in 1995, I was working with two groups in IBM in Manhattan. Both were using a measure they called the Net Satisfaction Index, or NSI. This index was an overall measure of customer satisfaction with IBM products and services. It was a combination of three hard measures of customer buying behavior and four soft measures of customer opinions. As I recall, the individual metrics were weighted as follows:

- Market share   20%   • Repeat/lost business   20%
- Mail survey   10%   • Telephone survey   10%
- Complaints   10%   • Focus groups   10%
- Growth in sales—existing customer accounts   20%

The index was a great example because it focused on one dimension of performance—customer satisfaction—and included a mix of leading and lagging indicators that were weighted unequally. It made sense to assign the greater weights to the measures of customer buying behavior, because this is a truer indicator of overall satisfaction.

Another company combines the attractiveness of each customer with their level of satisfaction with their loyalty to the company and its products. This measure turned out to be a great way of encouraging employees to focus on their most valuable customers and not worry about building high levels of loyalty from all of them.

GROWTH INDICES

Another company I've worked with was looking to expand into new markets. Simply measuring growth in sales could be misleading, because the growth could come from within existing markets. They decided to develop a growth index wherein a dollar in sales would be multiplied by a series of factors such as geography, new industry, new company, and new product to existing market. In other words, the value of a dollar in sales to a targeted market, geography, or customer would go up. This gauge turned out to be a good measure, and when salespeople's compensation was linked to it, the company experienced more rapid growth in its targeted area and industries.

PUBLIC RELATIONS INDEX

Public relations and image are considered important by most organizations, but few have developed good ways of measuring this aspect of performance. A federal government facility I've worked with for several years actually does a great job of measuring performance in this area. Included in its public relations index are the following metrics:

- Opinions of important politicians for or against their causes
- Votes in favor or not in favor of their causes
- Public opinion/image
- Positive or negative press and the publications it appears in.

The Public Relations Index was on the scorecard of the director and his direct reports as one of their key metrics.

A number of other examples of indices can be found in Chapter 11 and in the case studies in the appendices.

MIXING INDICES WITH OTHER METRICS

Scorecards for CEOs and other top executives tend to include more indices because people at this level are supposed to spend more time thinking strategically about the organization's future than managing the day-to-day operations. Performance indices make sense for executives who need to monitor performance, but usually not at the level of detail needed by lower-level managers. Executive scorecards tend to have more indices because lower-level metrics often roll up into these indices. It is permissible and actually recommended that your scorecard include a combination of discrete metrics and performance indices. Most well-designed executive scorecards I've seen contain no more than two thirds of the measures as indices.

For lower-level managers and individual contributors, no more than half of the scorecard metrics should be indices.

It's tempting to make all of the metrics for senior managers' indices, so as not to exclude any important measures. However, this is almost as bad as having 40 different measures on the scorecard—expressing all metrics as indices also becomes confusing. A person can remember the make-up of four or five indices, but probably not fifteen of them. Organizations that use one of the balanced scorecard software packages I review in Chapter 12 can handle more indices on their scorecards because scanning the detailed submeasures requires only a click of the button.

Tip: *Include a mix of performance indices and discrete metrics on your scorecard.*

THE DANGER OF PERFORMANCE INDICES

There are two major concerns with using indices to measure organizational performance. One is that an index may obscure important changes by folding data in with other measures. For example, a manager might not notice a big jump in turnover of middle managers if turnover is combined with a variety of other metrics to form an employee satisfaction index. Indices are summaries, and averages or summaries are sometimes not the best way of judging performance. For example, if we averaged all of the various measurements of a person's health, the readings might indicate a very healthy individual. This averaging may, however, lighten the emphasis on one specific problem area, such as a high cholesterol reading. Some of the software programs I review in Chapter 12 solve this problem by building "idiot lights" into the dashboard. For example, a gauge might show green, or healthy, performance, but if one of the submeasures or "under the hood" metrics is yellow or red, the idiot light will flash, alerting the manager to look beyond the gauge that shows the performance index.

Tip: *Dashboard software packages make performance indices more practical for and understandable by employees.*

A second, lesser concern with indices is that employees will not understand them. Many find the whole concept of an index a little complicated. People understand discrete numbers like sales or turnover better than indices, which combine a number of inputs. I know a lot of people who don't really understand the Dow Jones Index, or the Index of Leading Economic Indicators, but who do understand what it means when their stock drops $2 a share or when unemployment hits 6 percent. As stated, performance indices are more valuable for executive and upper-management scorecards, because at this level performance is analyzed from an overall, macro perspective.

Use the checklist that follows to guide your efforts to construct an effective performance index.

CHECKLIST FOR CONSTRUCTING A PERFORMANCE INDEX

When constructing a performance index, make sure that you:

☐ Limit the index to a single dimension of performance, such as customers, finances, or innovation/learning.

☐ Try to include no more than seven submeasures in a single index.

☐ Select submeasures that can all be measured with the same frequency.

☐ Use a 100-point scale for the index because it allows for enough variability in performance and is easily understood.

☐ Collect baseline data for several months or periods prior to setting targets for the submeasures.

☐ Assign weights to the submeasures based on their importance and their strength as indicators of overall performance in the area being measured.

☐ Try to include both leading and lagging indicators within your index.

☐ Don't put too much weight on the lagging indicators, or the index will not help to predict problems.

☐ Don't overuse this approach to measurement by making *all* metrics on your scorecards performance indices.

☐ Calculate the index score using several different weightings for a time in order to see which approach produces the most sensitive and best overall gauge of performance.

☐ Fine-tune the index as you gain more experience with it.

☐ Be careful of an index that never moves because submeasures tend to cancel each other out.

Vision: Deciding What You Want to Become

One of the keys to a good organizational plan is that everyone understands the company's vision of where it wants to be in the future. Whereas a mission statement is present-focused and defines an organization's objectives, a vision statement is future-focused and defines the organization's goals for the next three to ten years. The mission statement keeps an organization focused on its key customers, products, and services and helps to ensure that new business opportunities fit within the scope of that mission. The vision statement however, defines a *future* state, or a goal the organization wants to achieve. It is important to distinguish between mission and vision statements, because they have different purposes. Trying to combine both into a single paragraph leads to a garbled message and confused employees.

Most large companies and government organizations have developed vision statements during the past few years. Based on my observations and consulting experience, however, most of them are poorly written and fail to provide a clear description where the organization wants to be in the future; they are vague, unverifiable, unrealistic, and developed without much of a focus on the future.

A TYPICAL VISION STATEMENT

A typical approach to developing company mission and vision statements is to send the executive team off to a resort for a couple of days and make them work until they reach consensus on the key components of the strategic plan. None of the internal staff members wants the job of keeping all of the executives' big egos on task, so a strategic planning consultant is usually brought in from the outside to facilitate the meeting. The consultant gets the participants to brainstorm a list of 40 to 50 words that define the company's future vision. The list is then reviewed, prioritized, discussed, and distilled into a nice sentence that articulates the future vision of the organization. This statement is often wordsmithed to death by the group for four to six hours until everyone is tired enough to quit fighting or agrees the vision statement is complete. The end product is usually so filled with jargon and trendy catchphrases that, if questioned, the executives would have a hard time explaining it in plain language. The consultant likes it though, and everyone is too sick of the process to edit it any further. Most are anxious to get on to more important planning topics, like goals and strategies.

Tip: *Writing a vision statement with a team can be a painful experience that rarely produces a clear output.*

If you must go this route, why not save a day's meeting time and the fee you would pay a strategic planning consultant by using my Vision Generator in Figure 6-1 instead? I developed it after reviewing the convoluted visions of many business and government organizations. Using the words and phrases in the lists, string together appropriate choices from each column to construct your vision statement. Don't spare the adjectives, and feel free to add any buzzwords I may have forgotten.

Vision Statements That Say Nothing

The Vision Generator illustrates the pitfalls of relying on platitudes in place of a creative, germane, and achievable vision statement. Consider the examples in Figure 6-1, which might have emerged full-blown from the Generator.

VISION GENERATOR		
A List	**B List**	**C List**
World class	Producer	Leading-edge
Leading	Manufacturer	Innovative
Premier	Provider	Market-driven
Benchmark	Distributor	Value-added
Biggest	Developer	Benchmark-level
World's best	Processor	Highest quality
Preferred	Supplier	Cost-effective
Number One	Facilitator	Customer-focused

D List	**E List**
Solutions	Empowered employees
Products	Highest quality materials
Services	The best technology
Systems	High-performance teams
Data	New paradigms
Materials	Leading-edge systems

F List	**G List**
Synergistic fashion	Meet the real needs of customers
Total quality manner	Delight our customers
Reengineered processes	Exceed stakeholder expectations
Our core competencies	Deliver consistent profits and growth
Market-driven	Supplier of choice

Figure 6-1. Vision Generator

Our vision is to be the Number One manufacturer of the highest quality, most innovative products for the consumer products electronics industry, using the best technology and high-performance teams, capitalizing on our core competencies to consistently exceed all of our stakeholders' expectations.

Our vision is to become a world class, leading-edge supplier of benchmark-level systems for the financial services industry, using self-directed teams in a synergistic fashion to delight our customers, shareholders, and employees.

Our vision is to be the Number One developer of innovative, leading-edge solutions for the real problems of our customers, using leading-edge technology and our empowered workforce to produce consistently excellent financial results for our shareholders.

Tip: *Vision statements are supposed to communicate clearly to everyone where your company is going— so avoid jargon and buzzwords.*

Some companies prefer a vision that is terse and to the point. Yet, these are often no better or any clearer than some of the longer examples given. Some common ones I've seen:

- Simply world class
- To be the best
- Supplier of choice, investment of choice, employer of choice
- To be the benchmark
- Still here next year
- Still alive in 2005

Why Even Bother?

After reading such jargon-filled examples, you might wonder why an organization made up of intelligent people would bother wasting a day or more crafting a meaningless vision statement that mimics those presented here. Good question. The answer is that a vision is crucial for *any* organization's long term survival and success. Even a small business needs to have some sort of vision, which might simply involve staying in business for the next 10 years without changing, growing, or doing anything differently. A vision statement is the beginning step in any strategic plan. It should not only articulate what the organization is trying to accomplish, but also serve to inspire all its employees to help achieve the vision.

CHARACTERISTICS OF A GOOD VISION STATEMENT

Determining a vision for the future is one of the most important decisions a company must make. The absence of a vision can lead to constant haggling and a workforce that lacks direction. Investments are difficult to make without having a clear vision against which to evaluate each new opportunity or problem that inevitably arises. If you select the wrong vision and focus on the wrong aspects of performance, it could spell your demise. A chemical company that focused for years on its vision of providing the best service found out its customers did not really care about service—it was fine already—but they *were* interested in lower prices. Thus, achieving the vision—differentiating the company from its competitors through service alone—did not lead to the ultimate goal of gaining market share.

Defining your future vision requires careful thought and should not be delegated to consultants or anyone other than the senior leaders of the organization. If you think that it is difficult and risky to decide where the company is truly going in the future, you're right. There is a risk that you will establish the wrong vision. However, not having one, or having one that is vague, makes it almost certain that you will have future problems competing with other companies.

A good vision statement should be:

- Succinct
- Verifiable
- Focused
- Understandable to all employees
- Inspirational
- Memorable

A good vision statement paints a picture in every employee's minds of where the organization wants to be in the future. It is important that the vision be succinct, so that employees can remember it without having to refer to a poster in the lobby or a wallet card. Succinct doesn't have to mean stupid, however; Starbucks' vision states, "2000 stores by 2000."

A vision should also be verifiable. In other words, you ought to be able to tell whether or not it has been achieved. It would be hard to say, for example, when a company becomes "world class" or "the benchmark." A verifiable vision is one that 10 people could agree has or has not been achieved. The time frame for a vision is generally three to five years. It is hard for many organizations to visualize beyond that period.

The vision should also be focused on one or two aspects of company performance that are important for future success. Certain things like growth, profits, safety, and so forth should not all be addressed in the vision, or it becomes too cloudy. The vision should focus on the major goal the company is trying to achieve. For example, back in 1993, Ericsson's Cellular Phones division defined their vision as: "Number three in market share by 2000." At the time, they were number eight or nine in market share. Executives at Ericsson believed that the cellular phone business would belong to three or four companies by the year 2000, and they wanted to be at least number three. For several years, they focused their attention on this vision, developing strategies that focused on brand recognition and growth. In 1997, Ericsson became number three in market share—three years ahead of schedule—and they are now number two! Ericsson is now focused on a different vision that addresses financial results and product quality.

A vision should not stay the same forever. Once a vision has been achieved, a new one must be written to encourage the organization to continually improve.

An organization writes a vision statement in order to communicate direction to all of its employees. It is important for every employee to understand the vision so he or she can help the company achieve it. A major problem with many typical vision statements is that most employees don't understand them. You can see their eyes glaze over as executives roll out the vision in a series of companywide meetings, discussing their desire to become a world-class, leading-edge, customer-focused company. In my experience, most people don't use words and phrases like "world class" and "leading-edge" in daily conversation. Executives, consultants, and Dilbert might do so, but they are in the minority. One company, whose vision was "Simply World Class," conducted focus groups with employees, asking them what this statement meant to them. They received as many answers as they had employees; no one was sure what "world class" really meant, but everyone had a guess.

Finally, a vision statement should inspire employees. It ought to make them feel good about the direction of the company and drive them to excel. One of the best examples of vision statements I've read is Cargill's:

> *"We will raise the living standards around the world by delivering increased value to producers and consumers."*

Notice that this vision statement doesn't say anything about profits, safety, ethics, employee development, new products/services, or any of the many other things a successful business must focus on. It's not that these issues are ignored—Cargill certainly performs well in all of these areas. It's just that they want to keep their vision straightforward and focused on their major goals.

Tip: A good vision should be innately
memorable and inspirational.

THREE TYPES OF VISIONS

Based on my review of many good and bad vision statements, I have grouped them into three general categories:

- Growth visions
- Change visions
- Recognition visions

Growth Visions

Most publicly held companies, as well as a number of privately owned ones, desire to grow their business in the future. Growth might focus on a number of factors: sales volume, market share, number of facilities or locations, profits, stock price, or overall value. Before establishing a growth vision, think about whether bigger is better. Big companies and government organizations are often riddled with bureaucracy and waste, which only increase as they become even larger. Mergers and acquisitions often allow for economies of scale and greater clout with suppliers, but large organizations are often slow to change and adapt, and they lose any entrepreneurial spirit they may have had when they were younger and smaller. In many industries, a few big companies against which small companies cannot compete hold the market. For example, we now have only a few aerospace companies, when there were over a dozen a few years ago. The same can be said of telephone companies. The break-up of AT&T created a number of smaller companies that are now buying each other up and becoming vast enterprises with customers across many states.

If growth is the key portion of your vision that you want to emphasize, concentrate on one or two dimensions of growth and make sure that the vision follows the rules described earlier for being verifiable, brief, and focused. Growth visions alone are often not too inspirational to employees.

Tip: *Bigger is not always better, so be careful before settling in on a growth vision. Being a profitable, good place to work might be more important than getting larger.*

Change Visions

Another type of vision is to somehow transform your organization in the future. Change visions are appropriate for organizations that wish to develop new products or services, expand into new markets, change their position in the marketplace, eliminate existing aspects of the organization, or simply survive. Sears is an organization that had to create a change-focused vision in order to survive. The strategy they employed during the 1980s and early 1990s was no longer working, so they created a new vision that stated Sears would become a:

- Compelling place to shop
- Compelling place to work
- Compelling place to invest

Their vision also involved creating a different image for their stores; hence, the "softer side of Sears" ad campaign. They wanted to bring back the customers that they had lost over the years to Wal-Mart, Target, Penney's, and other competitors, and to attract new customers who had never thought of buying clothing, cosmetics, or other such soft goods from Sears. Although the Sears' vision is brief and addresses customer, shareholders, and investors, it is still quite vague and unverifiable. How will they know when Sears becomes compelling?

Change visions are also important for many government organizations today. The Internal Revenue Service has received a lot of heat during the last few years, along with talk of eliminating the IRS altogether by politicians in favor of a flat tax. I would think that a vision of business as usual, or growth, would be inappropriate for the IRS. It clearly must change or face dismantling. The American public seems to be clamoring for a "kinder, gentler" IRS, or at least one that will make drastically alter the way it operates. The Department of Energy is another organization that needs a change-focused vision—like the IRS, the very existence of the DOE is being questioned by the government. Neither of these federal agencies is likely to disappear soon, but they both need a vision that focuses on becoming a different type of agency.

Organizations that need to change in order to survive should not write a vision statement along the lines of "Still here next year." While this in fact may *be* the vision, it must be stated more positively and focus on exactly how you expect to survive and prosper.

Recognition Visions

The third and final category of vision statements focuses on recognition. For example, you might decide to focus on your employees and being recognized as one of the "100 best companies to work for in America" or some such similar distinction as bestowed annually by the likes of *Fortune* magazine. Southwest Airlines received the honor in 2000 of being the number two best company to work for in the United States, according to *Fortune* magazine (January 10, 2000). The Container Store was rated number one. It might be your goal to receive the same recognition.

Jamie Houghton, CEO of Corning, created a vision that his company would be among the most admired in America even though when he first took over as CEO, Corning was anything but that. He decided his vision would be verified by whether or not Corning was included in *Fortune* magazine's annual list of most-admired companies. He felt this was a good measure, because being listed required excellent financial results, stock performance, and a large number of CEOs from other large companies who believed that the company was well managed. Corning actually achieved this vision, and then some—it was listed by *Fortune* as one of America's most-admired companies, and it also won a Baldrige Award.

Recognition might also focus on safety, environmental performance, innovation, reputation, quality, or many other factors. Being recognized as the first choice of customers might be a suitable recognition vision. Rolls Royce or Rolex may have had a vision at one time to be recognized as the manufacturer of the best quality cars or watches in the world. Both companies have maintained this recognition over many years, in spite of attempts by competitors to steal it. Neither company seems concerned with market share, because their products will always be geared to a very specific, small market. Volvo had a different vision, which focused on being recognized for building the safest car. Although other automobiles have performed as well or better than Volvo in crash tests, Volvo still has maintained its association with safety.

DEVELOPING YOUR VISION STATEMENT

I emphasized earlier the folly of trying to write a vision statement by committee. But if a committee shouldn't write it, then how does it get crafted to ensure a broad range of input? Discover Financial Services used an approach that worked quite well. A market research professional spent about an hour interviewing each of the company's eight vice presidents, and asking them where they thought the company ought to go in the future. He asked open-ended questions, such as: "How do you think the consolidation going on in your industry will impact our future?" He also asked some close-ended questions, like: "Should we offer debit cards, or just stick with credit cards?" He summarized the results of the interviews with the executives and presented the information to the company's president. The president was asked to read all the input from his report directs and write a vision statement that was succinct, inspirational, verifiable, and memorable, without using any buzzwords. The idea was that the president would walk into the planning meeting a month later and lay the vision on the team—and that everyone would love it.

What actually happened was that the vision read more like a list of financial goals than a vision statement. The executive team offered some ideas on how to simplify the vision without losing its intent, and within 30 minutes the group agreed on a new vision statement for the company. It helped to have the president's first draft to begin with, and having the executive team contribute to simplifying the vision helped create their buy-in. I have worked with dozens of organizations to help them write vision statements, and the process we used at Discover worked better than any other approach I've tried. We duplicated this approach in each unit of the company to create additional vision statements, and it worked equally well. Everyone still had input, and we didn't waste hours in front of a flipchart wordsmithing a statement until it became meaningless.

We conclude this chapter with a checklist for thoroughly evaluating vision statements.

CHECKLIST FOR EVALUATING VISION STATEMENTS

A good vision statement should be...

☐ A single sentence.

☐ Inspirational—it makes employees feel good about working for the organization.

☐ Written in plain English, without any buzzwords.

☐ Clearly understood by all employees.

☐ Focused on one or two aspects of performance, versus many.

☐ Verifiable—you can tell whether you have achieved it or not.

☐ Linked/integrated with parent or related organization's vision.

☐ Cited by employees without their referring to wallet cards or gimmicks.

☐ Developed by the CEO or leader, not a committee.

☐ Examined each year to determine if it is still valid.

☐ Realistic, given the organization's current position and resource constraints.

☐ Subject to change, not carved in stone.

Situation Analysis: Identifying Strengths, Weaknesses, Opportunities, and Threats

An important aspect of any planning exercise is to evaluate your company's existing strengths and weaknesses to formulate a strategy for success. The problem with doing this sort of assessment yourself is that it's hard to be objective about your own organization. In this chapter, you'll learn how to conduct a comprehensive assessment of your organization using the Baldrige Award criteria. Most leading organizations today use the Baldrige criteria as an important component of their strengths, weaknesses, opportunities, and threats (SWOT) analysis (also known as situation analysis) done during the planning process. You'll also learn what the Baldrige criteria do *not* address, and how these other factors can help provide a more thorough assessment.

THE TYPICAL APPROACH TO INTERNAL ASSESSMENT

The typical approach to completing this step in the planning process is to appoint a committee to gather data on the organization's strengths and weaknesses, and then summarize this data in a report or presentation. The committee conducts interviews of management, reviews internal audit reports that may be relevant, and summarizes the company's strengths and weaknesses at the beginning of the strategic planning meeting. The typical agenda for such a meeting is shown in Figure 7-1.

**TYPICAL PLANNING MEETING AGENDA
DAYS 1–2**

• Review of past year's performance

• Review of industry trends

• Review of technology trends

• Review of competitive environment

• Review of product/service strengths and weaknesses

• Review of strengths, weaknesses, and trends in the human resources area

• Review of new product/service development progress

Figure 7-1. Typical Planning Meeting Agenda

The first two days of the planning process usually consist of a series of presentations on each of the topics listed above. Presentations are made by members of the planning committee, who are often asked to leave after their presentations in case any really sensitive information surfaces that only senior executives should discuss. Members of this committee are usually not, therefore, senior executives, but tend to belong to either the planning department or a cross-functional team of individuals from many different departments. The executives usually listen patiently to the presentation of the organization's strengths and weaknesses. When the presentation is over, however, the meeting often falls apart as the executives begin challenging the findings—are the weaknesses really *important* weaknesses? are the strengths *really* strengths? The committee often leaves the meeting feeling devastated and wondering how their thoroughly researched findings could be rendered so irrelevant. The problem is usually not that the findings are inaccurate, but rather that executives just don't like to see the weaknesses in their areas identified; and furthermore, executives as a group often tend to argue and debate.

Another problem with this agenda is that the first couple of days are spent listening to presentations. This gets boring, and it is not the best way of communicating the information needed to complete a situation analysis. One company I worked with streamlined the situation analysis phase of their planning process by writing a 20-page summary of the factors addressed in a situation analysis and sending it out prior to the meeting, insisting that each executive read it and understand it so that meeting time could be spent developing plans rather than listening to presentations. Members of the planning committee had one-on-one meetings with each executive to review the situation analysis report and answer questions prior to the major planning meeting. This proved to be an effective approach that not only shortened the length of the planning meeting, but also allowed the executives to spend their time developing goals and strategies rather than attending presentations.

Tip: *Do your situation analysis before the planning meeting, document it in a report, and briefly (e.g., for about an hour) review the findings in the planning meeting.*

Using Consultants

Rather than having the staff conduct an internal assessment, many organizations hire a consulting firm to evaluate their strengths and weaknesses. Consultants can often be much more objective and professional in this role because of their experience working with a number of different organizations. Also, as opposed to an internal group, consultants more confidently convey the plain truth. Furthermore, consultants have more credibility in general because they don't work for your company and thus lack biases.

There are, however, ways to use consultants wisely and ways to use them foolishly. The consultants' objectivity might be compromised if they represent a firm that specializes in selling a particular information technology system. For example, conducting a business assessment might involve a half dozen consultants working for four to six weeks, which might cost the organization $100,000 or more. However, designing and implementing an information technology system might go for a price tag of $10 million or more, and employ 30 to 40 consultants for longer than a year. I recommend finding a consulting firm that does not specialize in selling a particular type of intervention or system. Consultants will be much more objective if they are not using your assessment as an opportunity tool to sell you a big project.

USING THE BALDRIGE CRITERIA TO IDENTIFY STRENGTHS AND WEAKNESSES

In order to evaluate your strengths and weaknesses effectively, you must use a good assessment model. There is no better approach, nor one more widely accepted, than the criteria from the Malcolm Baldrige National Quality Award. The Baldrige criteria have been used by thousands of organizations since 1988 and have become accepted throughout the world as the model for organizational effectiveness. The stock prices of winners of the Baldrige Award from 1988 through 1998 outperformed the S&P Index by three to one! Even finalists for the award performed twice as well as the S&P Index.

The Baldrige criteria began as an attempt to identify companies that were doing a good job with the new management technique called Total Quality Management, or TQM. The Baldrige criteria changed significantly over the years, until they evolved into an overall model for assessing an organization's strengths and weaknesses. Most of the Fortune 500 use the Baldrige criteria for assessment, along with every branch of the U.S. military, other federal government agencies, schools, hospitals, and other nonprofit institutions. Roughly half of the Baldrige criteria (categories 1–6) addresses the approaches, processes, and systems the company employs to run its day-to-day business. The remainder looks at a company's results over the last five to seven years, including financials, market data, customer satisfaction, growth, employee satisfaction, and operational and regulatory data. Figure 7-2 outlines the major criteria in the Baldrige Award for 2000.

Tip: *The Baldrige criteria are the most widely accepted model for evaluating the health of any organization—use them as the template for your own SWOT evaluation.*

2000 BALDRIGE CRITERIA	
1. Leadership	**125 points**
1.1 Organizational Leadership	
1.2 Corporate Responsibility and Citizenship	
2.0 Strategic Planning	**85 points**
2.1 Strategy Development	
2.2 Strategy Deployment	
3.0 Customer and Market Focus	**85 points**
3.1 Customer and Market Knowledge	
3.2 Customer Satisfaction and Relationships	
4.0 Information and Analysis	**85 points**
4.1 Measures of Organizational Performance	
4.2 Analysis of Organizational Performance	
5.0 Human Resource Focus	**85 points**
5.1 Work Systems	
5.2 Employee Education, Training, and Development	
5.3 Employee Well-Being and Satisfaction	
6.0 Process Management	**85 points**
6.1 Product and Service Processes	
6.2 Support Processes	
6.3 Supplier and Partnering Processes	
7.0 Business Results	**450 points**
7.1 Customer Focused Results	
7.2 Financial and Market Results	
7.3 Human Resource Results	
7.4 Supplier and Partner Results	
7.5 Organizational Effectiveness Results	

Figure 7-2. 2000 Baldrige Criteria

The Leadership Category

The first category in the Baldrige criteria includes two items: 1.1 Organizational Leadership , and 1.2 Corporate Responsibility and Citizenship. The first item asks how you have designed a leadership system to provide the organization with direction, control, and clear values. Many successful companies have a charismatic leader but lack a good leadership system. The Baldrige criteria ask about succession planning, organizational structure, and other factors that ensure that your success is not dependent upon one senior executive. In order to receive a high score in this area, you need to demonstrate how you have cloned your CEO or CO and built a strong leadership team that works cohesively. Great organizations carefully select each member of their executive team, so that they all have the same basic values but complement each other's strengths and weaknesses. This first section also evaluates the organization's image in the community, and what it does to promote ethical behavior, volunteerism, charitable contributions, and development of products/services that don't harm people or the environment. Organizations that are effective in this area tend to go beyond legal and regulatory requirements and are proactive in their approach to charitable and community support. That is, these organizations do not wait for charities to request donations—they heartily focus on supporting a select few causes/groups.

The Strategic Planning Category

This second category focuses on having a systematic approach to planning (2.1) and a clear, well thought-out plan for achieving your vision and beating your competitors (2.2). Following the planning process suggested in this book is one way of achieving a good assessment on item 2.1; however, a different planning model may be just as effective. All that is required is for you to have a systematic approach to planning that has been evaluated and improved over the years. It is also important that planning is completed quickly, so most of the year can be spent running the business. Item 2.2 evaluates the quality of the current or last year's strategic and annual plans. Strengths and weaknesses will be identified relating to your vision, key success factors, targets/goals, and strategies. This item also looks at the communication of your plan throughout the organization. One of the best ways of accomplishing this is through regular review meetings, wherein the progress of the plan is discussed. Deploying scorecard software on your organization's intranet site is also an effective method for communicating progress toward your goals or targets. (Chapter 12 includes a detailed description of how software programs help you communicate performance data and plans.)

The Customer and Market Focus Category

Category 3 of the Baldrige criteria asks how well you have identified your various customers, segmenting them by common characteristics and recognizing their needs and priorities. This is particularly difficult for government organizations, which may have a variety of customers and stakeholders. Along with the thoroughness of your market research, this section also asks how you measure customer satisfaction and go about building strong alliances with important customers so that they remain important customers. Many organizations receive low marks in this area of performance because they rely on poorly constructed surveys to measure customer satisfaction and often cannot link customer satisfaction to buying behavior or loyalty. Even satisfied customers can be lured away by competitors through lower prices, new features, or novelty.

The Information and Analysis Category

This section of the Baldrige criteria focuses on collecting and using data in order to run your organization properly. The first item asks for evidence that a well-balanced set of performance measures have been identified that link into your strategic plan. This item also asks how you collect data on competitors and other comparable organizations. The second item in this section asks how you analyze and use performance data on your company and competitors to plan and make key business decisions. This section also asks for evidence of established correlations between leading and lagging indicators of performance—for example, being able to show the link between customer satisfaction and financial performance. (Most of the information in this book relates to categories 2 and 4 in the Baldrige criteria.)

The Human Resource Focus Category

This section addresses the strengths and weaknesses of your human resource systems. It asks about recruiting, job design, recognition, compensation, training/development, safety, and overall employee satisfaction/morale. The emphasis here is on linking together various HR systems to drive the right behavior from employees, and making sure that HR efforts are tied to company strategy and goals. Organizations that receive high scores in this category identify their key competencies and develop systems for acquiring or developing those competencies. This section also asks for evidence of a preventive-based approach to safety and employee well-being. Efforts to make your organization a great place to work are also examined. Companies like Southwest Airlines have found that delighting employees leads to happy and loyal customers, and that customer loyalty leads to consistent growth and profitability.

The Process Management Category

This section of the Baldrige criteria asks how you define and control your key work processes and thus ensure consistency in your products and services. It also asks how those processes are evaluated and improved, and how you select and manage suppliers and partners. This section is extremely important because it looks at how you run your operations and control variables that might lead to quality problems with your products and/or services. Many organizations assign much of their work to contractors or suppliers; this section asks about the criteria you employ to select high-performing suppliers and how you partner with them to achieve common goals.

The Business Results Category

The seventh and final category in the Baldrige criteria, which asks about your business results, is worth almost half the points. Results are divided into five separate categories, each asking about a different type of data. In each of the five items in this last section, the criteria call for evidence of positive trends over multiple years and evidence that your levels of performance are superior to industry averages, your own targets, and major competitors. Hence, having comparative data is critical in this category.

ASSESSING YOUR COMPANY AGAINST THE BALDRIGE CRITERIA

The most common approach to assessing your strengths and weaknesses against the Baldrige criteria is to prepare a 50-page application that summarizes your systems, processes, and results. The application is then evaluated by a team of trained examiners (external or internal), who verify the information in the application though an on-site audit. Telecommunication giant Ericsson has used the Baldrige criteria for assessing the strengths and weaknesses of each of its business units for the last few years. Ericsson picks a group of examiners, which includes some of the best people in the company. After extensive training, the 50 or so examiners spend several days evaluating each of the Ericsson business units and then do a follow-up visit for a few days to gather additional information. Each business unit receives a detailed feedback report summarizing its strengths and weaknesses in each of the seven Baldrige Categories, along with scores on each item in the criteria. These feedback reports are then used as part of the SWOT analysis that each unit does as part of its annual planning process.

Tip: Organizations that do Baldrige assessments and don't link them to the strategic planning process rarely get any benefit from the assessments. Make the assessment part of your SWOT analysis.

Cargill, a large corporation about the same size as Ericsson, uses a similar approach to evaluate its businesses. At Cargill the assessment is voluntary, and those that receive the best scores receive recognition in the form of awards from senior management. The "Chairman's Award" has become a coveted accomplishment over the years because it remains very difficult to attain. Executives in business units that win the Chairman's Award are often promoted to the best jobs in the company, so recognition is taken very seriously. Cargill trains a team of over 120 examiners each year to complete assessments of its business units. The criteria and application format are exactly the same as for the Baldrige Award process. About half the applicants receive follow-up site visits to gather additional data, and all applicants receive feedback reports that they use as input for their strategic plans.

The Focus Group Baldrige Assessment

An alternative to writing a 50-page application that summarizes your performance according to the Baldrige criteria is to evaluate your organization during a meeting of the senior executives. The assessment team will usually consist of the senior executive team with perhaps a few others less highly placed who are closer to understanding the real strengths and weaknesses of the company at a grassroots level. After being trained on the criteria, the team spends about a day or two identifying the company's strengths and weaknesses in each of the Baldrige categories and items. Discover Financial Services uses this approach; in fact, they have modified the Baldrige criteria by putting it into an easy-to-follow workbook. Internal facilitators lead the assessment meeting and prepare a feedback report at the end of the session. Sheraton Hotels uses a similar approach. They have taken the Baldrige criteria even further than Discover Financial Services by preparing their own list of hotel-specific criteria to supplement the 27 Baldrige assessment items. The Coast Guard has done its own interpretation of the Baldrige criteria as well. Customizing the criteria in the lexicon of your own industry makes the assessment much easier and more objective.

Tip: Focus group Baldrige assessments work best when
a draft list of strengths and weaknesses has been
prepared prior to the meeting.

STATE AWARD PROGRAMS

Just about every state in America has its own award program based on the Baldrige criteria. A number of companies with which I'm familiar, and many government organizations as well, prepare applications for their state-level Baldrige awards as a way to receive feedback from outsiders at a very reasonable cost. Applying for most state awards costs a few thousand dollars. For this investment, you will receive an assessment by a team of four to six individuals, along with a 25-page feedback report on your corporate strengths and weaknesses. The same sort of assessment from a consulting firm would cost between $15,000 and $25,000. In addition to receiving feedback from outsiders, many organizations find that they also receive an award, which helps to recognize the efforts of their employees. Most states distribute different levels of awards, depending upon an organization's overall score. For example, many states use the bronze, silver, and gold award strategy popularized by the Olympics. For information on state award programs and how they can be used to assess your strengths and weaknesses, contact the National Institute of Standards and Technology at (301) 975-2036.

Tip: Make use of state award examiners to get feedback on your organization's strengths and weaknesses at a very low cost.

ALTERNATIVE MODELS FOR ASSESSMENT

The Baldrige criteria represent the broadest and most widely accepted model for assessing an organization's strengths and weaknesses. Although these criteria provide a fairly detailed set of findings, your strategic plan may require a more detailed analysis of individual aspects of your organization. A number of companies follow the ISO 9000 or ISO 14000 criteria. An ISO assessment is done by a team of outside auditors who examine your manufacturing processes, quality systems, documentation, and a variety of other variables involved in producing consistently good products and services. The ISO 14000 standards involve an assessment of your systems for controlling environmental hazards and disposing of waste properly. The automotive industry has designed its own assessment criteria for assessing suppliers: QS 9000. The QS 9000 criteria incorporate much of the ISO 9000 criteria along with a few that are unique to the automotive industry. The Software Engineering Institute (SEI) evaluates the information technology functions in organizations using a process very similar to

the Baldrige Award and provides both feedback and levels of certifi-
cation based on the sophistication of an organization's systems.
Many IT organizations and companies in the software business use
the SEI model for evaluating their strengths and weaknesses as part of
their overall planning processes.

OTHER FACTORS TO EVALUATE

Performing a Baldrige assessment on your organization is a thorough
and often humbling approach to pinpointing strengths and weaknesses. Although the assessment is quite comprehensive, it does not
provide all of the information needed to develop a good strategic
plan. Some other areas of importance in the assessment process are
described below.

Product/Service Quality Assessment

Identifying the strengths and weaknesses of your entire product/
service line-up is an important dimension of planning. This assessment should look at quality, design, innovation, consistency, ease of
use, and any other factor that might be important in comparing your
products and services to others in the marketplace. Doing this sort of
assessment internally can be a problem because of a lack of objectivity. Quality measures like defects can be assessed using internal
data, but more subjective aspects, such as innovation and ease of
use, might be better evaluated by an outside expert.

Intellectual Capital

Evaluating the strengths and weaknesses of your human resources is
also crucial. The Baldrige assessment does examine HR planning,
work design, training, safety, and employee morale. It looks at the
degree to which you have systems in place for performing HR functions. In addition, it looks at HR results, but these results tend to be
measures of the past like turnover, accidents, or morale survey data.
 Intellectual capital has become a key differentiating factor for
many companies today. An objective evaluation of your core competencies—the major groupings of skills needed to perform your mission—is necessary. For example, a core competency for Toyota is its

manufacturing technology. A core competency for 3M is innovation and new product development. The degree to which you invest in and protect your intellectual capital may be an important aspect of your overall planning process.

Intellectual capital includes the collective brainpower of staff and partners as well as proprietary products and technologies. It does depend upon the business, however. If you run a chain of Laundromats, or a gardening business, intellectual capital might not be worth a separate assessment. However, in many business and government organizations, core competencies are even more important than products or services. High-tech companies whose products become obsolete in a year or two need to focus more attention on their ability to continue to churn out good products to meet market demands, rather than assess the quality of existing products. In an organization where intellectual capital is important, you need to evaluate your present strengths and weaknesses as well as your systems for developing and acquiring additional skills needed to meet future demands.

OPPORTUNITIES AND THREATS

Up to this point, we have been discussing only the first half of a situation analysis: strengths and weaknesses. A thorough analysis also includes an evaluation of threats and opportunities. This information must come from sources other than a Baldrige assessment.

Companies like Hertz, Sony, Microsoft, McDonald's, and others that are seen as leaders and pioneers in their respective industries have it tougher than those in the number two, three, or eleven spots. Some very successful companies sit back and wait for their competitors to take the risks and pioneer new products, services, and approaches. Once the new approach has proven to be successful, these companies rush their copycat products and services to the market, often selling them at a cheaper price than the originator. For example, a small motel chain didn't have a big budget for market research like some of their competitors, such as Holiday Inn or Hampton Inn, but it still needed a sound strategy for deciding where to locate new motels. This chain simply waited until Holiday Inn began construction of a new property and then located its motel around the corner. They assumed that Holiday Inn had done extensive research on the best locations for their new properties, and that they could piggyback on this research by locating their lower-priced motels very near to a Holiday Inn. Much to the dismay of Holiday Inn, this strategy has worked quite well for the smaller motel chain. They may not get their motels up and running as fast as Holiday Inn, but this chain has found that the copycat strategy works quite well and keeps their market research costs next to nothing.

Identifying and Studying Competitors

For some companies, simply identifying competitors is a challenge. In some high-tech industries especially, new companies pop up virtually overnight. It's important to constantly look for and learn about new competitors. Once you have identified your major competitors, you need to begin building a database of their strengths, weaknesses, product/services, pricing, and overall strategies. Leading companies develop comprehensive databases of competitor information and regularly update the information to keep it current.

Tip: Spending the time to build comprehensive databases on competitors is crucial to strategic planning, yet most organizations don't do it well.

At its corporate headquarters in Boston, Sheraton has an extensive database on the overall strategies of Hilton, Hyatt, Marriott, and its other major competitors. What's even more impressive is the competitor data that is gathered at the local level by each property. Each hotel has its own database on the four to six major competing hotels in its individual market. It is amazing how comprehensive this information is. For each major competing hotel, Sheraton knows its:

- Rate/prices for rooms, food and beverages, meeting space, etc.
- Room décor
- Meeting room space
- Staff to guests ratios

- Occupancy data
- Staff performance data (e.g., how long it takes to check in a guest, or cycle time for room service)
- Sales strategy–targeted groups, proposal content, etc.
- Renovation/improvement plans
- Corporate contracts coming up for renewal.

Hiring Competitors' Employees

Compared to other industries and companies I've seen, Sheraton is probably the benchmark for collecting and using competitor data. It is very common for hotel employees to have worked for many different hotel chains within a short period of time. Hotels understand this, and they have a systematic approach to picking the brains of new employees who previously worked for competitors. This process is not left to chance, but is pursued very systematically. The banking industry also effectively collects data in this way; many banking industry employees have worked for several different banks in their career, and they often delight in giving their new employer some useful insights into their ex-employer.

Tip: Most companies hire employees who used to work with competitors, but few interview these employees to uncover valuable competitor information. Don't let this opportunity go by.

Mystery Shoppers

Another way of collecting competitor data is to have your own employees pose as customers and collect first-hand data on competitor performance. This "mystery shopper" technique has been employed with great success for years by retail stores, airlines, and in other service industries. Employees of Sheraton hotels spend time as guests at Hyatt, Hilton, and other competitors. These visits are anything but a vacation, however—detailed data is collected, using comprehensive checklists; fed into databases; and used for both planning and evaluating Sheraton's performance against that of its rivals. For example, many hotels track the length of time it takes to check in a guest or to deliver room service. Knowing how local competitors perform on such key performance data can help in analyzing performance.

Testing Competitors' Products

Companies that manufacture products often buy their competitors' products and put them through rigorous tests and examinations to gather data. Car companies have been doing this for decades: they purchase their competitors' vehicles, bring them into the lab, and disassemble apart or subject them to durability tests to evaluate quality, workmanship, and a variety of other variables. Companies that manufacture high-tech electronic equipment have begun doing the same things in recent years.

Learning from Edge Competitors

According to author Alfie Kohn, the most important competitors to study are those he calls "edge competitors." Edge competitors are rarely mainstream companies that attend the trade shows, bid against you on big projects, and have a major share of the market. Edge competitors often break the rules and violate the conventional wisdom in your industry. For example, at one time, Domino's Pizza was a small chain of a few small stores in Ann Arbor, Michigan. Domino's changed the industry with their 30-minute delivery guarantee, making use of special, fast-cooking ovens and other techniques that had not occurred to other companies. Waiting an hour or more for a pizza seemed reasonable to most people until Domino's came along and set a new standard.

Campbell's Soup enjoyed about 80 years of market dominance in the prepared soups industry. When consumers began being more concerned with fat and salt intake, ConAgra's Healthy Choice Soups captured a small segment of the market, but did not pose a noticeable threat to giant Campbell's. In three short years, Healthy Choice became a major player in the soup market, taking a serious share from Campbell's (and also took away market share from them in the prepared foods category). By the time Campbell's introduced its own line of healthy soups and foods, these other companies had captured a significant share of the market.

Small companies are often quick to capitalize on changing market trends and often surprise their bigger competitors with a new approach or a product so revolutionary that it changes the way the industry does business. Internet book and music seller amazon.com is another example. The company came out of nowhere and has developed into one of the country's biggest distributors of books and music products. Barnes and Noble now also has an on-line bookstore, but amazon.com did to Barnes and Noble what Healthy Choice did to Campbell's.

As another example, consider the room service in most major hotel chains. Being on the road about 200 days a year, it's often hard for me to tell the difference between a Hilton, Hyatt, Sheraton, or Marriott. Although room service is not one of the aspects of room service that I would pick for improvement, Marriott did. A colleague explains that Marriott has managed to reengineer its room service process so that an order is delivered at exactly the time specified—for example, not two or three minutes before or after 6:30 A.M., but exactly at 6:30 A.M., when requested. After a couple weeks, he ended up back at a Hyatt or Hilton, and room service was usually delivered plus or minus fifteen minutes of the time when he requested it. Prior to his experience at Marriott, this would not have bothered him. However, he explained that this level of service had become an expectation after receiving it so consistently at the Marriott hotels and that he became disappointed in the service from Hyatt, Hilton, and even a Ritz Carlton he stayed at for a few nights. No other hotel chain could match Marriott's precision with on-time delivery or room service. He found out that technology was the key to Marriott's success. Room service personnel entered the order into a computer that would tell the cooks and servers exactly when to start preparing each item ordered, and even the most direct route to take in the hotel to get the cart there exactly when the guest requested it. Nothing was left to chance.

When one of your competitors advances the level or service to customers enough for people to notice a difference, this can sometimes be enough to change customers' opinions about your own company performance. As my colleague explained: "I was always satisfied with room service at Hilton and Hyatt until I received the higher level of service at Marriott."

Tip: The best companies pioneer innovations that surprise and delight customers, rather than simply giving them what they ask for.

Unsuspected Competitors

Your most threatening competitors are usually not the major companies against whom you currently compete. The real trick in building a solid competitor database is to collect data on those emerging companies that do not pose a threat today, but could become major players very quickly if their strategy pays off. Most large companies spend all of their time watching the other big players in their market, but finding unsuspected competitors is critical to an organization's success and often survival.

For example, Ericsson's Cellular Phone division has been watching Motorola and Nokia for years because these two companies held the number one and two market positions, and Ericsson wanted to become number three. They gathered data on a few smaller competitors, like Sony and Samsung, but neither were seen as much of a threat to Ericsson's goal of becoming number three. Qualcomm, a company out of San Diego, suddenly appeared, mimicking many aspects of Ericsson's products and strategy. In 1999, Qualcomm was the largest employer in San Diego, and its stock split several times, rising close to $300 per share. The company appears to have targeted Ericsson and has developed phones that incorporate many of the same features and designs that Ericsson's offer. Qualcomm even built its own football stadium in San Diego, gaining great exposure from its selection as the site of the 1998 Super Bowl. Many organizations fail to study adequately companies like Qualcomm.

Tip: Emerging competitors are the ones that pose the most serious threat, so don't fall into the trap of tracking only your current top three competitors.

Identifying Legal and Regulatory Threats

Part of a thorough planning process involves tracking government actions that might impact your organization. Government laws and regulations have been known to cripple businesses that were caught unaware. For example, the California law that forbids smoking in all bars and restaurants seriously hurt the business of a number of establishments. New, more stringent food safety regulations that the government issued in the mid 1990s resulted in the noncompliance of a number of food companies. Cargill, a company I discussed earlier, was one of the first companies in the industry to meet all the new regulations, which gave them an edge until competitors could catch up. Meeting the new, stringent regulations also made Cargill a more attractive supplier to picky customers like McDonald's, for whom Cargill now supplies eggs.

Regulations can also have a positive impact on a business. For example, my clients at Discover Card have been working with other credit card companies to ensure the passage of legislation that will make it more difficult for consumers to file for bankruptcy and walk away from their credit card debt. Losses in that industry were at an all-time high in 1998. The proposed legislation will have a big impact on how credit card companies assess risk and grant credit, so monitoring the vote can give a company an edge in the business.

Technology Threats

Technology threats often prove deadly. They can push huge companies into bankruptcy, because a change in technology can make current products or services obsolete or no longer in demand. Recall the story from the Introduction about the company that developed websites at $25,000 a piece until software appeared on the market that allowed people to develop their own websites for a few hundred dollars. Companies still exist that will design websites for you—and a complicated one still could be expensive, but usually not even close to the $25,000 it cost a couple of years ago for a very basic site.

High-tech organizations are usually very good at researching technological threats. They know what competitors are up to and generally do a good job surveying unrelated technologies for applications to their business. Lower-tech companies, though, often get caught by surprise. The example of Marriott's use of PCs in room service to allow for precise accuracy and on-time delivery of guest meals is an example. Hotels are a pretty low tech business, wherein the use of information technology has not been a big factor; however, many of them use technology creatively. The Sheraton Miramar in Santa Monica supplies potential meeting planner customers with an interactive CD that takes them on a guided tour of the property and answers common questions. This allows meeting planners to preview the property and view the meeting space without any travel expense.

The Ritz Carlton keeps a detailed database on each guest, which can be accessed by any property. If you request a nonallergenic pillow at the Ritz in Scottsdale, you will automatically have one placed in your room in any Ritz you stay at in the future, regardless of location.

Tip: Technological innovations can threaten the very
nature of any business, not just high tech firms.

The Perils of Success

I've been a consultant to many big, successful corporations and government agencies over the years: AT&T, American Express, IBM, Ford, U.S. Navy, Department of Energy, and others. I often find that these organizations start to think they are invincible. They get too cocky, and don't see any competitor as a real threat. Motorola, General Motors, Xerox, Dow, and many other respected corporations have had their share of problems because they did not pay enough attention to their competitors, failing to realize the real threats they posed. I don't find that small and medium-sized organizations are this way—they tend to be humble, a little scared, and always worried about the competition. Some fear is good, because it keeps you looking over your shoulder at what the other guy is doing.

It's hard not to become arrogant if you've been the biggest and most successful company in your market for years, but I've seen many such organizations brought to their knees in recent years because they did not pay enough attention to what going on around them. On the other hand, companies nowadays that spring up overnight become dominant in their industry within a few short years. For instance, circuit board manufacturer Solectron has gone from 1,800 to 18,000 employees in about 10 years, and Yahoo! has become a huge Internet player in a few short years.

PREPARING A COMPETITOR DATABASE

An effective database on edge competitors and up-and-coming companies is an essential tool in the planning process. You need to begin now filling in the blanks of what should become a comprehensive database. One excellent company used the following fields of information for its competitor database.

1. **Background/history.** Provide a narrative or bulleted summary of key events in the organization's history. Focus most of the information on the recent past (last 10 to 15 years) and how the products/services and strategies of the company may have changed.
2. **Products/services and pricing.** Include a list of the major products and services offered by the company, as well as how their pricing and features compare with your own products/services.
3. **Markets.** List the major markets to which the company sells its products/services with a breakdown of market share in each are compare
4. **Company values/philosophy.** List their overall philosophy, as well as any specific values they profess to or actually follow.
5. **Headquarters and locations.** Document the company's headquarters address, as well addresses of significant locations
6. **Partnerships/alliances.** List and describe any partnerships/ alliances with other companies, including key suppliers, and describe any issues relating to ownership of the company.
7. **Key officers and employees.** List the following information on each of the top executives: position, salary/ compensation, age, and background. List number of employees per location and employee type if available

(e.g., engineers, clerks, managers, IT professionals). Describe the company's overall approach to human resources management, including recruiting, training, compensation, and HR planning.

8. **Organization structure.** Draw the organization chart if possible, and indicate how the company is divided into business units.

9. **Results.** Provide a summary of key financial, market, operational, employee-related, and customer satisfaction results. Multiple years' worth of data are preferable to assess trends. Indicate how results compare with key competitors, including your own organization.

10. **Key strengths, weaknesses, and threats.** This information will be difficult to get from a D&B report or public database, but it is extremely important. Knowing precisely your competition's weakness can be of immense value in forging your own plan.

11. **Strategic direction.** Identify vision, key success factors, goals, and key strategies the company will likely use to succeed in the marketplace.

12. **Sources.** Identify the various documents and databases used to compile the competitor information. Include also a list of individuals who may be resources for further information—for example, consultants or employees who have insight into a competitor's business.

Use the following checklist to evaluate your own SWOT analysis.

CHECKLIST FOR EVALUATING STRENGTHS, WEAKNESSES THREATS, AND OPPORTUNITIES

When completing a SWOT analysis, make sure you:

☐ Complete the analysis before the planning meeting, and spend minimal time in the meeting highlighting the findings.

☐ Confirm your own findings with the use of outside resources where possible.

☐ Use the criteria from the Baldrige Award as the approach for assessing your organization's strengths and weaknesses.

☐ Identify the strengths, weaknesses, and strategies of major competitors using multiple and reliable source of information.

☐ Keep an eye out for edge competitors, and watch them closely.

☐ Identify current and potential threats to your organization, and develop action plans for addressing them.

Key Success Factors: Defining How You Will Achieve Your Vision and Beat Competitors

Key success factors (or KSFs) can be defined as the three to five broad areas on which your organization must focus in order to achieve its vision. KSFs should be specific; help identify performance measures and strategies; and help the organization prioritize its actions and investments.

Key success factors can be major weaknesses or deficiencies that must be fixed if the company is to achieve its vision. KSFs can be like very broadly defined strategies—for example, a KSF for a company in survival mode might be getting approval for a bank loan to fund company expenses for the next six months.

Although companies often confuse them, KSFs are *not* goals or even measures of performance. Achieving an 18 percent ROI is a goal, as is increasing sales by 22 percent next year. Goals address what you want to accomplish and/or are specific levels of performance for a particular metric.

Organizations also frequently confuse detailed strategies and initiatives with KSFs. KSFs do resemble strategies, because both focus on what you need to do or how you plan to be successful. The main difference between a KSF and a strategy is level of specificity. However, a KSF is a *broad area* of focus or action, whereas a strategy is a *specific* action. For example, a KSF might be to repair damaged product quality image with consumers; strategies to accomplish this might include better quality control techniques in the plants, increased inspection points in the new product design process, and a comprehensive advertising campaign that includes print, television, and other media. Another KSF might be to increase distribution points. Strategies could include opening eight new company stores, establishing partnerships with two new retail chains, identifying distributors in Asia, and increasing space in the company's own warehouses to allow more direct shipping of products to customers.

In short, KSFs specify broadly what you need to focus on to achieve your vision, and strategies provide the details of how this will be done.

WHAT DISTINGUISHES YOU?

In deciding on your key success factors, it helps to think about what your organization is known for, as well as what it is not known for. It is impossible to be successful if you try to be all things to all customers. Good organizations pick their niche and stick with it Some distinguishing characteristics to consider include:

- Lowest cost
- Easiest to do business with
- Largest distribution network
- Biggest selection
- Reputation
- Leading-edge technology
- Consistency—no surprises
- Customizing—
  "have it your way"
- Values/ethics
- Highest quality
- Timing—being first to market
- Unique product/service
- Location
- Size/buying power
- Image/prestige
- Best service
- Safest
- Styling/design

Successful organizations usually focus on, and become known for, one or two KSFs like these. Take for example two fashion designers who led their companies to become the most respected names in the business: Donna Karan and Gianni Versace. Versace concentrated on a unique look that was colorful, luxurious, and somewhat flashy. He wanted to differentiate his designs from Armani, who was known for more conservative cuts and subdued, solid-color fabrics.

Becoming associated with glamorous rock stars and movie stars was also a key to Versace's success. Donna Karan's designs are harder to differentiate from Armani's. She concentrated on creating an image for her clothing that was similar to Armani's, appealing to an older, more conservative audience. Donna Karan also did a better job of partnering with major retail chains like Saks, Nieman Marcus, and others to devote significant floor space to her apparel. Versace focused on selling his clothing through his own stores. A Donna Karan suit or dress would never be out of place in a corporate board-room; but only in the advertising or entertainment industries would most Versace clothing be appropriate. However, both companies have been quite successful in their chosen markets by concentrating on a few key success factors that differentiated them from their com-petitors. Certainly, style and design are key success factors, but so is the chosen marketing strategy.

Questions to Ask When Defining Key Success Factors

In trying to define your own KSFs, try to answer the following questions:

- Why do customers buy from us the first time—what draws them to us?
- Why do customers return or leave?
- What advantages do we have over our competitors that we could further exploit?
- What do we do that competitors will have a hard time copying?
- What words come readily to mind when people hear our name?
- What do we want to be known for?
- What problems do we need to fix that might jeopardize our future success?

Tip: Don't confuse business fundamentals with key success factors. Key success factors tend to change with time, while business fundamentals mostly stay the same.

Finding Data to Identify Key Success Factors

Most of the data needed to identify your KSFs should come from the situation analysis phase of your planning process. For example, one prime source of KSFs is knowledge of your competitors—analyzing their strategies allows you to select a strategy that will differentiate you in the marketplace. Another major source of information used to identify KSFs is market research on customer desires and needs. Understanding customer needs and projections of future requirements often helps a company to define success factors better than its competitors.

Charles Schwab

It is possible for several companies in the same industry to have the same key success factors or overall strategy and still be successful. For example, brokerage firms Morgan Stanley and PaineWebber might both have a KSF defined as an image of trustworthiness and shrewd financial decision making. Both firms must convince customers to trust them with their money. Image is a big KSF for many firms that sell intangibles.

But what if *every* major brokerage house is seen as trustworthy and shrewd? In order to differentiate yourself in such a marketplace, image is not enough and therefore is not a good KSF. Charles Schwab, perhaps realizing this, decided that one of the KSFs for his brokerage firm would be discounted fees but less service than offered by other brokers—kind of like Southwest Airlines' philosophy of low fares and less frills. Savvy investors, concerned about saving money on their transactions, have flocked to Charles Schwab. However, many investors will never become customers of Schwab because they prefer the better service they receive from more traditional brokerages, and they are willing to pay a little extra for it. Discount brokers like Charles Schwab are now being challenged by online trading companies like e*trade, where customers can do their own trading for less than $15.00 a trade and use the Internet to do their own research as well. Traditional brokers Morgan Stanley and PaineWebber were quick to not let this trend get the best of them, offering their own online trading services for customers. These firms now offer personalized service and advice from knowledgeable brokers, as well as access for their clients to research and trade via the Internet. Schwab's online trading has also become a big portion of their business and consistently gets high marks from investors.

Southwest Airlines

Southwest Airlines makes just about every list of the best companies in America, if not the world. In 2000 they were listed by *Fortune* Magazine as the number two company to work for from an employee standpoint. Every year they are number one or two in on-time performance and in delivering passenger luggage on time and to the right destination. Southwest has also performed extremely well for its shareholders, showing healthy profits in years when most other airlines lost money. Initially, they developed a number of KSFs that differentiated them from other airlines. They picked routes not serviced by the big airlines. They used one model of plane and standardized just about everything they did. They developed a procedure to board the plane more quickly than other airlines, and this allowed them to get one more flight per day from each aircraft, resulting in additional profit because of the increased productivity of their expensive fixed assets. Southwest also offered very low prices, convenient schedules, and employees who wore shorts and T-shirts and joked around with passengers to make them less nervous and help them better enjoy their trip.

The company concentrated on these key success factors for many years and saw impressive performance year after year.

Several years ago, United Airlines decided that they could do the same thing Southwest does, even better, and thereby take away a big chunk of Southwest's market. A new, subsidiary company, United Shuttle, was formed. The cross-functional team that designed United Shuttle essentially duplicated everything from Southwest, but differentiated themselves by offering passengers something they could *not* get on Southwest—an assigned seat.

Southwest uses a first-come, first-served system of seat assignment, whereby customers who check in first get to board the plane first. United thought that Southwest was discriminating against employed people—an important market segment. Most folks with a job usually cannot arrive the airport two hours before a flight, and thus they end up with "bad" seats on Southwest.

The launch of United Shuttle scared Southwest a little. This new company had copied many of Southwest's techniques and was eroding their market share. Herb Keleher, President of Southwest, was quoted as saying: "United has aimed a bullet at our heart and is trying to put us out of business." Several years later, Southwest is still in business, and so is United Shuttle. Although United was able to copy much of Southwest's' strategy and many of their KSFs, there was one thing that they could not copy: the culture. Employees who work for Southwest love their jobs, and this shows in how they treat passengers. Delighting passengers leads to high levels of loyalty and consistently healthy financial performance. United has not even come close to duplicating Southwest's wonderful culture. Many United employees are stockholders in the company and they *still* don't like working there. United Shuttle has had its share of labor troubles over the years, and their employees generally are better paid and have better benefits than Southwest, yet they still don't love their jobs like the employees of Southwest.

It appears that Southwest created this culture, which is the envy of many organizations, by using two major strategies. First of all, they are extremely careful about each individual they hire. I heard a representative of the company explain that they screen an average of 150 people for each person hired, and this is for entry-level jobs! Southwest not only screens for the usual criteria, but looks hard at personality, values, and other factors that are difficult to change. For example, a sense of humor is one of the major values of Southwest, and they try very hard to select people who possess it. The other secret to Southwest's culture is that their organizational practices are consistent with their values. They work diligently to reward values like efficiency and humor, and they celebrate successes in creative, fun ways. For example, to celebrate a newly formed partnership with a supplier, Southwest staged a mock wedding and invited employees from both companies to celebrate the partnership.

Southwest's wonderful culture is one of their most important key success factors. Not only does it bring them consistently high levels of customer satisfaction and financial performance, but it is also the one thing that no competitor can exactly capture. The best key success factors are those that the competition must struggle to steal from you.

For more information on this company, I suggest the book, *Nuts!: Southwest Airlines' Crazy Recipe for Business and Personal Success* (by Freiberg, Freiberg, and Peters; Bantam Paperback, 1998).

Tip: *Select key success factors that competitors will have a hard time stealing from you.*

Midwest Express: The Best Care in the Air

Midwest Express is another airline that has established a good set of key success factors, although by taking a very different tact than Southwest. Midwest Express *does* focus on people with jobs. Midwest Express is headquartered in Milwaukee and offers direct flights to 28 destinations around the country. Business travelers love Midwest Express because they receive first-class service for what they would pay for a coach seat on United, Delta, or Northwest. Midwest Express's strategy is to offer business travelers two-by-two leather seats, real glass and china, complimentary wine, and food comparable to first-class fare found on the major airlines. While many other airlines have tried to copy the no-frills approach of Southwest, Midwest Express adopted a formula that caused many other airlines to fail in the past.

MGM Grand Airlines used to offer outstanding service between LA and New York. Other airlines that tried unsuccessfully to focus on the business traveler with better service include the original Midway out of Chicago, Metrolink, Air One, Air Atlanta, and UltraAir. All of these other airlines are either gone or have adopted different strategies and now target a broader mix of passengers. Midwest Express and Southwest are the two domestic airlines that have shown the most consistent profit performance year after year, in spite of ups and downs in the performance of the other U.S. Airlines.

Midwest Express has made their formula work well by concentrating on keeping costs low, providing an outstanding product and service, and not being too aggressive in their growth. One of the company's key success factors in its formative years was access to capital at a low cost. Midwest Express started out as the internal airline for its parent company, Kimberly Clark, which has sales of over

$7 billion. Kimberly Clark has a triple-A credit rating, which gives them access to money at a very low cost. This gave Midwest Express an advantage over other airlines, which must pay much higher rates to borrow money.

Another factor that has made Midwest Express successful is that most of its flights are out of Milwaukee, which is not a hub for any of the major airlines. Northwest tried to gain market share in 1988 by establishing a mini-hub in Milwaukee, but gave up in 1992 after unsuccessfully trying to get Milwaukee-based passengers to switch airlines.

It is not coincidental that Midwest Express was rated as the number one domestic airline, according to a survey of 9,400 frequent travelers and travel agents conducted by Zagat. Northwest was rated as number 29 in the same survey. No other U.S. Airline received a rating in the top 10 of the Zagat survey. Delta, America, and United ranked 24, 25, and 26, respectively; Midwest Express ranked number 2—second to only Singapore Airlines.

Continental Airlines: From Worst to First

According to *Fortune* magazine (May 25, 1998), Continental Airlines was despised by its customers, shareholders, and employees and was about as close to the bottom of an industry as a company could be. In four short years, new CEO Gordon Bethune and President/COO Greg Brenneman have turned the company into one of the most respected names in the airline business. Stock has risen in value 1,700 percent since 1994, and both customer satisfaction and employee morale are at an all-time high. The approach Continental used to accomplish this miraculous turnaround was to create a clear vision and focus on four key success factors as part of their strategic plan.

The vision was to go from "Worst to First." This vision meets all the criteria outlined in Chapter 2: short, memorable, inspirational, and clearly important for the company's survival. The four key success factors identified by Continental were:

- **Fly to Win**—focus on building business in Houston, Newark, and Cleveland hubs, and concentrate more on

attracting lucrative business flyers; trade flip-flops and backpacks for suits and briefcases.
- **Fund the Future**—focus on gaining liquidity by restructuring the balance sheet, selling off nonstrategic assets, and abandoning unprofitable routes and schedules.
- **Make Reliability a Reality**—focus on the best on-time performance and providing consistent service to customers
- **Work Together**—change Continental's culture from one of fear, mistrust, cost-cutting, and millions of rules to one of fun, rewarding good performance, cooperation between departments, and empowerment of frontline employees.

For each of these key success factors, Continental developed a series of strategies or initiatives and metrics to monitor their performance. For example, the measures that related to "Make Reliability a Reality" were:

- On-time takeoffs and landings
- Baggage mishandles
- Customer complaints
- Involuntary denied boardings.

The strategies the company deployed that related to the key success factor of "Working Together" were:

- Financial incentives for on-time performance
- Consistent and reliable flight schedules
- Eliminate/change unnecessary rules, regulations, and procedures
- Open and honest communication with employees on good news and bad.

By following the simple planning approach outlined in this book, Continental's net income went from a loss of $613 million in 1994 to a profit of $385 million in 1997. Operational and customer satisfaction measures also show impressive levels of performance, placing Continental above roughly 80 percent of the airlines on most metrics.

The story of Continental Airline's turnaround is recounted in *Harvard Business Review* (Greg Brenneman, "Right Away and All at Once: How We Saved Continental," September/October 1998, pp. 165–179), and in an excellent book by CEO Gordon Bethune: *From Worst to First: Behind the Scenes of Continental's Remarkable Comeback* (John Wiley & Sons, 1998).

Ericsson Cellular Phones—James Bond's Brand

Ericsson, one of the largest telecommunication companies in the world, not only manufactures cellular phones but also makes the switching systems used by phone companies to handle calls, along with a variety of other telecommunication products, mostly sold to industry. Several years ago, the company decided that it had to become a major player in the competitive cellular phone consumer market. Back in the early 1990s, Ericsson was number eight or nine in market share. They eventually developed a vision that stated: "Become number three in market share by the year 2000." To go from number eight to number three is a major challenge for any company, especially within about five years, as Ericsson proposed. The company's executives brainstormed a list of about 50 possible KSFs. Because many of the executives had technical backgrounds, the majority of those suggestions were technology-related. The list of three key success factors the company finally settled on were more focused on other factors:

- Brand recognition
- Partnerships with retailers and carriers
- Development of new products focusing on digital technology and a broader array of price points

Brand recognition was an important key success factor for the company—no one buys a phone made by a company they've never heard of. Part of the problem was that Ericsson had been selling their phones with a GE logo on them. The company realized that the Ericsson name was not as widely recognized in North America as it was in Europe and South America. In order to become a major player in the cellular phone business, Ericsson needed to make Americans aware of who they were and what they did.

One of the smartest moves they made was to convince the parent company to give them the money to build a football stadium in Charlotte, North Carolina. Every time the Panthers played a football game on television, viewers would see the name Ericsson many times, because that is the name of the stadium. A lot of people then began saying that they had heard of Ericsson—but thought they built football stadiums! Ericsson then spent money on print ads, television commercials, sponsorship of sports teams, and a variety of other advertising strategies. Another smart move by Ericsson was to get the famous film character James Bond to use Ericsson phones and other products in the movie "Tomorrow Never Dies." (This same strategy had helped BMW sell their new convertibles when they appeared in "Goldeneye" a few years earlier. BMW ensured their cars were even more prevalent in "Tomorrow Never Dies": practically every mode of transportation seen in that movie is a BMW product. James Bond drives a new 750, which he controls while sitting in the back seat—using an Ericsson device. Even the bad guys drive black Range Rovers, another BMW product.)

Another of Ericsson's key success factors was to establish better partnerships with retailers like Circuit City and carriers such as Cellular One. Motorola had done a great job of getting their products to be pushed by both the retailers and the carriers through the use of price incentives, sales contests, promotions, sales literature, training for retail salespeople, and other approaches. Ericsson felt that their phones were so much better technologically than many of their competitors that they shouldn't have to resort to such techniques. Yet no one was buying their phones, so something had to change.

After I started consulting with Ericsson, I decided to buy one of their phones. The salesman in a local Circuit City at first said they didn't carry Ericsson products. When I pointed out one model on the bottom shelf of the display case, he admitted that they did carry that one item, but explained:

"You don't want to buy that phone anyway. First of all, it's expensive and an unknown brand. You want a phone made by a well-known, respected company such as Motorola or Sony. Besides, I can sell you this Motorola phone for one cent if you buy a two-year contract; the Ericsson phone will cost you about $300.00."

Ericsson wised up about working with retailers and carriers and began doing many of the things their competitors were doing, such as offering price incentives and sales contests, and training salespeople on the features, advantages, and benefits of Ericsson products as compared to their competitors'. They also invested significant sums in new product development, rounding out their product line with some lower priced models that appealed to a different market segment of consumers. The company also worked to improve their systems and processes, and they went from about 200 points on the 1,000-point Baldrige Award scale up to about 600 points in three years. Ericsson's cellular phone division was recognized as the best U.S. business unit on their internal Baldrige Assessment several years in a row.

Another smart move by Ericsson was investing heavily in the development of digital phones. Ericsson, Nokia, and San Diego-based Qualcomm have been the leaders in the development and sales of digital phones, which provide much better sound transmission than traditional analog phones. Motorola has been most hurt by a lack of digital products and saw their market share drop dramatically in a number of countries.

In 1997, Ericsson became number three in market share, achieving their vision three years ahead of schedule. As of the first quarter of 1997, Ericsson became number two, thanks to the James Bond promotional campaign and a few other well-chosen strategies. In 1999, the company experienced some new challenges. In the first half of the year, pretax profits plunged 44 percent, margins on mobile phones dropped to 1 percent, and cash flow turned negative. The company had become a big player in the market, but even market share was no longer improving in 1999, with a drop of 14.6 percent. Cost cutting appears to be a current key success factor for Ericsson. They are selling real estate and cutting 15,000 employees out of 120,000. The company is also working on cycle time for new product development. Ericsson has introduced a number of new products over the years, but they lag seriously behind Nokia. Ericsson's T28 is a flip phone based on a new platform with a lithium-powered battery. The phone, scheduled for release at the end of 1998, was released in the fourth quarter of 1999—a year after a similar Nokia phone was released.

Ericsson had a good clear vision, and key success factors that were appropriate and successful for a while. They managed to dramatically increase market share, partnerships, and develop a number of new products. The lesson to be learned from Ericsson is that a vision and key success factors need to be reexamined and often changed every few years as you own situation changes, and the strategies of key competitors change. Ericsson used to look at Motorola as the major competitor, but now Nokia has become the industry leader in cellular phone sales. Two of Nokia's key success factors seem to be creative product designs, and a research and development process that allows their products to reach the market much faster than their competitors. Nokia's market share grew 2 percentage points in 1998, giving them 23 percent of the market. Their revenue is expected to rise by 35 percent by the end of 1999.

BRAINSTORMING KEY SUCCESS FACTORS

While it's a mistake to assign a team or a committee to write a vision or mission statement, it is unwise to have a single individual develop an organization's key success factors. The best way to do this is to post the vision where all can see it, and have a small group of six to ten individuals brainstorm possible KSFs. I often do this with my clients on the second day of a two-day workshop on strategic planning and measurement. I ask the teams to brainstorm at least three flip chart pages or at least 50 possible KSFs before beginning to narrow them down. Several groups have managed to brainstorm over 100 KSFs in about an hour. The first page almost always includes a list of generic factors that are important for just about any company, such as:

- Motivated workforce
- State-of-the-art systems
- Value-added services
- Responsiveness
- Ethics/values
- High-quality products
- Risk taking
- Highly trained people
- Flexibility
- Being customer-focused

The problem with KSFs like these is that they are too vague and don't really help to identify specific measures and strategies. Every organization needs highly trained people, for example; identifying a particular skill or competency needed by your personnel in order to make your company successful is more what I would consider as a KSF. Nevertheless, these generic KSFs often help to stimulate thought that leads to more specific ones. In my experience, the best KSFs show up on the third and fourth flip chart pages, by which time the group is running out of generic ideas.

Tip: The best key success factors usually emerge
after the group thinks it has run out of ideas.

Prioritizing Key Success Factors

After brainstorming 50 or more possible KSFs, the next step is narrowing down the list. This is usually done by having each member of the team study the list on the flip charts and individually identifying his or her three to five top choices. Some thought should be put into this, so don't rush them. The group then considers those that received the most votes.

Sometimes the KSFs that receive the most votes should not make the short list, though. It is important to discuss this and to get the team to reach consensus on *the most important* KSFs for the company to focus on. The ideal number seems to be three: any more than that presents too much to focus on; and one or two usually represents too narrow of a focus. People need to understand that the KSFs are not supposed to focus on every single important aspect of running a business—i.e., fundamentals like growth, marketing, new product development, customer loyalty, and high employee morale. A good question to ask the group to help narrow down the KSFs is: "If we could only afford to invest in three broad strategies for the next couple of years, which ones would most help us achieve our vision?"

Defining Key Success Factors

Once the group has identified the high-priority KSFs, each one needs to be defined. Key success factors are often a little vague, and most need definitions that read somewhat like vision statements. One HR group came up with this KSF: Increase knowledge of internal customers' business needs and priorities.

This was defined as: We need to do a better job of researching the needs and priorities of our employees, managers, and corporate customers and learn more about the company's business to do a better job of linking HR initiatives to company initiatives. We need to stop assuming that we know what our customers need and want, and start listening more.

Lutheran Brotherhood, a financial services and insurance organization in Minneapolis, identified one of their key success factors as: Build affinity and loyalty. It defined this as:

> *LB needs to build greater loyalty from its members by offering them a higher caliber of personal service than they would receive from other financial institutions and by tailoring a unique combination of financial services and products to each member family's needs.*

Essentially, what LB is trying to do is build a stronger brand so as to create greater loyalty from its member customers.

Usually, the definitions for the key success factors are wordsmithed by two to four people on the planning committee, rather than the entire team.

---

*Tip: Key success factors need to be defined
clearly enough to be measured.*

IDENTIFING METRICS FOR KEY SUCCESS FACTORS

Along with defining KSFs, it is also important to identify the measures of your progress. You'll learn more about metrics in Chapter 9, but here we will focus on developing specific metrics linked to KSFs. The HR group I mentioned earlier came up with a leading and lagging metric that related to their KSF of becoming more customer focused. A leading indicator was the number of times the customer research questionnaire they developed was completely filled out at the start of an HR initiative or system design. This form forced the HR people to thoroughly interview their customers and document their requirements prior to the development of any new product (e.g., training course or benefit package) or service (e.g., online course registration, or benefits website). The lagging indicator was the level of customer satisfaction with their new and existing products/services according to ratings by employees and management. HR's products and services often received poor satisfaction ratings, and their new, more customer-focused approach was intended to result in better scores.

If you can establish a single metric that adequately measures a key success factor, you are better off. For example, Ericsson came up with a brand recognition index linked to its KSF with the same objective. This index told them how many people out of 100 had heard of Ericsson, knew of their products, and said good things about the company and its products. Sales would be the lagging indicator for this key success factor, and the company was already tracking sales.

Tip: Make sure that the metrics you identify directly measure the key success factors.

Once you've identified performance metrics that relate to your key success factors, you need to set targets for each metric and develop strategies to achieve those targets. Information on how to set targets can be found in Chapter 4 of this book; Chapter 9 addresses the development of strategies.

FINALIZING KSFs

After the team has identified the top three KSFs, it is a good idea to review them with a larger group to make sure that the majority agrees with the company focus. Often, lower-level employees can provide a level of realistic perspective lacked by the executives developing the overall plan. After obtaining input from numerous employees from different levels and functions, your KSFs can be finalized—for now. It's important to realize that KSFs should be reexamined at least once every six months to see if they still make sense. Very few organizations pursue the same KSFs for more than a few years. Some of them fall off the list because they are achieved or they solve a problem. Others may change because the company must alter its strategy to deal with a new competitor or changing customer/market requirements. It is also important to remember that KSFs are not supposed to address every aspect of your organization; rather, they tell you where to direct your focus while not forgetting the basics of running your company.

During this phase of the planning process, members of the team often become parochial in their interests, vying for their own special interests. The IT guy fights to have his area as a key success factor, as do finance and HR. Selecting the short list of KSFs often becomes an exercise in who can argue the most convincingly. The meeting facilitator needs to control this and ensure that the final KSFs will be those that enable the company to achieve its vision. If your function or area is not selected as one of the top KSFs, it probably means that it is currently quite successful and does not pose a major problem or need a change in approach.

Use the following checklist to evaluate your corporate KSFs.

CHECKLIST FOR EVALUATING KEY SUCCESS FACTORS

☐ Maximum of five key success factors; two or three are usually better.

☐ Key success factors do not all focus on one aspect of performance (e.g., financial results, customers, etc.).

☐ Key success factors are directly linked to the vision.

☐ Key success factors are not financial goals or measures and targets.

☐ Key success factors are not standard business fundamentals, but rather specific factors that will differentiate the organization from its competitors.

☐ Key success factors are clearly defined so that everyone understands them.

☐ Performance metrics have been defined for each key success factor.

☐ Only one or two metrics are listed for each key success factor.

☐ Targets have been set for each metric, and targets appear to be high enough to achieve the company vision.

Strategic Metrics: Identifying Measures Linked to Your Vision and Key Success Factors

Strategic measures are those that are derived from your vision and key success factors. They should be corporate priorities until the vision is achieved or the success factors are changed. One company selected sales growth in international markets as one of their key success factors to achieve a vision of growth in market share to the number three position. They developed an International Sales Index that measured sales, growth, and profits from international customers. This gauge was watched very closely for several years, until the company became a major player in the international marketplace. After a few years, the key success factor and its corresponding metric or gauge was no longer as important. The CEO and President did not watch the International Sales Index each month, but it remained on the dashboard of the Vice President of Sales, and certainly on the dashboard of the head of the international sales division. The status of this metric changed from one that was strategic in focus to a business fundamental.

Strategic versus Operational Metrics

It is important that your scorecard include operational measures that are linked to your mission, as well as a handful of strategic measures that tell you how you are progressing toward your vision. Figure 9-1 summarizes the main differences between the two types

STRATEGIC VERSUS OPERATIONAL MEASURES

Strategic Metrics	Operational Metrics
Link back to the vision	Link back to the mission and/or values
Are derived from key success factors	Are derived from business fundamentals or high-level goals
Are limited to 2-4 metrics	May include 12 or more metrics
Tend to change every few years	Tend to stay the same
Tend to be indices that consist of several individual metrics	May be a combination of indices and singular metrics
May be former operational metrics	May be former strategic metrics
Performance is reviewed by highest level of executives	Performance is reviewed by a wide variety of executives and managers
May focus on one or two aspects of organizational performance	Focus on all aspects of performance: financial, customers, internal, employees, innovation and growth, and supplier performance

Figure 9-1. Strategic Versus Organizational Measures

of metrics or measures that should be included on any organization's dashboard.

A good, balanced scorecard should include a mix of fundamental (or operational) measures and a handful of strategic metrics. The higher you go in the organization, the more strategic metrics appear on the scorecard. A CEO might have six strategic metrics and ten fundamental measures on her scorecard, whereas a less highly placed individual might have six fundamental metrics and one strategic metric on his.

The categories (or boxes) into which your strategic measures fall is secondary. Chances are that they will not all fall into a single category. I would be wary if all of your strategic metrics were in the financial box of the scorecard, for instance. Many financial measures involve looking at the past, so they tend to not make good strategic metrics. Nor should you try to force a strategic metric into each of the four or five categories on your scorecard in an effort to make it look well balanced. The metrics themselves are much more important than equally distributing them among the categories on your scorecard.

Tip: *It is not necessary to have a strategic metric in each of the scorecard boxes.*

Brand Recognition Index

Well-defined strategic metrics that tell you what you need to know start with well-defined key success factors.

An organization discussed in previous chapters, Ericsson's Cellular Phones Division, had identified brand recognition as their first key success factor back in 1993. Their definition of brand recognition went something like this:

"Everyone knows the Ericsson name, knows we are in the telecommunication business, and associates us with high quality, innovative technology, and exceptional customer service"

When it came time to identify metrics, most of the planning meeting participants felt that sales figures from both retailers and consumers were the best measure of brand recognition. Market share as compared to Motorola, Nokia, and others was also thought to be a good metric for assessing brand recognition. After further discussion, however, it was decided that none of these metrics directly measured brand recognition. Brand recognition was a *prerequisite* to sales and market share and should have been measured so as to evaluate the effectiveness of marketing and advertising programs. The Ericsson team created a Brand Recognition Index, which included metrics such as:

- Percent of consumers who had heard of Ericsson and knew what they did
- Percent of consumers who associated high-quality, innovative technology, and exceptional customer service with the company image

While it's true that sales data would have told Ericsson that they had managed to improve brand recognition, it is an indirect and lagging indicator. By measuring awareness of their brand, and the opinions of consumers and retailers, Ericsson created a better gauge for predicting future sales.

Tip: Make sure that the strategic metrics directly measure the key success factors.

Leadership Effectiveness Index

Another company selected "improved leadership" as a KSF. The executive team unanimously agreed that this was important, but it was a real challenge defining what it meant and how it might be measured. After discussing it for a while, the team decided that what they really meant was that the organization needed a consistent direction that was understood by all employees. Hence, they decided to measure two things that made up their "Leadership Effectiveness Index":

- Percent of employees that could correctly explain the company vision and their role in helping to achieve it
- Biannual employee ratings of the effectiveness of senior management.

Customer Relationship Index

Another company had a vision of improving its lagging profitability. One of the key success factors it selected to help achieve this vision was to build stronger relationships with targeted customers. The company had been spending too much effort catering to large customers that often provided slim profit margins and were difficult to work with. In this situation, sales from targeted customers again was proposed as a possible strategic metric. An increase in sales from a targeted customer might indicate a stronger relationship, but it might also mean that the customer just had a greater demand. Also, sales was a lagging indicator that would take too long to measure the effectiveness of account management strategies.

This company developed what they called a "Customer Relationship Index," which measured the strength of their relationships. The metric consisted of a 1-to-10 scale, with 1 indicating a new relationship (i.e., the customer was testing the company on a few small orders and was still using mostly other suppliers) and 10 being reserved for the strongest relationships (i.e., had been working together for many years, were a major supplier, had a long-term contract, had few problems) The ratings sound quite subjective, but they were determined using a wide range of objective factors, such as:

- Number of years doing business with customer
- Sales volume in dollars
- Pounds of product purchased annually
- Personal relationships with the customers' key executives
- Length and terms of contract
- Customer satisfaction data
- Number and severity of complaints

By way of communicating this metric to the staff, employees were told to think of a customer rated 10 as one to whom they were married for life and whom they loved eternally. A customer rated 1 or 2 was in the early stages of a relationship, which might be compared to casual dating or meeting for lunch. The trick was to move the customer up the chain in the relationship, so that the company could improve its profits and stability via long-term relationships with valued accounts.

The problem with any relationship is that you must be careful in choosing a partner. The company had in the past entered some "bad marriages"—accounts that they probably should not have been working with to begin with. Hence, their metric placed equal weight on the relative attractiveness of each account to the company. This aspect of the Customer Relationship Index consisted of a 1-to-10 scale by which the company rated its customers on their relative attractiveness. Customers that received a 10 rating were considered "beautiful" because they:

- Always paid their invoices on time
- Had a clear set of ethics that were consistent with the company's ethics
- Were pleasant and easy to work with
- Provided healthy sales and profit margins
- Forecasted their needs accurately
- Preferred partnering with trusted suppliers
- Manufactured products that were a good fit for the company's materials

The "ugly" customers—those rated a 1 or 2—had just the opposite characteristics.

Each of the factors listed previously was weighted based on its overall importance. For example, the dollars in sales and profits generated by a customer was worth 40 percent of their attractiveness score, whereas their ability to forecast their needs accurately was only with 10 percent.

The two factors in the index were multiplied together to come up with a total out of a possible 100. That is, a customer relationship rated 10 times an attractiveness rating of 10 equaled 100. A few examples of how the index was calculated are shown in Figure 9-2.

The objective of this metric was to drive behavior that would build the strongest relationships with the most important, or attractive, customers, while restricting the efforts expended on the least promising ones.

	RELATIONSHIP LEVEL	x	ATTRACTIVENESS LEVEL	
Customer A:	7	x	4	= 28
Customer B:	5	x	7	= 35
Customer C:	9	x	8	= 72
Customer D:	2	x	3	= 6
Customer E:	4	x	4	= 16
				157

157/5 Customers = 31.4 average relationship index score.

Figure 9-2. Calculation of Relationship Index Level

LEADING VERSUS LAGGING INDICATORS

The three example strategic measures just discussed are what I would call leading indicators because they should predict future outcomes. Leading indicators tend to be worthless by themselves, but they help to develop measures that possess true value. For example, if everyone in America knew the Ericsson name, and knew that they made wonderful telecommunications equipment, and still bought someone else's equipment, then Ericsson would be wasting their money on advertising and marketing.

Tip: Most strategic metrics tend to be leading indicators, and more of the operational or fundamental metrics are lagging (or outcome) metrics.

Lagging indicators tend to focus on valuable outcomes such as sales, profits, growth, retention of employees, and so on. The problem with lagging indicators is that they often don't detect problems until it is too late. For instance, a good lagging metric for a hospital is mortality rate. Someone must die to add a data point to the chart, however; and nothing can be done to save that person. A leading indicator for a hospital might be the number of mistakes made during surgical procedures, or the overall hygiene of the operating room. The test of a good leading indicator is that it predicts performance of a lagging indicator, and that trends in leading indicators may be detected quickly enough for corrective action to be taken. For example, dramatic, negative changes in a patient's vital signs might be considered a leading indicator of a major health problem. However, when this sort of change occurs, it is usually too late to do much to save the patient.

Figure 9-3 provides some examples of leading and lagging indicators that some organizations have found to be linked.

It would be wrong to assume that all strategic metrics are leading or predictive measures. Sometimes, the best way to measure something is to look at overall outcomes, or "water under the bridge" measures. For example, the International Sales Index described in an earlier example is actually a lagging indicator because it focuses on

EXAMPLE LEADING AND LAGGING INDICATORS	
Leading Indicator	**Lagging Indicator**
Customer satisfaction survey	Future customer purchases
Proposals written	Sales
Employee stress levels	Turnover or Illness
Dollars invested in R & D	New product sales
Safety audit scores	Lost time accidents

Figure 9-3. Examples of Leading and Lagging Indicators

sales that have already occurred. An insurance company that had a vision of becoming a more diversified financial services firm identified one of their key success factors as "Use of alternative marketing techniques rather than face-to-face selling." They could have tracked the number of direct mail pieces sent out, or the number of telemarketing calls made, but decided instead to measure sales of new products. Since the new products were all sold using marketing techniques other than face-to-face selling, this was a good way to measure the effectiveness of those alternative techniques.

THE DANGER OF FUTILE PROCESS METRICS

Ineffective key success factors surely lead to ineffective strategic measures, but sometimes a well thought-out and articulated KSF leads to a futile metric that drives the wrong behavior. For example, one HR organization had identified "Improving key work processes and increasing efficiency" as one of its key success factors. This was a government organization where much time in the HR function was spent collecting and circulating paper that added dubious value to the organization or its human resources. The measure selected for this key success factor was "Number of processes improvements completed," and the target was set at nine. Counting the number of process improvements turned out to be a bad metric, though. Each part of the HR organization made nine process improvements and thus achieved their goal; the problem was that they remained inefficient paper-pushers because the processes they selected to improve often consisted of changing who processed what paper, or merely changed the sequence of steps in a process that should not have been performed in the first place.

Another organization decided that a key success factor was to improve the overall safety and health of its workforce. Rather than focus on traditional safety metrics like lost time accidents, the organization chose to measure the implementation of a new safety program called "Integrated Safety Management," or ISM. Implementing the ISM approach required many new forms, meetings, committees, and in general added more bureaucracy to an already bureaucratic government organization. The organization also decided to measure all of its prime contractors on this new ISM index because it wanted to make sure they implemented the new safety program. Because ISM was not an option, everyone did it and made sure they got a good score on their ISM index. The problem with this measure was that it showed no correlation to decreased hazards or accidents in the workplace. One lagging indicator that it did correlate with, however, was increased costs. Implementation of the new safety program clearly was costly, yet there was no data to indicate that it did anything to make the workplace safer.

The measures discussed in both of the preceding examples would mislead an organization into believing that it was making good progress on its key success factors and coming closer to its vision. Both served to drive the behavior of employees and contractors; however, it was not clear that this behavior led to improvements in any of the organization's overall performance measures.

STRATEGIC MEASURES THAT ALLOW CHEATING

A strategic metric used for years by the Navy, Air Force, and other branches of the armed forces is the "Readiness Index." The measure is strategic because it looks at how prepared the armed forces are to respond to a conflict. The index includes both equipment and personnel. Conceptually, it is a great metric for predicting a response to a real emergency or conflict. The problem is that the data in the overall metric reviewed by the brass is often fudged by lower-level personnel. Of course, no one I talked to confessed to doing this, but they all had some good stories about how others had slightly modified the score on readiness assessments to receive a passing grade.

The Coast Guard is the only branch of the military I've worked with that has a good check on their readiness data because they can compare it to actual performance data. The Coast Guard doesn't just practice; they go out on real missions every day to save boaters, catch drug runners, and protect the marine environment. The integrity of the Coast Guard's mission readiness data is evaluated each day in a busy Coast Guard location like District 7 in Miami. District 7 (and others I've worked with to help develop scorecards) have found a very strong correlation between mission readiness measures and mission performance measures. Other branches of the military have a tougher job finding lagging indicators because they don't wage war every day.

Customer satisfaction is another common leading indicator that appears in the strategic section of organizational scorecards. Customer satisfaction surveys measure customer opinions, which should predict buying behavior. The problem is that they don't in most cases. How customers rate an organization on a survey seems to have little bearing on their likelihood of doing business with the organization in the future. Because customer satisfaction scores are so important in many organizations today, and it is hard to make the average score improve much, some organizations have learned to cheat.

Some car companies use customer satisfaction scores as one factor determining dealer car allocations. Those with lower scores get fewer of the choice cars. Rather than concentrate on improving service, which is difficult and expensive, dealers have figured out that it is easier to cheat. One car company explained that it caught over 50 dealers doing things like calling up customers about a week before the J.D. Power survey was due to arrive in the mail. Customers were told that if they would give the dealer all high ratings and bring in a photocopy of the survey, the dealer would give them a free oil change or detail the car for free. With this sort of thing going on, it is little wonder that the car companies see only a slight or no correlation between survey data and owner loyalty.

IMPROVING AND MAINTAINING CORE COMPETENCIES—MEASURING INTELLECTUAL CAPITAL

The employee or human resources box on a company's scorecard is often the least sophisticated and most likely to include meaningless metrics that are not really correlated with important outcomes like growth, profitability, or even customer satisfaction. Yet, just about any company you encounter today will tell you that people are their most important asset. The problem is that the metrics they have on the human resources aspect of the business tell them little about the value and performance of this asset.

Common HR Metrics of Limited Value

As a consultant reviewing the scorecards of many large government and business organizations, I see mostly the same metrics in the HR section.

Turnover

Just about every medium to large organization tracks attrition or employee turnover. The problem with this as a metric is that it may not tell you much. If you turn over 20 percent of your new employees each year, this could be a good sign if the ones who leave are those whose performance does not meet your standards.

Many big accounting/consulting firms lose 80 to 90 percent of their new hires over a five-year period. Two such firms that I worked with, however, do not see this as a problem. They invest a fortune in training new employees, even though they know that most of them will depart in a few years. Many of those employees get hired away by the firms' own clients, and in turn become the firms' good customers. In this case, turnover is not an indication of a problem—it is expected, and often positive in that it keeps labor costs low by always providing a stable of new recruits.

Another problem with turnover as a metric is that whether it is positive or negative depends upon the person leaving. When some people quit, everyone breathes a sigh of relief: "Thank God he finally left, he's been retired at his desk for the last five years!" When other people leave, you realize that they are irreplaceable. You might lose a seasoned employee who's been with the company many years, is one of your best managers, and is being groomed to take over as president someday. It can be devastating to have a competitor steal this person away. Yet, on the turnover graph this person will appear as just one more dot on the chart—the same as the kid in the mailroom who left after six months because he had not been promoted yet.

Turnover is a crude measure that does not tell you much about how well a business is managing its human assets.

Education Level

A common metric in educational, technical, and R & D organizations is the average education level of the staff. These firms count advance degrees and believe that the value of their intellectual capital increases with the number of Ph.D.s and others graduate degrees. While this is certainly easy to measure, the number of advanced degrees held by an organization's staff can also be a misleading metric. I might end up trading someone of the caliber of Bill Gates or Steven Jobs for 50 Ph.D.s.

The problem with education is that it is no guarantee of competence. We've all met folks with advanced degrees from impressive universities who are not our brightest coworkers.

Hours in Training

A common HR metric I've seen on many corporate and government scorecards is average number of training hours per employee per year. Some big companies brag that their employees receive 80 hours of training per year on average. The problem with tracking how many butts sat in how many classroom chairs is that it tells you nothing about the overall competence of the employees. Training attendance, or BIC (butts in chairs), as a metric does not tell you whether the employees needed the course, whether they learned anything, or whether it improved their job performance or value to the company.

Meeting Developmental Plan Objectives

A new HR metric I see cropping up on a number of scorecards is the percentage of employees who have met developmental objectives that were agreed upon at the beginning of the year. Most companies include a developmental plan as part of the performance management/appraisal process, whereby an employee negotiates with the boss on skills he or she will improve or acquire during the following year. At the end of the year, the company measures the extent to which these developmental objectives have been accomplished. The problem with this as a metric is that the developmental objectives are often stated as activities to be pursued (such as attend this or that course) rather than specific competencies to be acquired. Another frequent problem is that the skills or knowledge acquired are not the key competencies needed by the company to improve its future.

A Simple Human Capital Index

A simple way of calculating the value or strength of your staff is to create a human capital index that is made up of four submetrics:

- Number of years in the business/field
- Level in the company (by job grade or organizational chart level)
- Performance rating
- Number and variety of positions/assignments held

Each of these four factors needs to be weighted based upon its relative importance. For example, you could make each submetric worth 25 percent, or weigh them as follows:

- Level in the company   35%
- Performance rating   25%
- Variety of positions   25%
- Years in field/business   15%

Each individual would then be given a score once a year based on these four factors. Three of the four metrics are hard, objective measures; performance rating is a subjective measure derived from a performance review and might be based on peer evaluation, superior evaluation, and measurable performance on key objectives (sales, profits, etc.) Using such a system, a vice president of marketing who has been with the company for 18 years, has worked in manufacturing and other divisions, and is consistently rated as superior in performance might receive an overall score of 88/100. A new worker who takes phone calls in the customer service center, is two years out of high school, and is an average performer, might receive a score of 7/100.

Such an index monitors the strength of a company's personnel and gives it a way to calculate the true loss of a key person to turnover. Every person who quits the company is ranked based upon his or her "Human Capital Score." Similarly, when a new person is hired, that person's score goes into the index. (In this case, one would have to guess on the performance rating or take the word of previous employees. Another alternative is to rate performance as a zero until the person has been on the job a year.)

What this approach does not measure is the knowledge or competencies of your employees. It also does not measure values, ethics, or managerial expertise. Hence, it does not really provide data on the overall brainpower of the employee base. However, if that brainpower is not is not translated into value for the organization, it is of little use to track it. The advantage of this approach is that it is incredibly simple to execute, easy to understand, and fair, because most of the index is based upon hard, objective measures.

A More Complex Human Capital Index

An organization interested in measuring the level of competency or skill mix of its workforce might want to create a human capital index that looks at experience and competencies. The previous example simply looked at experience and job performance ratings. To construct a more complete index, you would first decide how to weigh the two dimensions of skills/competencies versus experience/performance. A good mode might be:

- 60 percent experience/performance and
- 40 percent competencies/skills.

The weights might be reversed in an organization that needs to work on acquiring many new skills or competencies and is not as concerned with having seasoned employees. Once you've decided on the weights of the two factors, you can compute the experience/performance side of the metric using the approach I previously outlined. In other words, you measure things like years of experience, variety of experience, performance ratings, and job level. The competency side of the equation is a little more challenging.

Types of Skills/Competencies

The overall mix of skills needed from employees can easily be separated into two types, technical and nontechnical.

Technical skills are those that pertain to your industry or field and include a wide variety of technologies, such as engineering disciplines, hardware platforms, system engineering, marketing, legal, human resource development, contracting, or any field of knowledge that is important to your organization today and in the future. Start out by listing all of these broad disciplines or fields of knowledge, and weighting their importance on a 1-to-10 scale. This will be hard to do because they are all important. The weightings should be done by a cross-functional team that can be objective in looking at their entire organization rather than their own function/discipline. The competencies that end up with 10 ratings should be the ones that are most closely correlate with current and future company success. Make sure that there is a relatively even distribution of scores. In other words, they can't all be rated 7 to 10, or the system will not work.

Next, you should do the same thing with nontechnical skills/ competencies. Many companies already have a list of these "generic" competencies. For example, Nortel developed a list they call "Core Values" that includes:

- Leadership
- Quality
- People Growth
- Customer Orientation
- Teamwork
- Risk Taking and Innovation

Your list might not be as concise as this one, and also might include 15 to 20 nontechnical skill that you consider important. Some other examples might include:

- Project Management
- Verbal Communication
- Planning
- Conflict Resolution
- Relationship Management
- Listening
- Written Communication
- Coaching/Mentoring
- Negotiating
- Providing Feedback

As with technical skills, each nontechnical skill must be weighted based on its importance. The weightings can be done overall, for the entire company, or for each position. (The same sort of thing could be done for technical skills.) Certainly not every technical skill will be appropriate for every employee. The more rigorous you make this index the more complicated it becomes, however, so I recommend not making it too complicated to begin with.

Once you've identified all the skills and competencies important to your organization, you need to rate each person's level of proficiency in each area. This rating should also be 1-to-10 scale, with 10 indicating a world-class expert, and 1 indicating a complete beginner or novice in the area. A zero rating would mean that the person has absolutely no knowledge or skill in the area. The ratings of skills and competencies can be done using a variety of methods. Companies that employ 360-degree appraisals can use this process to do the competency assessment. In 360-degree appraisals, employees get feedback from their customers, suppliers, bosses, and peers. A simpler approach is to have a person rated by himself and his peers. The more people who have input to the ratings, the more complicated and bureaucratic the system will become, so select an approach you can really commit to. When you are all finished, each employee will have a competency score that ranges from 0 to 100. A high score indicated a high degree of competency in highly weighted skills.

To calculate the overall human capital score for each employee, you would take the competency score multiplied by the weight and the experience score multiplied by the weight to arrive at the final number. A couple of examples are shown in Figure 9-4.

Final Recommendations

The most important aspects of an organization are hard to measure objectively. Competitors can steal your products, services, distribution channels, and often just about anything you do except in "fuzzy" areas like your culture or your personnel. Traditional HR metrics fail to inform an organization about the level of performance or knowledge of its employee base. The two examples of human capital indices provided here are not intended as ironclad models; rather, they are designed to stimulate you to develop your own index, incorporating whatever makes sense for your organization. Some of the best metrics I've have been custom-designed for a particular company, not taken from a book or from another, similar company. It is

CHIEF INFORMATION OFFICER		
Competency Scores		**Experience Scores**
Technical	82 × 60% = 49.2	Job Level	88 × 35% = 30.8
Nontechnical	49 × 40% = 19.6	Per. Rating	65 × 30% = 19.5
		Variety of Exp.	30 × 25% = 7.5
		Years of Exp.	55 × 15% = 8.25

Totals	**68.8**	**66.05**
Human Capital Score	68.8 × 60% = 41.3	
	+ 66.05 × 40% = 26.4	
Total	**67.7/100**	

JUNIOR MARKETING EXECUTIVE		
Competency Scores		**Experience Scores**
Technical	18 × 60% = 10.8	Job Level	10 × 35% = 3.5
Nontechnical	12 × 40% = 4.8	Per. Rating	72 × 30% = 21.6
		Variety of Exp.	35 × .25% = 1.25
		Years of Exp.	5 × .15% = .75

Totals	**15.6**	**27.1**
Human Capital Score	15.6 × 60% = 9.4	
	+ 27.1 × 40% = 10.8	
Total	**20.2/100**	

Figure; 9-4. Examples of Human Capital Indices

often useful to calculate indices several different ways for a year or two to find the right formula that best depicts overall performance levels.

It is also important that your employees accept the index as being valid. You would not want to set it up so that an employee whom everyone knows is extremely valuable gets a lower rating than an average employee. Be prepared to do some evaluation and refinement of the index over time. It's worth the effort if this type of data can help you make more balanced management decisions regarding your human resources.

EMPLOYER OF CHOICE

A key success factor for many of today's companies is the ability to attract and retain the best people. Organizations are now very competitive in their approaches to becoming great places to work. Special accommodations, like day-care, health clubs, flexible hours, and working from home offices, have become commonplace. When *The 100 Best Companies to Work For in America* was first published by Robert Levering and Milton Moskowitz in the early 1980s, only 2 of the 100 companies in the book offered flextime. On the current list, 70 percent offer some kind of flextime, and 89 percent offer compressed work weeks. If being the employer of choice, or being regarded as one of the best companies in America, is a key success factor, it is important that some of the metrics on your corporate dashboard monitor your progress toward that goal.

A client of mine recently established a vision to become one of America's best companies to work for. Their biggest competitor was among the top ten in that category in 2000, and they were not even on the list, according to *Fortune* magazine (January 10, 2000). They can easily measure if they make it onto the list next year, and also measure their rank relative to competitors who also make the list. However, a measure that changes once a year is not too meaningful. They need to devise metrics they can track at least monthly to determine if progress is being made.

Fortune Magazine's Metrics for the Best Companies

The criteria for making *Fortune* magazine's annual list of the 100 best companies to work for are largely based on a comprehensive survey that consists of 57 questions about how employees rate their experience at the company. In fact, two-thirds of the points for making the list are based on employee survey data. The other third are based on the existence of policies, practices, and services that are employee-focused. In listing the 100 best companies to work for, *Fortune* looks at several key metrics:

- Job growth—number of new jobs created per year
- Applicants—number of applicants in relation to number of positions open

- Diversity—percent of women and minorities in the workforce
- Voluntary turnover
- Number of hours of training per employee

These are all good metrics for assessing whether or not your company is viewed as a good place to work, and they can all be tracked at least once a month. Some other good metrics to consider that relate to being a good employer are as follows:

- Offer to acceptance ratio—percent of candidates that accept job offers
- Best practices index—employee benefits and services offered versus best-in-class companies in same field
- Employee morale data gathered via focus groups
- Absenteeism or sick time used
- Participation at company events after work
- Percent of employees with stock options or retirement benefits that they would stand to lose if they left (exit barriers)

If becoming a great place to work is part of your vision, or a key success factor in achieving another vision, it is important that you develop a gauge on your dashboard that provides information on your progress toward this goal. It is unlikely that a single metric will do the trick. No single measure will verify that a company is a great place to work; rather, an index that combines a number of the individual metrics listed previously must be utilized. (Refer to Chapter 5 for more information on constructing a performance index.)

METRICS FOR THE DOT-COMS

As companies develop metrics to better assess their performance, the financial section of the scorecard is often the least subject to change. Sales, ROI, EVA, cash flow, profits, and similar metrics appear on most scorecards I've seen recently. Yet, it appears that many of these traditional metrics don't apply as well to Internet companies in today's New Economy. Yahoo! reports better-than-expected earnings in the first quarter of 2000—and their stock drops by $5.00 a share. AOL reports that they are merging with Time Warner—and their stock drops about 10 percent in one day. Eventually, all e-firms will have to become profitable if they want to survive, but their price-to-earnings ratio seems to have no correlation with stock prices, as is the case for more traditional companies. It appears that the dashboard for an Internet company should include some unique gauges.

First-Generation Internet Metrics

The first new metric for Internet firms is number of website hits. This measure was initially used to help determine growth, value, and the prices Internet firms like Yahoo! were able to charge for advertising. The belief was that website hits would translate into sales for the advertiser. Formulas were being created to equate web site hits (a leading indicator) with purchases (a lagging indicator). Measuring the number of exposures of a given advertisement is not a new idea. Billboard companies can tell advertisers how many people drive by their advertsiements on the freeway each day, and this helps determine prices for placing billboards in various locations. The television and radio industries both measure the number of people in their audiences (or share points) as a major factor in determining their overall success and advertising revenues. Based on their traditional use in these established industries, it would seem that website hits would be a great metric for Internet firms, and indeed website hit counts are frequently used by corporations to evaluate the success of their websites.

The problem with tracking website hits is that they don't necessarily predict buying behavior. The Internet is filled with window shoppers who don't buy anything from the sites they visit. I recently sold a collector car on eBay and had over 400 website hits. No car lot in the world would have attracted that amount of attention to my car in a week's time. A more telling metric was the number of bids I received. The first time I ran the auction, I received 55 bids but none of them met my reserve price. The second time I ran the auction, I received only 42 bids, but one was $2,500 over the reserve price. In my evaluation, eBay turned out to be a great way to sell a car, and I believe that the number of bids received on auctions is probably an excellent metric for an on-line auction company like eBay.

Second-Generation Internet Metrics

A new more sophisticated set of metrics is being used by some of the larger internet firms of today. Website hits are easy to track, but the measure turns out to not be too useful. Some of the second generation metrics include: number of new visitors, length of stay, click-throughs, and repeat visits. The two metrics that are monitored closely by investment professionals are number of new visits and length of stay. The first measure is called "eyeballs" in the industry, and the second one is referred to as "stickiness." Direct mail firms probably wish they had a measure like this that told them how much time we spend looking over the mailing piece before we toss it in the trash. Many I don't even open, whereas others get opened and even saved sometime. A metric that could be quantified that seems to directly influence stock prices of internet firms is the comments made by investors on stock chat boards. These comments are particularly influential prior to or directly after the company has some sort of announcement or news release. It would be possible to monitor major sites where securities are discussed each day and count both the number of positive and negative comments, and the potential impact of these comments on the stock price.

Investigating the New Dot-Com Metrics

A professor at McMaster University in Hamilton, Ontario set out to find out if these new internet metrics actually prove to be reliable predictors of organizational health. In a recent article in the *Toronto Globe and Mail* (April 11, 2000, p. B-15), Dr. Nick Bontis explains how he tracked the stock performance of 15 major internet firms for a year. Yahoo had the most number of "eyeballs" with 40 million unique users. Dr. Bontis tried to find a correlation between the growth in number of unique users and stock price. Over the 12 months in his study, eBay's performance showed the strongest correlation. Number of unique visitors grew 367 percent, and stock price rose 430 percent in the same time period. On the other end of the spectrum, Infoseek added 83 percent new visitors, and its stock rose only 13 percent. Overall, the 15 companies in the sample did show a fairly strong correlation between growth in "eyeballs" looking at their sites, and increases in stock price. Dr. Bontis explains: "The number of unique visitors was a positive and significant predictor of stock price fluctuations, whereas traditional financial measures such as revenue and gross margins acted in an inverse relationship with stock prices."

The 1100+ point drop in the NASDQ during the week of April 10, 2000 would not seem to have been predicted by looking at these new internet metrics, however. The only one that might have given some warning was comments on stock chat boards, that typically convey the feelings of investors, and are a good gauge of their sentiments.

The new internet metrics proposed here are, at best, leading indicators of growth and demand for the information on a web site by customers. It does make sense to include them on the dashboards of dot-com companies to supplement some of the more traditional measures. One of the best things about these metrics is that they can be tracked every day, or even every hour. Financial, customer, or employee measures cannot usually be tracked that often. These metrics can and should be monitored on a daily basis to help predict the future success of the internet firm. What this points out is that the traditional measures of the health of an organization may not apply as well to internet companies. I would not recommend abandoning the traditional metrics like sales, market share, and profits, but to supplement the internet scorecard with some of the measures discussed here. Time will tell whether these metrics actually predict organizational success, but the jury is still out. There is not enough history on these firms or the new metrics to validate their ability to predict financial results.

MEASURING INNOVATION AND RISK TAKING

Another important strategic metric for many organizations today is one that looks at their ability to be innovative with product/service designs, and to take risks. As organizations become larger and develop greater resources for dealing with failure, they seem to also become risk averse. It's almost as if they now have so much to lose that they are afraid to take risks. It's rather strange that an organization can start out being quite innovative and unafraid of taking a worthwhile risk, yet end up ten years later being afraid to try anything new. Perhaps it has something to do with age. Organizations are merely collections of people, and people tend to take more risks and be more creative when they are young. A few companies manage to maintain an innovative, risk-taking culture, but most lose their edge with time.

While everyone agrees that a certain amount of risk taking is important, and that innovation is critical to being a leader in any industry, I have not seen many organizations that know how to measure this important characteristic. Most have taken a stab at measuring something in this area, but most have also found that the metric did not drive the sort of culture and behavior they were looking for

4 Types of Metrics That Examine Innovation and Risk Taking

As with most sections of the scorecard, there are four general types of data that can be collected:

- Attitude or opinion data
- Behavioral or process data
- Output data
- Outcome data.

Attitude and behavioral metrics tend to be leading indicators, and outcome measures are lagging indicators most of the time. Some examples of the four types of metrics are shown in Figure 9-5.

As you can see from the table, there are many ways to measure whether or not an organization promotes risk taking and innovation. The attitudinal metrics might be an important part of the index because employees need to feel that innovation is desired and that risk taking is OK. As a manager in one company remarked to me, "Risk taking is rewarded around here as long as you succeed—failures are not tolerated."

METRICS THAT FOCUS ON INNOVATION AND RISK TAKING	
Attitude/Opinion Metrics	**Behavior/Process Metrics**
• Employee survey about how the organization encourages innovation • Customer survey rating creativity of products/services • Employee opinions about how the organization deals with failures	• Number of new product development teams • Percent of time spent on new products/services • Levels of authority/empowerment of employees • Use of cross-functional teams to design new products/services
Output Metrics	**Outcome Metrics**
• Number of publications • Number of patents • Number of new products/services • Awards received from professional associations/ societies	• Dollars in sales from new products • Percent profit from new products/services • Cost reductions due to process or design innovations • Products/services copied by competitors

Figure 9-5. Examples of Four Types of Metrics

This company did not have a culture that encouraged risk taking, because failure often cost someone his or her job. If these sort of attitudes pervade your organization, you will have little luck with a strategy that focuses on being more innovative and taking more risks.

Ineffective behavior measures or process metrics can drive the wrong behavior. A group of car dealers I worked with almost went broke because one of their key measures was percent of employees on improvement teams. While everyone was in team meetings, customers were walking out of the car lots because no one was around to help them. Another company measured the extent to which a new product design process had been followed, and whether or not the right people were on design teams. Because this was how they were measured, everyone followed the new product design process, and it took them longer to produce products that no one wanted. The cost of new product development also rose because of all the additional meetings and documentation generated by the "new and improved" product design process.

Output metrics also tend to drive the wrong results when organizations attempt to measure innovation and risk taking. A common output metric for R & D organizations is number of patents generated. A new idea needs to be truly unique to receive a patent. Not all patented products will sell well, but it is important to encourage new ideas and to have a constant pipeline of new products. One problem with number of patents as a metric is that patents are expensive. Motorola calculated that the work needed to receive a patent averaged $70,000. If most patented new products don't make it to market, this metric could encourage the wasting of a lot of money.

Another common output metric used in R & D and academic institutions is publication. Publish or perish is still the law in academia, and you get what you measure. In the field of business alone there are over 1,000 new books published each year, and the vast majority sell less than 500 copies during their entire print cycle. Writing a book that sells is often not part of the criteria, because academic institutions don't want to encourage commercialism from their professors. In fact, scientists like Carl Sagan, who have written bestsellers, have often been scorned by their colleagues for chasing royalties.

Measuring awards received from professional societies is another metric associated with innovation. Films that receive Academy Awards are considered better than others that may have been commercial successes but were artistic failures. Every field has its own version of the Academy Awards that it bestows for accomplishments in that field. The problem with counting trophies and plaques is that earning them becomes an end in and of itself. Some organizations get very good at figuring out how to win various trophies and honors, and devote far too many of their resources to the pursuit thereof.

Outcome metrics are probably the best way to measure innovation and risk taking. If innovative new products produce huge sales volumes and profits, this is a pretty clear indicator of success. Having your new product or service ripped off by competitors is also a very clear measure of success in this area. While outcome measures are the strongest indicators of innovation and risk taking, they are lagging measures, and too much focus on them may actually discourage risk taking. If you measure the success of a new product or service solely based on the revenue it generates, some will clearly be labeled as failures. One organization gets around this by measuring and actually celebrating its biggest failures at an annual awards banquet. Their belief is that if they are not failing at a number of things each year, they are not taking enough risks. Furthermore, each failure usually provides a lesson to be learned. What a great way of encouraging risk taking and innovation. These awards are not an attempt to publicly roast or humiliate the employees involved with the failure; rather, it is all done in the spirit of fun and learning.

What Becomes of Strategic Metrics?

The strategic measures on your scorecard should be subject to periodic review and change, depending upon how you progress in achieving your vision. Some strategic measures fall off the scorecard completely; some have their status changed from strategic to fundamental metrics; and some evolve into different metrics or involve different data-collection techniques.

You should expect to drop some strategic metrics entirely from your scorecard. For example, Ericsson no longer tracks brand recognition as even a fundamental metric—they have now achieved it and are satisfied that enough people know who they are and what they do. Similarly, IBM does not track telephone quality anymore. They have learned how to handle voice mail and telephone calls well and simply don't need to measure this aspect of performance any more. Once you accomplish one of your key success factors, or solve a problem, the measures associated with the key success factor may no longer be necessary.

Other strategic measures don't get eliminated, but their dashboard status gets reduced from speedometer to, say, oil gauge. In other words, what was once a key strategic metric now becomes a business fundamental or a mission-related metric. For example, a company with an aggressive cost-cutting effort in place might measure reduction in operating expenses as a strategic measure for a couple of years, until they get their costs down to where they should be. The cost-reduction gauge never vanishes entirely, but it might transition to a measure of overall operating expense versus budget, which is a fundamental measure that the company will always have on its dashboard.

The third thing that tends to happen to strategic metrics is that their definition changes, and perhaps the methods used to collect the data change. This is common, as organizations find better, more sophisticated methods of measuring different aspects of performance. The example mentioned earlier of the company that looked at the attractiveness and loyalty of each of their customer accounts was originally a strategic metric that looked at loyalty only. Through experience in monitoring the loyalty metric, the company came to realize that all customers were not equal, and they needed to add a dimension to the measure that looked at the relative importance of every customer before deciding on the appropriate level of loyalty each one warranted.

Use the checklist below to assure that your strategic metrics are precise and valid.

CHECKLIST FOR EVALUATING STRATEGIC METRICS

Strategic metrics should be:

☐ Directly linked to key success factors.

☐ No more than one-third of the total number of measures on your scorecard.

☐ Leading indicators (usually).

☐ Examined at least once a quarter to see if they still make sense.

☐ Refined as you learn to improve the measure and/or data-collection methods.

☐ Mostly on the scorecards of senior executives and upper-level managers.

☐ Linked to the accomplishment of your vision.

☐ Correlated to key outcomes or financial measures where possible.

☐ Predictive of future success.

Strategies: Developing Actions, Projects, and Initiatives to Reach Your Targets

The most difficult part of the planning process is figuring out how to achieve your vision, key success factors, and performance targets. No matter what they may be, there are always many different ways of reaching them. This chapter will focus on the process for determining strategies. There is not much science involved in developing strategies, but even the most well thought-out plans must be tested before their effectiveness is known. As with many things in life, the key to developing effective strategies is having the right information to use in making decisions. Much of this information should have been gathered in the situation analysis phase of your planning process, where you looked at your competitors, customers, and your own strengths and weaknesses.

KEY SUCCESS FACTORS AND STRATEGIES

As you learned in Chapter 8, a good plan is to identify the three to five key success factors that will most help you achieve your vision. Key success factors are like a broad collection of strategies, without specifying the details. For example, I discussed how one of Ericsson's KSFs for its cellular phones division was brand recognition. There are many different ways to gain brand recognition. Building a football stadium in Charlotte was a specific strategy, as was getting Ericsson's phones featured in the James Bond movie, "Tomorrow Never Dies."

Once you have identified key success factors and metrics for evaluating your progress in achieving them, the next step is to develop action plans, initiatives, or strategies.

AVOIDING POORLY DEFINED STRATEGIES

Organizations often develop failing strategies because the decision-making process is too clouded with politics, self-interest on the part of individual executives, and an unwillingness to take risks for fear of failure. One company I worked with decided that a key success factor for market-share growth was to improve service to existing customers in order to build greater loyalty and encourage referrals for new business. A strategic planning meeting to decide on the best strategies for achieving this goal was held at a nice resort away from the office. Each executive believed that his or her function was the key to market-share growth and argued strenuously for the resources and support needed.

The VP of information technology believed that improved technology and systems were the primary strategy the company needed to deploy to achieve customer loyalty and growth: "Our systems are seriously out of date compared to the competition." Building detailed customer databases and updating our phone system will enable us to provide the customized service necessary for improving loyalty and getting more referrals."

The VP of marketing objected, explaining that a comprehensive marketing strategy was the essential element: "Better information technology and phone systems will do little to improve our market share—new systems will only increase our costs. We need to do thorough market research on potential customers and those of competitors to segment them by key characteristics and develop a multi-tiered marketing strategy aimed at the priorities of each group."

The VP of human resources disagreed: "What we really need to do is upgrade the qualifications of our customer contact personnel, make an increased investment in training, and reduce turnover through better compensation and employee services."

The consultant leading the planning meeting was far from objective as well. She thought the strategy ought to center around a solution that her company specialized in providing. Of course, it would require at least 20 consultants on-site for a year or more, but this approach had helped many other companies increase customer loyalty and grow market share.

The bottom line is that often everyone has his or her own interests at heart, rather than the overall good of the company. Each individual has a hard time forgetting the function he or she represents and feels obligated to the staff to fight for resources and linkage of the function to the company's overall strategic plan.

Tip: *Beware of politics in the selection of strategies.
It helps to include someone from the outside in the
planning meetings who has no interest in selling
a particular strategy or program.*

The President or CEO may be more objective than the others because he or she does not represent a particular function, but often this is true only in theory. Usually, one or two senior executives will devote time throughout the year to convincing the boss that his or her pet project is the best way to achieve the company vision. Deciding on strategy becomes a game of politics, and decisions are often made based on who can argue the most effectively for their own interests.

Poorly defined strategies are not just caused by political games among executives. Vague key success factors are often the cause. For example, one company I worked with brainstormed a list of over 100 possible KSFs in a planning meeting. After much discussion, they narrowed down the list to four, one of which was "Leadership."

Everyone agreed that the company had a problem with leadership—which, of course, meant *them*. After identifying that leadership was important, a small group worked on a definition of this key success factor and came up with something like this:

*We need to work in a collaborative fashion to achieve the
company vision and goals and communicate a consistent set
of values and expectations for all company employees and
stakeholders.*

Based on this definition, the group identified a few key metrics to assess leadership. One was how employees rated leadership performance on an annual survey. The planning team then proceeded to brainstorm possible strategies for improving leadership. The list ranged from moving some of the executives into different jobs, to a team-building exercise in the woods for a few days, to having everyone complete a personality evaluation. The strategies the team eventually selected skirted the real issues—a lack of leadership at the top, and a team of senior executives that were fiercely competitive with each other.

One of the strategies that made the short list was changing the organization structure. Redrawing the organizational chart is probably one of the most common and least effective ways of improving organizational performance. It's hard to tell if the company's strategies for improving leadership were effective, because they had not clearly defined the key success factor and had not developed good metrics for tracking improvement.

Tip: Failure to clearly define key success factors, and a lack of good performance metrics for key success factors, are among the most frequent causes of bad decisions regarding strategy.

PRODUCT STRATEGIES
Apple's iMac

Some organizations differentiate themselves from competitors by offering a unique product or service. For example, Apple computers have always been unique in their ease of use. The company has had its share of colossal failures and successes over the years, but has maintained a very loyal base of customers. The iMac computer, released in 1998, appears to be just the ticket for once again restoring the company to health through innovative product design. The company hired industrial designer Jonathan Ive to create a PC with the futuristic design. (Ive made a name for himself designing tubs, toilets, and sinks for a London design firm.) The distinctive, clear, blue-green plastic top on the iMac lets people see that it is just as elegant inside as out. Of course, innovative design is not the only reason the iMac has been successful. It is very fast, attractively priced, and even easier to use than previous Apple models.

Yet there are many low-priced, fast, user-friendly PCs on the market. As with most things in business, it doesn't take long for someone to copy your strategy or product design. A firm I've never heard of is now offering a PC that looks almost exactly like the iMac for about 50 percent lower price (if you sign up for two years service from an internet service provider). However, Apple is staying one step ahead of their competitors with the regular release of new and better iMacs, including a laptop version.

The New Volkswagen Beetle

The new Volkswagen Beetle is one of the most successful cars the company has introduced. Yet if its designers had listened to corporate headquarters, the vehicle never would have existed. The company was interested in going forward, not backward. Initial proposals for the car were quickly squashed. Designers worked in secret in California for several years on the project. One Volkswagen executive believed in it, but knew the company would never fund it, so he secretly funneled money to the project from his budget until he felt the political climate in the company would be more receptive to the idea. Volkswagen executives believed that their cars should always be forward-looking in design and that a return to old, albeit classic, designs was a mistake. By the time the executives found out about the secret project, it was so far along and had received so much positive feedback that they agreed to continue to support it. The success of other car companies with retro designs may have had something to do with their change of sentiment, as well. Jaguar had returned to the classic lines of the E-Type sports car with its new XK8, and DaimlerChrysler had introduced some successful products with retro styling, such as the Plymouth Prowler, and the new PT Cruiser.

Designers at Volkswagen used the same basic, round shape of the old Bug, but made it more muscular and modern than its predecessor. The shape of the car evokes delight in almost everyone. The front-end view is designed so that the hoodline looks like a smile, with headlights as eyes. The spartan dashboard is both futuristic and nostalgic, with its unique bud vase. The car has done better in the marketplace than anyone expected, with 40,000 units sold between March and October, 1998. The company has easily surpassed its sales goal of 50,000 units for the first year; its biggest problem now is keeping production up with demand—customers have to wait up to 16 weeks for a yellow Bug. Volkswagen has recently come out with a Turbo model of the Bug, and plans to release a convertible model in the next year or two. The company is also selling limited edition colors exclusively via the Internet.

As with the iMac, styling appears to be a key factor in the Bug's success. There are many well-made, inexpensive cars on the market, but none that look anything like the Volkswagen Bug.

SERVICE STRATEGIES

Products are often easily copied and, in most industries, pioneering companies get their designs ripped off by competitors who change them just enough to avoid being sued and often offer very similar products at lower prices. One way of ensuring competitive advantage is to focus on service. A company that does this better than most is the Ritz Carlton hotel chain. Every point of interaction between a customer and a Ritz employee is carefully engineered so that the guest always has a pleasant and consistent experience.

Ritz Carlton is in a very different league than McDonald's, but the two firms are both known for amazing consistency of service and product. One of Ritz Carlton's closely guarded secrets is how they find such intelligent, well-mannered, good-looking people to work in their properties. Competitors have no idea how Ritz finds and manages to hang on to these people in an industry known for high turnover. McDonald's approach is to standardize and automate everything they can to ensure consistency. They also have exceptional employee training, and employees receive a great deal of supervision. As with most fast food companies, McDonald's has fairly high turnover, but still manages to maintain consistency in service. Ritz Carlton is also known for consistent service, but it is not achieved through automation and close supervision of employees. In fact Ritz Carlton employees are given broad levels of authority to do whatever it takes to satisfy a guest. Like upscale retailer Nordstrom, Ritz Carlton carefully selects each member of its staff. By hiring carefully and treating employees well once they come on board, both companies do a better job of retaining staff than many of their competitors. It would seem as if this strategy would be fairly easy to copy, but I've yet to see a hotel chain or retail store that has the caliber of service found at Ritz Carlton or Nordstrom.

CUSTOMER RELATIONSHIP STRATEGIES
United Airlines

Another strategy that many organizations have employed successfully is built around successful relationships with key customers. The airlines are masters at this. For example, United segments its frequent-flyer customers according to the number of miles they fly each year and the average ticket price paid. The highest tier of customers achieve "1K" status if they fly 100,000 actual air miles in a year. These are the most profitable customers for United—they often spend over $100,000 a year on airline tickets and usually pay full price. 1K customers receive the highest priority for first-class upgrades and double frequent flyer miles for most flights; are able to board the plane first; get first choice of meals; and receive mileage bonuses for each 10,000 miles flown. They have access to a special 800 number that is answered immediately, a special check-in desk at the airport, and a host of other special services.

The remaining frequent flyers are sorted into other categories: Premier Executive, Premier, and Mileage Plus.

Airlines segment customers and develop special services for their high-end customers to ensure loyalty from them. Since these customers are their most profitable, losing just one can cost the airline thousands of dollars in profits. This special treatment approach works extremely well, because customers become accustomed to the high degree of service and begin to expect it. As the special treatment becomes the passenger's standard, the regular service from other airlines appears below par, and thus loyalty is fostered.

Dayton-Hudson and American Express—Using Customer Data to Build Loyalty

Dayton-Hudson chose a similar approach, but instead of concentrating on the top 25 percent of their customer base they chose to focus on the top 2.5 percent, who generated about two-thirds of their sales. The company made use of a detailed customer database that tracked purchasing trends and preferences of individual customers and used it to tailor awards to each individual customer. American Express, one of the better companies at making use of customer data, has done the same thing. They might notice that you like to shop at Nieman Marcus, so as an award for using your American Express Card they might send you a gift certificate from Nieman's. If your lifestyle changes, and you move from the city to suburbia and start spending more money at Home Depot than at Nieman's, American Express will start sending you gift certificates to Home Depot. This approach—tailoring awards to customer preferences—goes a long way toward building loyalty.

Tip: Service companies like United Airlines and American Express have found that it is important to build the highest levels of loyalty from the most desirable customers; not necessarily from everyone.

OPERATIONAL EXCELLENCE STRATEGIES
Discover Card

Another way to differentiate your organization from competitors is to be the most efficient or lowest cost provider. One company that has chosen this strategy is Discover Financial Services. Of all the credit card companies in the United States, Discover Card does the best job of card member service. Most employees in credit card companies work in cardmember services or the call center, and Discover outperforms them all in both service and costs. If you call 1-800-DIS-COVER, you will get through to a live person in 30 seconds or less and have all of your questions answered in a single call. The company had always been known for excellent cardmember service, but until 1998 had no evidence that they were also the most efficient operation in the business. An independent study done in 1998 revealed that the company also led the field in operational efficiency: their transaction costs were among the lowest of all credit card companies in the service side of the business.

Shea Homes

Shea Homes is another company that focuses on efficiency and quality service as key success factors. Shea builds homes in Arizona, California, and Colorado, and does almost all of their work through outside contractors. They are known for reducing cycle time and building homes that have close to zero defects. Shea can build a home from start to finish in much less time than many of their biggest competitors, and when you move into a Shea home, you will have a hard time finding anything wrong. They measure quality of workmanship by listing the number of items, if any, that are noted by the homebuyer at the time of orientation (the acceptance of the home).

The list usually consists of minor repairs needed, like leaky faucets, uneven caulking, paint drips, cracks in cement, and the like. While Shea has an average of .5 items per orientation, it is not uncommon in the industry to have as many as 20 to 30 items on an orientation list. Shea's target is that they will build 80 percent of their homes with zero defects by the year 2000. All indications are that they will make this goal—they were at 76 percent zero defects at year-end 1999.

Shea also measures customer satisfaction by number of referrals. They use a stringent measure, in that referrals are determined by the number of Shea homeowners who refer others to Shea; many other homebuilders track referrals from others, not just those who already live in their homes. Shea's referral rate in Arizona was at 20 percent at year-end 1999.

An amazing 95 percent of its homebuyers would recommend Shea Homes to their friends! Shea has accomplished this largely by narrowing down their contractors from about 800 many years ago to around 100 today. They have partnered with these 100 or so suppliers, working together to better manage their businesses. Shea teaches their suppliers to evaluate their businesses against the Malcolm Baldrige criteria, and 12 of their contractors won the Arizona State Quality Award in 1997. The company is a role model for the use of the planning principles outlined in this book. Another testimony to their success is that Shea just purchased their largest competitor in the Phoenix/Scottsdale area: UDA Homes. Shea is now the largest home builder in the area, as well as being the best in quality. (Incorporating their operational excellence strategy with the new acquisition should not be difficult, as the president of UDA Homes used to be an executive at Shea Homes.)

STRATEGIES FOR DEPARTMENTS AND SUPPORT FUNCTIONS

Plans are made at various levels in an organization: business unit plans, facility plans, even plans for support departments. It is important for departments in an organization to have their own vision, key success factors, measures, targets, and strategies. Several years ago, I worked with a finance function in IBM that had a vision of changing their role from data collectors and reporters to financial consultants. Achieving this vision would not only help them add more value to their organization, but also make their work more interesting and challenging. They devised a strategy that eliminated unnecessary reporting and data collection, thus freeing up time to spend consulting with internal customers on their financial results and helping the group achieve its vision.

The only way to ascertain if you have selected an appropriate strategy is to try it out and see if it works. Before spending a lot of money and time on a strategy that you're unsure of, you want to at least review how other organizations may have used the strategy effectively, or how and why some may have failed. Another effective technique when evaluating potential strategies is to describe exactly how the strategy will affect the metrics or gauges you have identified for a given key success factor. For example, a team might be called upon to explain how improving service by investing in more customer-contact personnel would lead to greater loyalty from customers (a KSF). It's a good idea to have individuals who were not involved in the planning meetings review the strategies, and to get their input on the likelihood of success.

If there is time, it is often wise to "preflight" a given initiative or strategy in a single business unit or facility before rolling it out to the entire company. Timing often makes this impossible, however—by the time you find out whether or not the strategy is effective, you might need a new one.

STRATEGIES AND METRICS

In the previous chapter, you learned how to develop metrics that provide information on your progress toward achieving your vision. These strategic metrics link back to your key success factors and provide executives with information on how various strategies are working. Strategic metrics linked to key success factors tend to appear on the dashboards of upper-level managers and executives.

Each individual strategy also needs its own set of metrics. For example, one company that was looking to change its image from traditional and conservative to leading edge and innovative created a good strategic metric that looked at its overall image with clients and potential clients. In order to change its image, it developed a new advertising campaign, new marketing materials, new service offerings, training for staff members based around a new service model, and a variety of other strategies. Each of these individual strategies needed its own metrics that evaluated the cost and effectiveness of communicating the new image. Internal process metrics were also tracked for each strategy, which looked at the level of creativity of marketing materials, the extent to which the new brochures were completed on time and within budget, and so on.

The Danger of Simply Measuring Strategies

I've reviewed a number of strategic plans for large federal organizations, and all of their metrics focus on the completion of specific projects or strategies. I reviewed one that contained a list of over 100 projects or initiatives, each with its own set of metrics. This approach creates far too many metrics, and, though the project or strategy may look healthy, the organization may still fall short of its overall goals.

For example, the Department of Energy's strategic plan lists one of their objectives as "improving international nuclear safety." Supporting this objective is a series of projects or strategies, such as: "Promote nuclear safety culture improvements internationally by providing strong leadership in international nuclear safety organizations and centers." Missing from this plan is a gauge for the Secretary of Energy that measures overall levels of international nuclear safety. Without such a metric, it is impossible to tell whether or not the various strategies are helping to achieve the objective.

It is important to measure strategies, but first make sure that there are gauges on your dashboard that link back to major goals or key success factors. Measures of individual strategies are subordinate to these higher-level metrics.

The Danger of Benchmarking to Define Strategies

One conclusion you should draw from this chapter is that there is no one recipe for success—there are as many good strategies as there are types of organizations. Benchmarking, the practice of studying the best companies and adopting their practices, has peaked in popularity but is still a widely used shortcut for defining successful strategies. The idea is to copy successful strategies from other companies who have already evaluated them and perhaps learned from many years of failed attempts using other strategies. Benchmarking can leapfrog a company way ahead of its competitors—if the right strategies are chosen. The folly of this approach is that what works in one company may fail in your own organization. In fact, this is usually the case. There are no universally successful strategies. The success of a given strategy depends upon timing, resources, competitor strategies, competencies, and a variety of other variables that all must be properly aligned.

The chances of all these variables being identical in your organization and another are very remote. Therefore, it is unlikely that copying another company's strategy will provide yours with the same level of success. However, benchmarking is a useful way to generate alternative strategies: successful practices of similar companies should be examined and considered, but not adopted without thoroughly evaluating the likelihood of their success within your organization.

Tip: Using benchmarking to identify your strategies will always make you the follower, never the pioneer.

The checklist below will help you to assess the strategies your company develops in order to achieve its goals.

CHECKLIST FOR EVALUATING STRATEGIES

Decisions on the right strategy should be made by asking the following questions of each of the proposed alternatives:

- ☐ What is the probability that this strategy will allow us to reach the desired target/goal?

- ☐ What evidence do we have that this strategy has worked for others?

- ☐ Is this strategy different from our competitors' or simply copying theirs?

- ☐ What are the risks associated with this strategy?

- ☐ Do we have the capabilities to carry out this strategy?

- ☐ Is this strategy going to be politically acceptable—will senior management and/or board members buy it?

- ☐ Can we afford this strategy?

- ☐ What is the likelihood that a competitor will copy this strategy and perform better than us?

- ☐ Are we thinking outside of the box, or taking the safe route as we often do?

PART 3

IMPLEMENTING THE SCORECARD

Instrumentation: Designing Data-Collection Strategies

Designing the scorecard is actually much easier than figuring out how to collect the appropriate data. During this phase of the process, changes often are made to the original plan and metrics. Reality sets in when the organization discovers the cost and time involved in data collection. In this chapter, we will demonstrate how to execute a data-collection plan. Much of the chapter is devoted to measuring the process metrics that will help you predict output performance and outcome measures. Many organizations do a good job measuring their outputs, but these are mostly lagging indicators.

MEASUREMENT PERSPECTIVES

Any organization can be conceptualized as a system with inputs, processes, outputs, and outcomes. Figure 11-1 depicts such a systems model of organizational performance.

The ideal measurement system will include measures of all four perspectives: inputs, processes, outputs, and outcomes. Examples of these metrics are shown in Figure 11-2.

Outcome measures are usually highly important to an organization because they clearly tell it how it's doing on achieving its mission and vision. However, simply measuring the outcomes is of little help in better managing the organization. This is why the scorecard

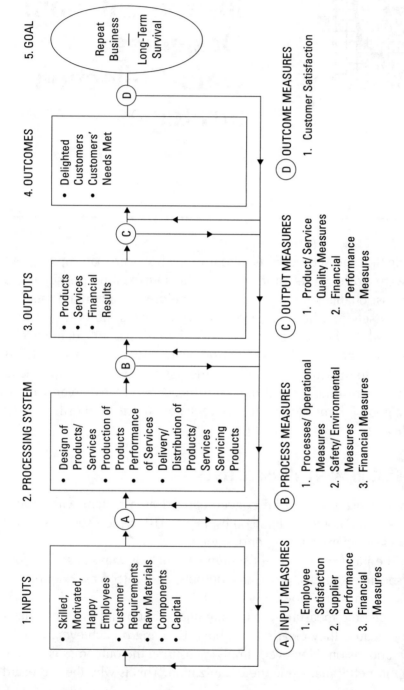

Figure 11-1. Systems Model of Organizational Performance

	EXAMPLES	**EXAMPLE METRICS**
Inputs	Components or parts	Defects, returns, damage
	Market research data	Completeness Accuracy in predicting customer buying behavior
	Building specifications	Completeness
	Film script Marketability	Human interest
	Customer-reported problems	Clarity
Processes	Baking bread	Time and temperature
	Making a sales call	Number of objections raised
	Completeness of proposal questionnaire	Correct sales process followed
	Handling a customer inquiry	Cycle time Completeness of data Correct probing process followed
	Troubleshooting a mechanical problem	Use of correct diagnostic tools and equipment Cycle time Safety guidelines followed
Outputs	Audit report	Thoroughness Accuracy Customer feedback
	Car repaired	Accuracy of repair Timeliness Work clearly documented Customer feedback
	Stranded boater rescued	Property saved Safety of boaters Cost of mission
	Sale made	Dollar value of sale Terms and conditions New or existing customer Margin $ of sale

Figure 11-2. Example Metrics Sorted According to System Components

Figure 11-2 – Continued

	EXAMPLES	EXAMPLE METRICS
Outcomes	Happy customers	Repeat business Increase in $ spent Referrals
	Successful company	Return on investment Rise in stock price Growth Market share
	Recognition	Awards received Benchmarking visits Positive press Able to attract top talent to work in the company

needs to be a mix of measures covering inputs, processes, outputs, and outcomes.

> **Tip:** Make sure your scorecard includes metrics that examine inputs, processes, outputs, and outcomes.

While it's true that all four measurement perspectives are important for any organization, your scorecard may differ in its focus depending upon your level in the organization. If you are a CEO or president, most of your metrics should focus on outcomes such as growth, financial performance, satisfied loyal customers, and making the organization a great place to work. If you are a first-level supervisor, your scorecard should focus more on input and process metrics, along with a few of your own team's outputs. It is important that, across an entire organization, adequate data in each of the four perspectives is collected.

> **Tip:** Scorecards for senior management focus more on outputs and outcomes; scorecards for lower-level managers and individual contributors focus more on inputs and processes.

INPUT METRICS

Input measures are crucial because they tend to have the most influence overall on the quality of an organization's outputs and outcomes. Inputs consist of data, raw materials, people, equipment, facilities, and anything else needed to perform the mission. Inputs, such as components or raw materials in a manufacturing organization, are usually precisely measured. Similarly, equipment is closely evaluated before purchase to ensure it will perform according to the organization's needs. Other important inputs are often not measured well—for example, the quality of new hires. Rarely do organizations follow through on 90-day probation reviews, and the screening of potential new hires is often anything but thorough. For instance, one service company with 50 percent turnover checks only to make sure potential employees don't have a drug problem and then puts them right to work.

An increasingly common approach among organizations today is to stop measuring upon arrival the quality of goods and materials purchased from suppliers. This inspection process is expensive and shouldn't be necessary. Rather than measure the materials or parts as they arrive at the dock, leading organizations ask their suppliers to provide process data each day, so they know that the material that gets delivered will meet their standards. For example, Coca-Cola buys much of its fructose from Cargill. Rather than inspect the fructose when it arrives at its plants, Coke asks Cargill to provide data on key process variables in the fructose manufacturing process. The data are actually linked to Coca-Cola's computers, so they can monitor the fructose production the same way Cargill does. Focusing on the supplier's process metrics ensures that Coca-Cola is getting quality corn syrup every day, and it saves them the time and money once spent on inspections.

Identifying Process Metrics

Process metrics are either incredibly simple to identify, or exceedingly difficult. In the bakery example from Figure 11-2, time and temperature of the oven are two obvious process metrics. Even someone who has never baked could probably figure out that these are the two most important process variables to track and control. In most manufacturing businesses, the process measures have been identified based upon solid research that shows the correlation between certain process parameters and the quality of the outputs produced. This same level of precision process metrics is often lacking in service or government organizations.

Consider a group of employees whose job is to detect and rectify fraud in a credit card company. Their output can be measured easily each day by the dollar amount in fraud detected and recovered and the number of alleged criminals reported to law enforcement authorities. Each investigator gets a "report card" every week showing performance on these key output metrics. Some investigators are much better than others, though. If the manager of this unit wanted to improve *everyone's* performance, he or she would need to look into developing process metrics. The problem is, investigating fraud is not like baking bread. Each case is a little different. Sometimes the card member, who wants to avoid paying for a legitimate charge, perpetrates the fraud. Other times, someone at the merchant organization has put through a fraudulent charge. In other cases, a criminal has stolen a card or obtained the number and put through fraudulent charges. While it is true that each case should follow a step-by step process, mindlessly following this process does not lead to better results.

In talking to some of the top investigators in this unit, it became apparent that the timeliness with which they gathered important details about each case had a direct bearing on the likelihood of resolving it. The longer a case stayed on the books, the less likelihood there was of resolving it. Therefore, a relevant process metric was the cycle time required to gather important facts about the case by interviewing the individuals involved and gathering documentation. The total cycle time for solving the case was not a great process metric; what was important was how quickly the investigator was able to gather and document all the important data about a case.

Most work processes today are more like the fraud investigation unit than the bakery. When job tasks are performed identically every time, we tend to automate them so that we don't, for example, need to constantly adjust the temperature of the oven—something called a thermostat does it for us. In any job that involves a little thinking and creativity, coming up with the right process measures is a challenge.

When I got out of college and began work in a training and consulting firm in Detroit, my first assignment was a project with Hart Schaffner & Marx, one of the country's premier men's suit manufacturers and retailers. This was back in the days when just about everyone wore a suit to work every day. Our challenge as consultants was to help the company improve sales in its retail stores. We looked at all sorts of sales models that claimed to be the formula for improving sales. We interviewed many great and mediocre salespeople in Hart Schaffner & Marx stores and in other industries like car dealerships. Every salesperson had a theory on what it took to be good. The problem was, everyone also had a different idea of what constituted important metrics in the selling process.

After several days of interviewing, we still did not have a clue as to how to improve sales. We decided to visit the stores for hours at a time and watch some of the company's master salespeople at work. We recorded their behavior on worksheets and later looked for similarities in what they did. We also spent time observing some of the less successful clothing salespeople and recorded their behavior, looking for differences between the great and the mediocre. They proved to be subtle but extremely important.

Among several other things, we noticed that the successful salespeople never accepted a customer's word on his correct suit size. Great salespeople mentally sized up the customer (i.e., 42 long, 38 short), selected a high-priced jacket in the approximate size and slipped it on the customer. Many almost had heart attacks when they looked at the price tag, but it did feel and look great—nothing beats the feel of a hand-tailored jacket made out of the finest fabric. The superstar salesman would then take the customer over to the rack of lower-priced suits, and get the customer to try on a few. The suits in this price range, though, just didn't look or feel like the more expensive ones. All the while, the salesman would talk about how a good, expensive suit will last 15 years or more and is a great investment, and how less costly suits don't stand up to repeated dry cleaning. By teaching this and other subtle techniques to all salespeople, Hart Schaffner & Marx was able to significantly increase the average amount of sales in their stores. One of the key process measures that became standard and was taught to all salespeople was to size-up a customer using the most expensive jacket in the store before asking what price range he was interested in. Beware the next time you go shopping for a new suit: once they get you to try on that Armani, the Perry Ellis will never feel the same.

The point of this example is that process metrics are important to any organization, but they must lead to important outputs like increased sales. The challenge in coming up with good, behavior-based process measures is finding the right behaviors that actually lead to success. When it comes to human behavior, you get what you measure, most of the time.

Process Measurement Techniques—Employee Behavior

The absolute best way to gather data on any process metric is to use automation to monitor the process parameters constantly. Examples of such measures can be seen in paper mills, steel mills, chemical plants, or similar manufacturing businesses. Many of these types of factories almost run themselves today. Process metrics are constantly monitored, and these data are fed into a computer that adjusts the manufacturing processes accordingly to keep everything within certain standards. The end product comes out the same every single time because all the right process variables are monitored and controlled. If you can apply such an approach in your organization, you don't even really need process variables on your company dashboard because the automated systems will ensure good performance with little or no human intervention. Most systems like this have built in alarms or "idiot lights," to alert operators when process parameters fall out of the control limits.

Sadly, most readers do not work in organizations where this type of precise process measurement and control is possible. Most employees today work in organizations where people, not machines, perform the major work processes. When human behavior is the major component of a work process, measuring the right process variables becomes more of a challenge. All process measurement techniques that focus on recording human behavior can be classified into four basic approaches:

ASKING	WATCHING
• Interviews	• Direct observation
• Surveys	• Indirect observation

Most organizations I've worked with rely more on the asking techniques because they are simple and inexpensive. We can conduct individual interviews and focus groups, or conduct a survey and ask people about their own behavior or the behavior of others. For example, a common way of evaluating whether or not a manager's behavior has changed after a leadership course is to survey subordinates before and after the manager attends the course to see if they sense a change in his or her managerial behaviors. The same approach is used to survey bosses after their employees attend a training program to see if the employees' behavior has changed.

There are a variety of asking techniques that I have seen used in organizations:

- Self-assessment surveys, whereby employees evaluate their own behavior
- Surveys in which bosses evaluate employee behavior or employees evaluate their peers' or bosses' behavior
- Surveys asking customers to evaluate your employees' behavior
- Surveys in which you evaluate supplier or partner behavior
- Focus groups in which a team of people are asked questions about another group of people
- Individual interviews in which questions are asked about your own behavior or the behavior of others.

Trying to gather data on behavior in the workplace by using these techniques, however, is mostly a waste of time. There is a great deal of evidence that shows that people are terrible observers of their own and other people's behavior. Three people can all witness the same exact events and yet see them completely differently.

If interviews and surveys are so unreliable, why are they so widely used? I think you know the answer—because they're cheap and easy, and they make it appear as if we are using scientific data-gathering techniques.

Tip: *Don't waste your time trying to gather data on human behavior using interviews and surveys.*

The only reasonably reliable way to measure human behavior is through observation—having a trained observer watch employees and record their behavior.

There are two basic ways to measure behavior through observation techniques: direct observation and indirect observation. In other words, you can put an observer or auditor in the workplace and tell people they are being watched, or you can never reveal that they are being watched. The problem with direct observation techniques is that when people know they are being watched, they generally do all the right things. As soon as the observer leaves, the behavior reverts back to previous patterns. Thus, direct observation can be flawed, because people behave differently when they know they're being watched. The only situations where this approach works well is when there is always close supervision and the supervisors are the ones observing the behavior. Close supervision and monitoring of employee behavior is one of the reasons McDonald's does such a good job on service. However, most organizations don't have the level of supervision you find in a McDonald's restaurant.

I've now pointed out the problems with three of the four approaches to measuring behavior-based processes in the workplace. The fourth approach, indirect observation, is the only one I recommend. I've seen many companies effectively use this approach to monitor employee behavior. Some service companies, like retail stores and airlines, use mystery shoppers. These mystery shoppers pose as customers and record data on the behavior of service employees. Employees never know when they might encounter a mystery shopper, so they always have to be on their toes. Most call centers monitor the phone calls of their customer service representatives on a regular basis. Employees cannot tell when the supervisor might be listening in on the line, and supervisors use detailed checklists for evaluating the interaction between the employee and customer.

Another company I worked with used videotapes of employees to measure safety. Employees knew that they could be videotaped, and the tapes were very revealing in demonstrating some of the unsafe behaviors and practices that went on in the workplace. A government organization I worked with monitors employee use of the Internet, trying to catch people accessing inappropriate sites (e.g., pornography or chat rooms) during work hours.

If you think that all of these indirect observation approaches seem deceptive and smack of Big Brother, you are right—so do I. But, you also have to agree that the only reliable way of monitoring behavior is to observe people when they don't know they are being observed.

Tip: Use indirect observation techniques to gather data on employee behavior that is critical for work processes.

TECHNIQUES FOR MEASURING OUTPUTS

All organizations have outputs. Outputs can be products manufactured or services performed. Most organizations already collect good data on the quality of their outputs. FedEx tracks package delivery on a daily basis and can even track a package's progress from one part of the country to another, using their sophisticated tracking system. Auditors get their work papers reviewed repeatedly by a hierarchy of supervisors and managers before they are prepared in final draft for a client. Most of these measurement approaches are very thorough, objective, and do not need to be changed in a balanced scorecard implementation project.

Counting versus Judgment

The outputs of most organizations cannot be adequately measured by simply counting them. Even an organization that produces thousands of the same part each day must evaluate these parts using a judgment system. I remember working with a plant that manufactured plastic bottles to be used for IV solutions. The machines produced several bottles each minute and dumped them into large bins. Quality inspectors removed random bottles from the bins every few minutes and evaluated their quality using mostly observation. They were looking for various types of flaws in the product. This was a judgment measurement technique. Employees did not have to count how many bottles were produced—the equipment did that. The equipment did not monitor the quality of the bottles, however, and some came out with flaws. So, even though the plant *counted* the number of defective bottles it produced, the counting data were based on a *judgment* measurement system wherein inspectors evaluated the bottles against specific criteria.

Tip: *Most output metrics should be based on judgments using specific criteria.*

The work of some organizations is difficult to measure daily. A scientist might work on a project for several years before a prototype is ready to be tested. On long-term projects or work, sub-outputs need to be identified and measured throughout the course of the project. For example, an R & D or new product development project might have a number of sub-outputs that get evaluated and measured before the project can proceed to the next phase. A conceptual design document might be the first output, which is evaluated for technical feasibility, marketability, and a variety of other factors. The point is that all work outputs are measurable, but that most outputs must be measured using some kind of judgment. The key is to be able to quantify judgment measures so they can be graphed, analyzed, and compared over time. Qualitative data are informative, but do not allow managers to evaluate trends and levels of performance.

MEASURING OUTCOMES

The big difference between outputs and outcomes is that outputs are mostly an internal measure. In other words, the organization itself evaluates what it produces or accomplishes. In order to measure outcomes, we must look outside our own company. We need to go to customers, the community, the market, and regulatory groups. Outcomes include a safe work environment, a great place to work, loyal customers, rising stock prices, increased company valuation, and reputation or image.

Financial outcomes are usually measured very well and need little or no adjustment. Outcome measures might relate back to your mission or your vision. For example, a major airline might have a measure of customer loyalty that links back to their mission of being an airline that builds loyal customers through better service than their competitors. A mediocre company might have a vision of becoming the most respected and copied company in their industry in five years. Hence, they would develop outcome metrics that focused on being recognized (awards received, positive press, etc.) and the number of their products, services, and practices that have been copied by competitors.

Tip: Outcome metrics need to address all major
stakeholders: customers, investors/owners,
employees, and the community.

Measuring Outcomes for Government Organizations

Since the Government Performance and Results Act (GPRA) was passed a few years ago, all Federal Government organizations now have metrics. Many began the scorecard design process by identifying process metrics and measures of outputs. The problem with many of these metrics is that they did not link back to the organization's mission and did not provide information on whether or not the organization really provided any value to taxpayers. The second draft of measures that followed focused more on outcomes. For example, the Department of Transportation is held accountable for the outcome of safe highways. Since they build and maintain these highways, this makes sense as an outcome over which they have some control.

The metrics associated with this outcome need some work, however. One of the key metrics is the number of traffic fatalities. This metric is not a good one for the DOT, however, because alcohol, speeding, or both cause most traffic fatalities and the DOT does not control laws for driving under the influence of alcohol or set fines for exceeding the speed limit. Nor can they reduce the likelihood of these crimes through better deterrents and penalties. A metric like traffic fatalities can only lead to frustration on the part of DOT personnel because there is not much they can do to improve performance on this measure.

It is a good idea to make government organizations accountable for their outcomes. In fact, we should evaluate every government organization by the value they provide to taxpayers and others. However, holding them accountable for metrics over which they have little control is not the answer. The answer is to define meaningful outcomes that they can influence through their actions. For example, the New Mexico Department of Transportation measures the quality of their state roads using a fairly sophisticated index. Maintaining high-quality highways is an important metric for a DOT organization, and one they can exert much control over. The New Mexico DOT is also concerned about their public image as an important outcome. Image is hard to measure, but they measure it by tracking press clippings in which they are mentioned and coding each article as to whether it is positive, negative, or neutral. Of all the government organizations' scorecards I've seen, New Mexico's DOT metrics stand out as being exemplary.

Measuring Outcomes in Support Departments

Support departments like human resources, information technology, procurement, and finance also sometimes find it difficult to identify meaningful outcome measures. These departments often identify outcome measures over which they have little control, or that they can control or influence but are unimportant. For example, an HR department I worked with wanted to measure overall employee satisfaction in the company as one of the key outcome measures on their scorecard. While employee satisfaction certainly passes the importance test, HR cannot do much to influence it. Employee satisfaction is determined by a wide variety of variables that have nothing to do with HR policies or pay and benefits. In fact, I attended a conference presentation recently where data was presented indicating that an employee's relationship with his or her supervisor is the most important factor that determines job satisfaction.

In another organization I worked with, the finance department wanted to put overall return on investment for the company on their scorecard because they helped managers make better decisions about ROI by providing them with accurate data. Yet, ROI for the company was not a good metric for the finance department because their sphere of influence on this measure was too limited. A good outcome metric that they did track was timely delivery of financial data to all internal customers.

Tip: Outcome measures should focus on important variables over which you have some degree of influence and control.

WHO MANAGES THE METRICS?

Most metrics involve some sort of judgment, and it is important to select the right person or group to perform that judgment. The advantages and disadvantages of various approaches are discussed below.

Using Managers/Supervisors to Measure Performance

One task faced by most managers and supervisors is to evaluate the work of employees and make judgments upon it. A project manager on an audit reviews the work papers of individual auditors, for example, and provides feedback on their work. A construction foreman monitors both the construction processes used by his team and the workmanship of their outputs. Using managers and supervisors to perform judgments and collect data on employee performance makes sense because they are probably doing it anyway—it is already part of their job. A new scorecard might involve new rating forms, the use of sampling, or new criteria for making judgments about employee's work.

While there are many advantages to having managers collect performance data and perform the evaluations/judgments, one big disadvantage is that they often focus on aspects of performance other than quality and workmanship. Managers and supervisors are often more driven by cost and schedule than by quality. This might cause them to approve of an employee output and give it a good rating because it is judged to be "good enough to get by." Problems might show up later and be noted by either the next group in the organization to receive the output, or by the customer. For example, the dry wall foreman might approve of a job, even though there are some minor surface defects, because of a desire to meet deadlines and get on to the next job. The painter then has to correct the surface defects before doing his job, or he simply paints over the defects and the problem remains unnoticed until the customer moves into the new office building.

Tip: When using managers/supervisors to evaluate outputs and collect data, make sure that their priorities are properly balanced.

Using Peers in the Next Function to Measure Performance

Another common approach to judgment and data collection is to use the function that receives the outputs from the previous function to do the measurement. In our construction example, this would mean that the painters evaluate the performance of the drywall team, and that the drywall team evaluates the work of the framers, and so on. This can be an effective approach, because these people often know what to look for and have built-in consequences for letting shoddy work pass—i.e., *they* have to deal with it.

One problem with this approach is that judgment and data collection is not often a formal part of the function, as it is in the case of the supervisor. Consequently, time must be allocated for evaluating the performance and perhaps filling out rating sheets. People who are paid based on the outputs they produce have no interest in wasting time filling out rating sheets on the previous group's work. Another concern with this approach is that collusion sometimes occurs. In other words, the teams get together and decide to be easy on each other so they can all get the job done quickly, get paid, and move on to the next assignment. This is not common, but I have seen it occur in a few industries and organizations.

Using Inspectors to Measure Performance

An approach common to manufacturing organizations is to use quality control inspectors to evaluate work outputs and record performance data. The advent of the quality movement in the late 1980s changed the role of some of these inspectors, and workers were made responsible for self-inspection. This approach had mixed success, however, because production was often considered more important than quality, so outputs were often "passed" with known defects. Using trained inspectors to evaluate performance and record data is one of the best approaches in terms of thoroughness and objectivity. These inspectors are usually well trained in what to look for, and as inspection is their full-time job they are not distracted by other competing priorities, as are supervisors or managers.

In some organizations, inspectors are hired from outside the organization. For example, the Department of Energy chooses to do most of its work with outside contractors. DOE personnel serve as inspectors of the contractors' work processes and outputs. Other organizations hire consulting firms to serve as inspectors, assessing their performance and recording performance data. Outside inspectors are usually even more objective than internal ones. However, they are sometimes biased by a desire to sell you solutions to the problems they uncover. Have you ever heard of a consulting firm that evaluated an organization and told them they didn't need to do anything to make improvements? Coincidentally, the consulting firm always seems to have the appropriate solution to sell to you.

The only real downside to using inspectors to monitor and record performance data is the cost and the perpetuation of the idea that workers are not responsible for the quality of the work they do—in other words, that the inspector is responsible for finding defects.

Using Self-Inspection for Performance Measurement

A simple and sometimes appropriate way of measuring performance is to have employees record data on their own outputs. Pilots use a checklist whenever they fly, for example, as a way of ensuring that all important process and safety standards are followed. Putting supervisors or inspectors in the cockpit does not make sense, so the airlines count on the pilots and co-pilots to monitor their own performance. With other professionals, self-inspection might not be appropriate. Having doctors supervise their own surgeries might be a bad idea, for example.

Although objectivity is certainly the biggest downside to this approach to measurement, it does offer a number of advantages. First of all, it makes people more responsible for the quality of their own work if they know they have to measure and record data on performance. Second, this approach adds no extra cost or staff, because the employees are already doing the work and having them periodically monitor performance is not a big intrusion on their time.

Using Customers to Measure Performance

Customers are the ultimate judges of an organization's outputs and services. Internal inspectors might give high marks on the same performance that customers grade poorly. The best feature of using customers to measure performance is their objectivity and their vested interest in buying high-quality goods and services. Since customers are the ones paying for your outputs, they are often the best judges. They will also evaluate what is important, whereas internal inspectors or supervisors might evaluate factors that are easy to perform well on but are not very important. Using customer feedback alone might be inadequate in most professions, however, because customers are not as thorough as internal evaluators might be. Another concern with using customers to measure performance is that poor performance is best detected *before* products or services reach customers.

A good example of using customers to measure performance is Shea Homes asking homeowners to rate the workmanship of their homes. Through a homebuyer survey after the close, homeowners rate each process, from sale through close of escrow. Another method to obtain feedback is through their "Intro Cal Process." A third party calls every homeowner 30 days after close of escrow to ask specific questions about the orientation process. The homeowner has had an opportunity to live in the home and may find areas of concern. This allows Shea an opportunity to regain confidence by a quick follow-up to any outstanding issues.

A home is the biggest purchase most people make, so they are usually very interested in providing the builder with feedback. This approach works well for both Shea Homes and the people who buy their homes. Over 60 percent of the homeowners return the home-buyer survey sent to them shortly after the close of escrow.

Summary of Advantages and Disadvantages of Measurement Perspectives

Figure 11-3 presents a summary of the pluses and minuses of using various groups of people for evaluation and data collection. This information should help you in preparing your data-collection plans. It often makes sense to use several different sources of data to maximize the reliability of your data. For example, many organizations use both internal inspectors and customer feedback as measures of the work they do.

DESIGNING A DATA-COLLECTION PLAN

Once you have identified the measures that you want on your scorecard, the next step is to put together a plan for collecting the data. A useful format for such a plan is shown in Figure 11-4, along with an example of what a portion of the plan might look like.

A measurement plan like that in Figure 11-4 represents the highest level of planning needed to be done in order to identify how things will be measured, how often, and by whom. The last column shows how the metrics link back to goals or key success factors.

Data-Collection Perspective	Objectivity	Thoroughness	Cost
Supervisor	Medium	Medium	Low
Peers/Other functions	Medium	High	Low
Inspectors	High	High	High
Self-inspection	Low	Medium	Low
Customers	High	Low/medium	Medium

Figure 11-3. Data Collection Perspective

Measures	Data-Collection Method	Frequency	Owner	Link to Goal or KSF
Customer				
Loyalty Index	Rating of relationship based on multiple factors	Quarterly	Marketing	1.2,3.4,6.1
Customer Satisfaction	Random telephone surveys	Monthly	Customer Service	1.2,3.3,3.4, 5.3,6.1
Daily Defect Index	Sampling of output measures	Daily	Operations	2.1,2.3,8.2
Employee				
Attrition Index	Turnover + value of individual to org.	Monthly	Human Resources	4.1.4.2,6.3 7.1.8.1
Employee Satisfaction	Survey + other hard data on well being	Quarterly	Human Resources	4.1,4.2,6.3 7.1,8.1,8.3
Human Capital	Assessment of compe- tencies and value	Quarterly	Human Resources	1.1,1.2,3.3 5.2,5.3,6.1

Figure 11-4. Measurement Plan

Numbering or coding them is important, so that you don't have to spell them out in the measurement plan.

Evaluating Potential Data-Collection Strategies

Collecting data can be both expensive and time consuming. I've seen a number of balanced scorecard initiatives end up being canceled because the data-collection strategies ended up taking so much time that several clerks had to be hired to collect and report all the data. It is important to design your data-collection strategies around your resource constraints and your organization's level of tolerance for data collection and reporting. Some factors to think about when evaluating potential data-collection strategies are:

- Can we purchase this data or data-collection instrument from an outside company?
- Do we have this data somewhere in the organization already?
- Who will be responsible for gathering and reporting the data?

- How often will we collect data on this metric?
- If a sample will be used, what is the sample size?
- What format will be used to report the data?
- How much time will be required to gather and report the data?
- Will the data tell us anything we do not already know?
- Is there a less expensive way to gather the data that will not involve a major sacrifice of its integrity?
- Can we collect the data less frequently or use a sample?
- How will we ensure reliability and integrity of the data-collection processes/instruments?
- Who will design/build the instruments?
- If judgment is involved, who will do the judging?
- Can automation be used?
- How important is this metric in relation to others on the scorecard?
- How do others collect data on this type of metric?

Figuring out the mechanics of data collection for every metric on your new scorecard is the part of the project that takes up the greatest amount of time. Use the following checklist to simplify the task.

CHECKLIST FOR EVALUATING DATA-COLLECTION STRATEGIES

In assessing your data-collection strategies, make sure that you have:

☐ Considered a variety of different approaches before settling on one method.

☐ Evaluated the cost of collecting data via the methods identified in your plan.

☐ Considered collecting the data less frequently, but not so infrequently as to make the measurement less useful.

☐ Consulted with internal and external resources to decide on the best data-collection methods.

☐ Used the best data-collection instruments and methods you can afford.

☐ Built in appropriate controls to avoid cheating on metrics.

☐ Used the appropriate groups and/or individuals to collect the data.

☐ Built in reliability checks to ensure consistency where judgment is involved in measurement.

☐ Used appropriate techniques for measuring process or behavioral variables.

☐ Made use of appropriate sampling techniques.

Dashboard Design: Systems for Communicating Performance Data

One reason many people hate performance data is that they are often difficult to read and interpret. Studying 18 columns of numbers on a spreadsheet is not something that most of us relish. The challenge with any performance measurement system is first to get people to look at the data, and second to take appropriate actions and make decisions based on that data. This chapter is about reviewing data, understanding what it tells us, and accurately analyzing it in order to improve plans and decisions.

TYPICAL REPORTING PROBLEMS

Every week I sit next to executives on airplanes, watch them remove large, 2"-thick binders from their briefcases, and open them up to reveal a couple hundred pages of data displayed on spreadsheets, with scores of figures on every page. I watch them squint trying to read the numbers and refer to other sections of the binder for additional data that might explain the data on another page. It appears that their companies have chosen to include *all available data* in the big binders, even though much of it is irrelevant to executives at this level. Other executives open laptops rather than binders, only to look at the same confusing array of spreadsheets on their computer screens.

In addition to these complex spreadsheets for reporting performance data, most companies also hold monthly management meetings to review performance data. I've sat in on a number of these meetings, and usually they are deadly boring. Each executive gets up and reviews his or her charts of performance data. Most charts are in different formats, and most of the meeting time is spent in getting the attendees to understand the charts and making excuses for negative trends or levels of performance. Obviously, this is not an effective approach, but it is nevertheless repeated hundreds of times in organizations all over the world.

BALANCED SCORECARD SOFTWARE: THE MISSING LINK IN THE SCORECARD SYSTEM

My first exposure to balanced scorecard software came at a conference about three years ago, put on by the International Quality and Productivity Center in Washington, D.C. An organization called the Soft Bicycle Company had a booth at this conference. At first glance, I couldn't imagine what a bicycle manufacturer was doing at a balanced scorecard conference. Approaching their booth, I saw no bicycles, but rather graphics showing gauges on a simulated car dashboard. This company had actually developed software that allowed for the presentation of performance data using color-coded gauges and graphs that resembled a car's dashboard dials. This was exactly the type of thing many of my clients had been seeking for years—a simple, effective way of displaying performance data on the computer! What made this product even more exciting to me was that it could pull data from existing databases and allowed users to "drill down" into other metrics to analyze the causes of performance problems or look for trends in related measures.

Upon further investigation, I learned that a few other companies also have created software for displaying and analyzing performance data. A company called Panorama out of Toronto offers a product called PB Views, which is ideally suited to the communication of balanced scorecard data. A third company, CorVu, out of Minneapolis, also sells a balanced scorecard software program, which has increasingly impressed me over the last year. Hyperion, headquartered in California, markets yet another excellent product. Each of these firms is a solid organization, staffed by top-notch professionals who provide follow-up support for buyers of their software.

These software packages represent the most exciting development in recent years to help communicate performance data in a simple, graphic format and provide tools for analyzing it that help managers make better decisions. There are a couple of other products on the market that can be called balanced scorecard software, but I have chosen to review only these four, which I think are the best. Clients of mine have purchased these products, and their feedback generally has been good.

If the tone of these descriptions sounds like a sales pitch, it's because I am excited about the many features of these software packages and how organizations can use them to analyze and improve their performance!

I'll proceed by discussing each of the programs in detail and describing their capabilities. At the end of the chapter, I present a comparison of these products, which you might find useful in selecting the one that best fits your organization (see Figure 12-1). I have not included pricing information because prices are subject to change. Each of these companies also has a website where you can demo their software; the website addresses are included. I urge you to take advantage of these product demos—they provide the visual counterparts to the desciptions that follow.

PB Views

In 1993, Panorama Business Views out of Toronto introduced an exciting line of balanced scorecard software products called PB Views. PB Views has been a groundbreaking product from the beginning, allowing organizations to create a customized set of performance metrics, including financial and nonfinancial, that provides management with a complete diagnosis of organizational health. The PB Views system allows companies to understand, measure, and communicate their operational performance in the context of their strategic objectives and key success factors.

One useful feature of PB Views is that you can use any measurement framework—such as Kaplan and Norton's four categories of data, ISO 9000, the five categories of metrics in the Baldrige criteria, or your own customized model—for sorting performance metrics.

This flexibility makes PB Views an excellent choice for organizations that do not want to be constrained by designing their scorecards around a generic model.

PB Views Graphics

PB Views displays data in a series of colored boxes, typically green, yellow, and red. By scanning the number of the various boxes, managers can tell which areas of performance have problems and which do not. Within each colored box that represents a specific metric, the actual level of performance appears in numerical format. Red means performance is in trouble; yellow indicates that targets are not being hit, performance is probably mediocre; and green shows performance that is at or above the goal or target. A red arrow indicates that the manager should drill down deeper into the data because one of the submeasures is red. A yellow arrow means that one of the submeasures shows yellow performance or "danger," and a black arrow means that the submeasures are all showing green levels of performance. If a box doesn't contain an arrow, there are no submeasures.

It is possible to show one metric at a time, with all of its subsidiary measures underneath it. One of the nice features of PB views is that it also shows a trend in performance over time, along with notes that help explain current performance. When looking at any measure of performance, there are usually three important factors to evaluate: levels, trends, and variability. Colored boxes and arrows provide information on current levels of performance in relation to targets or goals. Bar charts or line graphs provide information on trends and variability in the data. This is important, because the boxes might show that performance levels are green, but the trend chart could show a declining trend that could soon become yellow if action isn't taken.

PB Views also allows users to view the entire "dashboard" at one time to get an overview of performance before drilling down into specific performance measures. All screens allow the user a variety of choices for viewing other data, or looking at the existing data in different formats.

Briefing Books

Another excellent feature of this software is that it allows you to display "Briefing Books," which can be easily created to display measurement information in an easy-to-read format. This feature also allows users to drill down into greater detail and links to other reports, websites, e-mail messages, and so on. Briefing Books can be private or shared with others. In fact, all data in PB Views can be coded for protection or access to certain levels of individuals in the organization.

Other Features of PB Views

Multilocation Module

PB Views Enterprise Edition is an exciting new feature that enables managers to track, consolidate, and manage performance across a number of locations. This gives users the ultimate flexibility and allows performance metrics to be defined differently for some or all locations. Performance metrics and scorecards can easily be tracked and consolidated at each level within an organization.

Internet Publishing Module

Panorama has recently developed an enhancement that allows users to publish business performance information from the user-friendly Briefing Books, using browser readable formats. With the Internet Publishing Edition, users can operate their mainstream PB Views application exactly as they do now, entering or importing data, providing performance commentaries, and so on. When they want to publish one or more of their Briefing Books to a website or network, they can simply choose those they want to publish and identify the location for publishing.

Compared to the Competition

Panorama is a quite cost-effective performance management solution, even though it offers the most comprehensive, user-friendly system available. Its affordability makes it stand out above the competition, providing organizations with optimum bottom-line value in return for a reasonable investment.

Other systems are awkward and lack the flexibility of PB Views. The reason is that other products are limited by some of the following issues:

- Locked into specific frameworks, like the balanced scorecard
- Created as rudimentary add-on applications to traditional warehouses; it's usually necessary to adopt the underlying data warehouse technology
- Inability to input data manually—modifications to measures require technical assistance
- Poor visualization of performance information
- Allows users to quantify their own performance

Because PB Views is not an add-on product but was specifically designed to offer users the best performance measurement system with the latest technology, it offers maximum flexibility. Data can easily be imported from other applications, or input manually without technical assistance. PB Views supports numerous well-known frameworks, enabling organizations to customize it. Performance information is simple to understand, with color-coded performance indicators giving the user an immediate review of performance. PB Views uses actual data to indicate actual achievement.

Some of the strongest positive feedback I've heard about Panorama regards their service after the sale and their willingness to incorporate customer-requested improvements into new software releases.

How to Contact Panorama

Panorama Business Views, Inc.
6 Pardee Avenue, Suite 103
Toronto, Ontario, Canada
M6K 3H5
Phone: (800) 449 3804
Email: info@pbviews.com

Panorama Business Views Ltd.
1 Pickford St. Aldershot
Hampshire, UK
GU11 1TY
Phone: +44 1252 338991
Email: pbviews@compuserve.com

Website for demonstration: www.pbviews.com

The CorVu Integrated Business Intelligence Suite

CorVu Corporation is another leading international provider of integrated business intelligence, performance management, and balanced scorecard solutions. The CorVu product, which was launched in 1993, has always been designed as an integrated suite, combining end-user query, production reporting, executive alerting, on-line analytical processing (OLAP) analysis, forecasting, "what-if" analysis, and business performance management applications.

To be successful, a decision support system must meet the information needs of its end users. While some may only need static reports, others require extensive analysis capabilities. Still others need to interact with the data to determine "what-if" situations. Mobile users may need to work with data off-line. Satisfying the demands of such a diverse user community typically requires a number of different tools, often from multiple vendors. However, administering a multitool decision support environment can be both complex and costly. What is needed is an integrated suite of tools that can be managed together. The CorVu Integrated Business Intelligence Suite is designed to do just that.

Views of Performance

CorVu allows organizations to display their performance data using a wide variety of graphics and formats. Color-coded, "dashboard-type" gauges can be used, along with a color-coded box format similar to PB Views. CorVu also allows trend charts, bar charts, pie charts, and briefing books, like the Panorama product. Both CorVu and PB Views use a red, yellow, and green color scheme to display performance data. Graphically, the gauge format in CorVu makes the data more like a real car dashboard, a format with which most people are familiar. I like these gauges because you can see how far off you are from yellow or red.

What I prefer about the PB Views format is that arrows show potential "under the hood" problems. The CorVu system does not have this feature. However, it does allow you to display data in a hierarchical organization chart format like PB Views, along with the option of using the gauges.

Other Features of CorVu

Communication and Feedback

One nice feature of CorVu is that it not only provides static information, but also allows managers and employees to exchange comments or provide answers to questions about the performance data. This feature can be extremely useful for determining the root cause of problems and identifying corrective actions. For example, a manager might notice that sales are down in the Midwest region for the month of June. Upon further drilling down of the data, it is revealed that software sales are not up to goal, but that other products and services are selling at goal level. Drilling even further down, the manager discovers that the decline in software sales can be traced to four specific customers. She then sends a message to the Midwest sales manager, asking what is happening with these four accounts and why software sales have been lower than forecast.

Robust Information Analysis

CorVu users can interactively analyze a variety of factors relating to business performance, using graphs, gauges, and reports. Visual comparisons between actual performance and targets, industry averages, or benchmarks is possible, enabling users to analyze performance effectively. Performance results are directly linked to the business processes that drive those results. Critical to this capability is strong database connectivity. For the vast majority of measurement metrics, CorVu is able to automatically retrieve data from existing databases. This eliminates the need to manually enter performance data each month or week. This is a huge advantage in cost and labor savings. CorVu can interact with many different data sources, pulling data from your financial, marketing, HR, or customer databases. Data sources may include relational and/or multidimensional databases, flat files, and even proprietary files.

Forecasting and Impact Analysis

While the core modules of CorVu provide users with an interactive window into corporate information warehouses, CorVu also includes a forecasting module. Unlike many query and reporting tools that simply tell users what has happened in the past, this tool allows them to predict more accurately future developments. The CorVu forecasting module examines the past and applies selected statistical methods, strategies, and parameters to predict trends and events. Users can perform "what-if" analyses to determine what would happen if they improved performance on a leading metric and how that might impact a lagging measure's performance. These analyses or forecasts help to dramatically improve the accuracy of planning and decision making. Thus, the balanced scorecard becomes much more than a tool for reviewing past performance—it allows one to more accurately craft the organization's future.

Internet Enabled

The delivery of timely information throughout the enterprise has become more critical than ever before. Toward that end, businesses in every industry are increasingly turning to Internet/intranet technologies. Corporate intranets provide a high degree of platform independence, along with a familiar browser front-end. As a result, corporate intranets provide a powerful vehicle for deploying the balanced scorecard approach to performance measurement.

Through CorVu, administrators can create reports, graphs, and other analyses which can be scheduled to run at desired intervals. These data can then be easily published on the web server, where users may access and analyze them interactively from their browsers. Administrators control access and distribution of information to specific users and groups. The CorVu web server is installed at a central location where all administrative tasks are performed. When a new release is installed at the central site, it is automatically delivered to users, providing a single point of installation and deployment. This allows for rapid deployment of performance information, along with the much needed control over distribution and access.

Whether users need full business intelligence capabilities, or simply static reports and graphs, the CorVu web server provides the means to deliver both. While delivering scorecard information via the Web offers tremendous power, not all users are on-line all the time. For this reason, the CorVu web server delivers objects to the users' browsers. Users may then employ CorVu's complete suite of business intelligence products from within their browser, even without a web connection. As web-based deployments increase in popularity, many organizations find that a combination of web-based and client/server deployment is necessary to meet the needs of all users. CorVu's client interface is identical in both the web server and client/server implementations, eliminating the need for additional training. This enables browser-based users and client/server users to easily share information and analyses for more productive, workgroup-style computing.

How to Contact CorVu

North America and
Latin America:
CorVu North America, Inc.
3400 W. 66th Street Suite 445
Edina, MN 55435 USA
Phone: +1 612 944 7777
Email: sales@corvu.com

Australia, East Asia, Africa,
Middle East:
CorVu Australasia Pty. Ltd.
Level 4, 1 James Place
North Sydney, NSW 2060 Australia
Phone: +61 2 9959 3522
Email: sales@corvu.com.au

UK, Europe:
CorVu Plc.
Craven House
40 Uxbridge Road
Ealing
London, W5 2BS United Kingdom
Website: www.corvu.com

DASHBOARD @NYWARE™ (FROM THE SOFT BICYCLE COMPANY)

A Washington, D.C.-based company called Soft Bicycle has a great product that performs most of the same functions as the previous two. (I never did discover why they chose this name. Perhaps it is to illustrate that their software can go anywhere with a minimum of effort.) As you might expect from its name, Dashboard @nyWARE™ uses color-coded gauges to display performance data. Similar to CorVu's, these graphics are even better in that they closely resemble real automotive dials and instruments. As with the other packages, you are not limited to using just the gauges; data also can be displayed in trend charts to evaluate performance over time and in a variety of different formats.

The Soft Bicycle Company has developed an Internet-based performance measurement system called Dashboard @nyWARE™. This system was designed to show four metrics at a time, in line with the balanced measurement approach set forth in Norton and Kaplan's *Balanced Scorecard.* The Dashboard @nyWARE™ software allows viewers to display any number of measurements in a variety of different displays and clusters, such as gauges, line charts, and pie charts, for every measure. In addition, the software provides the ability to review related documents, such as policies or regulations and detail reports for the measures. Dashboard @nyWARE™ was also designed to support collaboration of performance measures by integrating email to the measurement displays. Dashboard @nyWARE™ is an extremely lightweight tool, installed on one web server, so multiple installations are not necessary. The principal design criteria for Dashboard @nyWARE™ was ease of use—to enable fast access for viewers to see status information about their organizational or individual performance.

Business leaders understand the value of sharing information about their organization's performance with staff and employees. By using the familiar and engaging metaphor of an automobile dashboard, Dashboard @nyWARE™ software makes it possible for organizations to display critical, up-to-date metrics on every computer desktop. Initial implementations of Dashboard @nyWARE™ indicate that an organization performs significantly better over time, because people correct and manage their work better when they have knowledge of their organization's lagging and leading metrics.

How Dashboard @nyWARE™ Works

Dashboard @nyWARE™ runs on a Window NT server and can be accessed by any number of users who have password access through Microsoft Internet Explorer browsers. It allows an entire organization to monitor performance in relation to specific objectives, such as customer satisfaction, finance, and personnel. Measures are designed through an easy-to-use design interface, and data for the measures can be loaded manually or uploaded automatically from multiple database sources, all at intervals specified by the user. Dashboard @nyWARE™ makes accessible and explicit an organization's performance measurements—including goals, actual performance, trends, and internal policy documentation. The product supports a firm's quest to operationalize quality. It also helps organizations to conduct strategic conversations about performance through integration with their email systems.

In the past, performance measurement systems were not explicit or accessible to all employees, which hindered organization decision making and learning. Since change does not operate on a schedule, an organization must be prepared to respond whenever a shift in the landscape occurs. Dashboard @nyWARE™ was designed to allow employees at any level of the organization to share the corporate vision and strategy and enable individuals to respond to change as it occurs. Traditional management reporting styles are time- and labor-intensive and often render the report inaccessible for the short term. Reports that lack graphics can be difficult to interpret and often bury key performance indicators within extensive statistical listings.

Dashboard @nyWARE™ provides graphical depictions of current and historical performance that are fast and easy-to-understand. Information about organizational performance must be linked to corporate objectives, departmental goals, company policies, and best practices for all employees to see—which is where Dashboard @nyWARE™ excels. Whereas traditional reporting tools do not provide contextual cause-and-effect relationships to understand the implications of change and decisions in the organizations, Dashboard @nyWARE™ makes those implications perfectly clear and concrete.

Performance measurement systems are inherently rich and dynamic because they tend to involve technical systems (software, hardware, networks), business systems (operating principles, structures, frameworks, and implicit and explicit incentives) and social systems (individuals, teams, and organizations).

In order to enable organizational learning, leadership development, and constructive feedback, and to implement and make effective use of performance measurement systems, the Soft Bicycle Company followed a set of philosophies and guiding principles while building the framework of the Dashboard @nyWARE™ system.

Performance measurement systems should incorporate collaborative technologies. The purpose of a performance measurement system is to help executives and managers participate in useful strategic conversations. Therefore, the traditional monitoring and display system will be most effective when it is tightly integrated with a simple, elegant, collaborative technology. Dashboard @nyWARE™ links to your existing email system and allows collaborative features that enable simple, structured conversations and can be linked to a specific measure.

How to Contact the Soft Bicycle Company

The Soft Bicycle Company
1000 Thomas Jefferson Street NW, Suite 100
Washington, D.C. 20007 USA
Phone: 1 888 565 BIKE
Email: info@softbicycle.com
Website: http://www.softbicycle.com

HYPERION PERFORMANCE SCORECARD

As this book was going to press, I came across a fourth scorecard software program that I believe is worth discussing. The company is called Hyperion Solutions Corporation, headquartered in Sunnyvale, California, with offices in Manchester, U.K., and in Singapore. The scorecard product, Hyperion Performance Scorecard, incorporates most of the same features as the other three products discussed in this chapter. Like the others, it allows employees and managers to view performance data in easy-to-interpret charts and graphics, and includes a number of features for evaluating and analyzing performance data.

Hyperion Performance Scorecard lets users select from such popular scorecard frameworks as the Balanced Scorecard, Arthur Andersen's Vital Signs, and the Baldrige Criteria. The balanced scorecard framework helps managers guide their organizations through a common set of key success factors, providing predictive, forward-looking views of the overall business that go beyond a focus on short-term, bottom-line results. If users prefer, they can create a custom scorecard methodology to address the organization's unique requirements.

Benchmark and Communicate Targets

Organizations must research and understand world class performance levels in order to evaluate the business and reward managers competitively. Hyperion Performance Scorecard provides direct web access to leading benchmarking services for establishing effective targets. Variable targets allow users to set different goals for any period of time. To close the gap between today's performance and tomorrow's achievement, users can formulate specific milestones as tangible expressions of commitment.

Monitor Progress toward Goals

Compiling and monitoring performance measures enables organizations to stay on course and drive change to achieve business goals. Hyperion Performance Scorecard gives decision-makers the ability to respond quickly, accurately, and completely to opportunities with customers, suppliers, employees, and other stakeholders. It delivers actionable business information to executives, management, and line managers through web-based scorecards, reports, and dashboards. Graphs and tables provide a visual guide for all measured date, to facilitate the comparison of information across critical business areas, targets, external benchmarks, and time. Hyperion Performance Scorecard also stores text and file attachments—such as the organization's mission, values, goals, and objectives—to aid in the dissemination of information throughout the enterprise.

Leverage and Maximize Technology Investments

Hyperion Performance Scorecard lets organizations leverage and maximize their sizable investments in enterprise resource planning (ERP) and transaction-processing systems. Users can build and report a comprehensive, balanced, and up-to-date view of the organization's performance through manual input or by importing data directly from external systems. The process is seamless, allowing organizations to realize greater returns on technology investments.

Connect Each Enterprise Desktop

Visionary organizations often deploy applications across all functions and levels of the organization to hundreds or thousands of users.

Diversity in the information system landscape places new and important demands on performance measurement systems. These enterprisewide initiatives are a natural fit for web-based deployment strategies. Hyperion Performance Scorecard's web-centric design promotes cost-effective Internet and intranet distribution of information throughout the organization.

Leverage a Proven Business Analysis Platform

Hyperion Performance Scorecard delivers functionality and extensibility into reporting, analysis, modeling, and planning. Users can combine business-critical data from corporate ERP, customer relationship management, and financial management systems to establish a complete picture of strategy through to execution.

Graphics/Views

- Strategy map displays the entity modeled, strategic objectives, critical success factors, and multiple layers of actions (terminology is customizable) and links them to accountable parties.
- Accountability map defines the parties responsible for each strategic objective, critical success factor, and action. Accountability maps are user-defined and can be set up in several ways: by reporting hierarchy, by products/service/project, by virtual team, or any combination.
- Traceability map shows the entire defined organization's health at a glance using traffic lighting as well as scores. Red and yellow alerts invite users to drill down to get more information on what measure or measures might be causing the alert.
- The scorecard view (for any accountable party) displays the measures, strategic objective, perspective, result, target, and score for the time period chosen.
- Trend analysis allows you to plot multiple measures for multiple time periods on a single chart, and/or compare multiple charts. Users can choose a variety of ways to display graphs, including bar, line, three-dimensional, and area charts.
- Reports provide a listing of all measures, results and targets, and status symbols for fast review for the period chosen and the previous period.

- Web reports also include personalized views of selected scorecard information. The "Scorecard Central" report displays all scorecards that the user is an owner or a member of, including the total score, perspective score, actions, owner, members, results, targets, upper and lower limits, alerts for good and bad performance, and the top three measures with the greatest variance (users can navigate to the full variance report from here).

How to Contact Hyperion

Headquarters
Hyperion Solutions Corporation
1344 Crossman; Avenue
Sunnyvale, CA 94089
Phone: (408) 744-9500
Fax: (408) 744-0400
Email: info@hyperion.com
Website: www.hyperion.com

European Headquarters
Hyperion Solutions Europe
Enterprise House
Greencourts Business Park
333 Styal Road
Manchester M22 5HY
United Kingdom
Phone: 44 161 498 2200
Fax: 44 161 498 2210

Asia-Pacific Headquarters
Hyperion Solutions Asia Pte. Ltd.
#24-01 IBM Towers
80 Anson Road
Singapore 079907
Phone: 65 323 3485
Fax: 65 323 3486

COMPARING THE FOUR PROGRAMS

I recommend taking a look at all four of these programs before deciding to buy one. Clients of mine have said that they are all around the same price and have many of the same features. There are some slight differences that might sway your decision one way or another, however. Figure 12-1 presents a summary of the major features of these programs.

Feature	PB Views	CorVu	Dashboard @nyWARE™	Hyperion Performance Scorecard
Present any number of performance measures	Yes	Yes	Yes	Yes
Red/yellow/green color-coded performance levels	Yes	Yes	Yes	Yes
Primary graphics used	boxes like an org. chart	gauges	gauges	org. chart, gauges, scorecard
Capable of showing trend charts	Yes	Yes	Yes	Yes
Perform analyses using "drill down"	Yes	Yes	Yes	Yes
Shows "idiot lights" regarding lower-level metrics	Yes	No	No	Yes
Pulls data from existing data bases	Yes	Yes	Yes	Yes
Allows a wide variety of graphics	Good	Best	Better	Best
Displays reference documents associated with measurements	Yes	No	Yes	Yes
Link measurement displays to email	No	No	Yes	Yes
Trigger external applications	No	No	Yes	Yes
Allows for notes for discussion of performance	Yes	Yes	Yes	Yes
Allows any scorecard design	Unlimited	Kaplan & Norton	Unlimited	Unlimited
Allows "what-if" simulations with additional software	No	Yes	Yes, simulations with additional software	Yes, simulations with additional software
Allows forecasting	No	Yes	No	Yes
Report writer	Yes	Yes	No	Yes
Web viewer	No	Yes	Yes	Yes

Figure 12-1. Dashboard Design: Systems for Communicating Performance Data

ALTERNATIVES TO BUYING A SCORECARD SOFTWARE PROGRAM

About the only downside to these software programs is that they are expensive. On a per-user basis, the cost is typically less than $500.00. But in a large organization, this can add up very quickly. Some organizations have found that they need system engineers to help link the software to their existing databases, which adds to the cost of the installation. One alternative is to develop your own software. Both the Army Rock Island Arsenal and Coast Guard District 7 in Miami (discussed earlier in the book) decided to develop their own scorecard communication tools. The army program makes use of red, yellow, and green color-coded charts and has many of the same features as the packaged programs discussed here. In organizations that have more time than money, developing the program in house might be the best approach. Keep in mind, however, that this could take several years to design, test, and implement.

Another client of mine had a couple of summer interns design a program for displaying performance data. Raw data, entered into the system once a month, are displayed in color-coded graphics. Their system is not as slick as one of the packaged programs, but for the salary of two interns for three months, it is great! The disadvantage to using this system throughout the company is that data still has to be manually entered; the system doesn't talk with any existing company databases. Thus, the program is practical for updating the CEO's scorecard, but could involve many clerks spending hundreds of hours each month entering data once the company develops scorecards for others in the organization

A low-tech alternative is to not use computers at all for displaying performance data—simply continue to use paper reports, bulletin boards, and overhead transparencies in meetings to communicate the data. This might be a wise approach for a small to medium-sized organization that cannot afford to put everything online. Through the use of color graphics similar to the ones described in this chapter, even a paper-based, static system can be a good way of communicating performance data. Just don't use the spreadsheet format of 28 columns of numbers in 6-point type! You can create your own gauges or graphics on paper like the ones described in this chapter. One of my clients actually uses the format of a baseball scoreboard to display performance data in their call center. The scoreboard actually has lights and looks just like the ones you'd see at a baseball stadium.

Use the checklist that follows to help you select the best option for your organization.

CHECKLIST OF QUESTIONS TO ASK WHEN
EVALUATING SCORECARD SOFTWARE PROGRAMS

☐ Can we preflight the software in a segment of the organization without spending $100,000?

☐ How much work and expense will it take to integrate the software with our existing databases?

☐ How much should we budget to spend on maintenance each year?

☐ Is it possible to include qualitative data on the software?

☐ How would qualitative data be displayed?

☐ Is it possible to customize the categories we use for sorting our scorecard data, or do we have to adapt to a generic model?

☐ When we look at performance, can we see all the high-level metrics on one screen?

☐ Can we design the format of the data displays to look like an airplane cockpit, a ship control panel, baseball scoreboard, or other theme?

☐ Must we stay within the red/ yellow/green color scheme, or can we use other colors?

☐ If we don't have an intranet site, can we still use the software?

☐ How long will it take to get all of the users online and using the software?

☐ How easy is it to add or delete metrics from the software?

☐ Can we make some gauges larger than others to show priorities, or must they all be the same size?

☐ Can the software be used to show performance on process metrics where stability is the most important dimension of performance?

☐ Can we program in correlations between leading and lagging metrics to do "what-if" scenarios?

☐ What new releases are planned, and what will be the new features you plan to include?

☐ What are the costs of new releases?

Integration: Linking Your Scorecard to Other Organizational Systems

The best-designed scorecard in the world, by itself, will not do much to improve an organization's performance. The performance metrics that a company examines on a regular basis provide only the framework for an effective performance management system. In this chapter, I'll discuss how these other organizational systems might be integrated with the scorecard:

- Performance appraisal/management
- Developmental planning
- Compensation
- Recognition/rewards
- Organization structure

I'll also discuss the importance of demonstrating links or correlation between leading and lagging indicators to improve planning and decision making.

WHY MANY SCORECARD INITIATIVES FAIL

You no doubt realize by now that designing an effective scorecard is a challenge. Making sure that all the metrics are well balanced and linked to strategic plans or business fundamentals is simple to understand, but hard to implement. Scorecard initiatives that fail are not always due to bad metrics, however. I've seen some good scorecards fail because they were not linked to other systems in an organization. Following are some of the most common problems I've seen in organizations that have had trouble making the balanced scorecard approach work.

Keeping Two Sets of Books

In one common scenario, senior management uses a scorecard to report company performance to employees and management, but uses a different set of measures to report performance to the Board of Directors, shareholders, or other stakeholders. Two sets of performance measures are tracked and reported. Board members, and others who may not have been exposed to the balanced scorecard approach, historically have judged companies on traditional, past-focused financial metrics. As you know, there is still a place on the scorecard for traditional financial metrics. However, keeping two scorecards and reporting different data to different audiences only helps to ensure that the scorecard will eventually be dropped. The "real" scorecard is the one presented to the Board and shareholders, and executives learn that the nonfinancial metrics on their own scorecard are not the truly important ones. Hence, they revert to their previous approach of managing by looking in the rearview mirror.

Several companies I have worked with avoided this dilemma by involving the Board of Directors and other key stakeholders in the scorecard design process early on. Lutheran Brotherhood, the financial services firm mentioned several times previously, is one example. LB involved their Board at the very beginning of their scorecard project, making presentations to them on the approach, getting their buy-in, and using the new scorecard as the format for performance presentations given at periodic Board meetings. Board members have come to expect reports on all the measures on the company scorecard, not just the financial ones.

Stanislaus County, in California, also has done a good job of involving Board members up front. The county is run by a CEO and staff, like a corporation, but is also governed by an elected Board of Supervisors that functions like a corporate Board of Directors. County CEO Reagan Wilson had me conduct a one-day workshop for his Board of Supervisors before they were very far along in their scorecard project to familiarize them with the approach, and to convince them that it was important to study a range of performance metrics to evaluate county performance. This helped board members understand the new scorecard the county had begun implementing.

Tip: Involve your Board of Directors and other key stakeholder groups in the scorecard design process early on to ensure their support and understanding of the new performance measurement approach.

Following One Set of Metrics but Rewarding Another

Another company, with whom I had worked for several years, put a great deal of effort into designing a good, balanced scorecard for several levels of management, starting with the CEO. Performance on scorecard metrics was reviewed at monthly management meetings throughout the company, and the scorecard was well communicated through bulletin boards, newsletters, and reports. The nonfinancial measures simply never got much attention, however. Monthly management meetings were spent, for the most part, discussing financial performance, because that was the aspect of performance everyone felt was still the most critical.

It turned it out that there was good reason for everyone to believe in the importance of financial results: 95 percent of an executive's bonus was based on the financial metrics on the scorecard, and 5 percent was based on all other metrics. The company talked a good game about the importance of service, customer satisfaction, employee morale, and new product development, but they only paid bonuses for sales, profits, and growth. Hence, the nonfinancial measures did not really matter to anyone, and the balanced scorecard effort never had much impact in making the organization more forward thinking.

Setting Individual Performance Objectives Without Considering Scorecard Metrics

Almost every organization has some kind of performance appraisal system that involves a planning session, wherein objectives are set, and a review session at year-end. Often, these objectives have little or nothing to do with the scorecard. (This, too, comes down to keeping two sets of books.) The importance of scorecard metrics is drummed home, but at the end of the year, employee appraisals are based on very different factors. Since raises, promotions, and recognition are usually tied to performance review feedback, we know which set of metrics gets the attention.

In organizations with well-integrated scorecards, the scorecard metrics are the very same as those used for performance planning and appraisal. The only issues typically discussed in performance appraisal sessions that do not appear on scorecards are behavioral issues. A performance appraisal discussion might include a review of performance against targets on scorecard metrics, along with a discussion of softer issues, such as behavior consistent with the company values or the development of key competencies.

One company I'm familiar with has gone so far as to include the softer, behavioral dimensions of performance on all of their scorecards. One portion of their scorecard looks at performance, and the other portion looks at leadership behaviors, or competencies that the company has found are highly correlated with success as a manager. Thus, their scorecard and their appraisal systems derive from the same information. Even though the behavioral dimensions are based on subjective judgments and selective memories of events and situations, the scorecards present a good balance—a mix of hard, objective measures and softer ones that are considered no less important.

Linking Consequences Prematurely to Scorecard Metrics

Once you start measuring and holding people accountable for performance, many will seek a short-cut. It's human nature to find the easiest way of accomplishing something. For example, losing weight through diet and exercise is hard, unpleasant work for most overweight people. When someone markets a pill that claims to curb appetite and burn fat, or an exercise device that promises a toned body with only 15 minutes per day of exertion, they sell like hotcakes.

I have emphasized all along that it is very important to link consequences to performance on your scorecard metrics. However, it is equally important not to do so prematurely. Linking bonuses or compensation to metrics that are not tried and tested can be a recipe for disaster. A real estate company I worked with began rewarding high customer satisfaction scores with trips before the bugs had been worked out of their data-collection system. By having their agents personally hand out customer satisfaction surveys and explain them to customers, they were giving the agents too much room to stack the deck in their favor. The company ended up refining their data-collection methods in order to gather more objective feedback, but they gave away a number of undeserved free trips before doing so.

Tip: *Refine your metrics and data-collection processes before linking performance to rewards/consequences.*

BUILDING LINKS BETWEEN SCORECARDS

It is important to ensure linkage between the scorecards for different levels and functions in your organization. Much of this has to do with where the scorecard project is initiated. Another important dimension is in how much collaboration exists between individual departments that are developing their own scorecards. Rarely does an organization begin the scorecard effort at the CEO level. Even when that is the case, at some point in the initiative different units or departments begin designing scorecards simultaneously. While this is appropriate and often necessary so that the project does not take three years to complete, I often see major disconnects between metrics at different levels and functions. To avoid this, it is crucial that you build in sufficient review and evaluation steps in the process and follow a sequence in the design of metrics. An example of a successful approach is shown in Figure 13-1.

The process outlined above ensures appropriate linkages by developing scorecards in a top-down fashion and reviewing the drafts at each level before proceeding to the next. The executive's scorecard and guiding documents (i.e., mission, vision, and values) are the inputs for the design of the scorecard for the unit managers, and so forth. This approach sounds as if it could take many months to complete, but it actually proceeds quickly once the first two levels of metrics are defined. On a current project, we defined the metrics for

Phase I: Executive Scorecard Design

- Draft scorecard and guiding documents for executive
- Review with executive and staff
- Prepare second drafts of guiding documents and scorecard for executive

Phase II: Unit Scorecard Design

- Draft scorecard and guiding documents for manager of one unit
- Review with unit manger and staff
- Prepare second drafts of guiding documents and scorecard for unit manager
- Repeat process with other units

Phase III: Department Scorecard Design

- Draft scorecard and guiding documents for manager of one department in one unit
- Review with department manager and staff
- Prepare second drafts of guiding documents and scorecard for department manager
- Repeat process with other departments

Phase IV: Staff Scorecard Design

- Draft scorecard and guiding documents for staff members
- Review with department manager and staff
- Prepare second drafts of guiding documents and scorecards for staff
- Repeat process with other departments

Phase V: Develop Data-Collection Plans

- Draft data-collection plan for executive
- Review with executive and staff
- Prepare second draft of data-collection plan
- Repeat process with unit managers, department managers, and staff

Figure 13-1. Sequence in Design of Scorecard Metrics

the vice president, revised them, prepared a second draft, and then found that many of the same metrics fit on the scorecards of the unit managers and department managers. For example, we developed an overall project management index that told the vice president how all of the functions for which he was responsible were performing on their projects. Each unit manager also had a project-management index on his or her scorecard, as did department managers and staff members who managed the projects. In fact, we found that about 60 percent of the measures were common across all four levels in the organization. Therefore, we were able to spend much less time developing scorecards for the lower levels than for the executive level.

Tip: Performance on lower-level scorecards should predict performance on the metrics the next level up in the organization.

Using Logic to Find Potential Disconnects

Following a top-down process and building in sufficient reviews in your project plan will help weed out some linkage problems, but not all of them. Some will not be apparent at first, and will require more analysis to be identified. At Discover Financial Services we used a large group to help us find the disconnects in their metrics before we got too far along in the scorecard design process. We developed an exercise called "Find the Disconnects," which was kind of like the *Where's Waldo?* book series, wherein you need to find the character Waldo hidden in complicated drawings. For the exercise, we created a case study that was very close to Discover Financial Services' actual business practices. (In fact, the exercise included actual drafts of scorecards and guiding documents that the participants themselves had prepared prior to the meeting. We presented it as a case study so as not to embarrass participants whose scorecards needed major work.)

The case included an overview of the company and its situation, a description of its vision, mission, key success factors, and values, and scorecards for the president, vice presidents, and several unit managers. Also included was information on targets for each metric and broad strategy. Using small teams of five to six people, each group had to comb through the case material and find the following types of disconnects:

- Lower-level metrics that didn't link to upper-level metrics
- Leading and lagging indicators on the same scorecard that didn't link
- Inconsistencies between targets across levels
- Inconsistencies in metrics that should have been common across levels and functions
- Key success factors for which there were no metrics, and strategic metrics that were not effectively linked to KSFs
- Mission or business fundamental metrics that were inconsistent across functions or levels

The exercise turned out to be a bit more complicated than we anticipated, and it turned out that there were too many disconnects and too much material to review for the time we had allotted for the process. Regardless, the exercise drove home the importance of checking for linkages across different levels and functions in the organization. Using the feedback from the teams in the exercise, we were able to improve the metrics and linkages between the scorecards.

Finding Linkages between Leading and Lagging Indicators

A major premise of the balanced scorecard approach to measurement is that an organization will manage better by looking at predictive metrics that indicate potential future performance problems before they turn critical. Conceptually, most people buy into this, but the majority of organizations I've seen with balanced scorecards have not defined these correlations and are still making poor business decisions based upon their scorecard metrics.

The Employee-Service-Profit Chain at Sears

Sears has had it rough in recent years. Once one of the most successful companies in America, Sears underwent a major restructuring that involved selling off many successful parts of the company, such as Budget Rental Car, Allstate Insurance, and Dean Witter/Discover, and closing their catalog division. As part of the turnaround strategy developed in 1995, a new balanced scorecard was put into place, to help Sears focus on employees, customers, and profits (see "The Employee-Service-Profit Chain at Sears," *Harvard Business Review*, January/February 1998). Their new vision, referred to as the "3 C's," was to make Sears a:

- Compelling place to work
- Compelling place to shop
- Compelling place to invest

The scorecard Sears developed was designed to tell them how they were progressing towards this vision. They developed thorough measures of employee morale, because according to their research employees were the first link in the chain of success. Detailed employee surveys were conducted monthly, asking large samples of employees how they felt about working at Sears. Focus group and survey data were collected from customers just as often, to see how shoppers felt about their experience with Sears. Finally, leading and lagging financial indicators were put into place to see if the company was turning the corner on its financial results. Management believed that by making Sears a compelling place to work and shop, they would indeed become a compelling place to invest. In other words, financial success would follow if they concentrated on making the measures of employee and customer satisfaction look good.

Rather than rely on previous research that showed this to be the case, Sears decided to conduct some research of their own to determine if correlations existed between these three scorecard perspectives, and if so, how strong they were they. The research revealed that the three metrics were linked, but not strongly. Sears found that they needed to get an expert to evaluate their specific data. Consultant Tom Buzas found the following correlations in Sears' data:

	Drives	**Drives**
5-point increase in employee morale	1.3 unit increase customer satisfaction	0.5% increase in revenue growth

While this analysis makes for good reading in *Harvard Business Review*, it does not seem to provide much information that would help the company improve. A 5 percent improvement in employee morale could take an enormous amount of effort and require a significant investment. According to these statistics, this would result in a 1 percent improvement in customer satisfaction, leading to a .05 percent increase in sales revenue. Later in the *HBR* article, the authors explain that for every dollar in revenue Sears takes in, they keep about 2 percent in profit.

Let's look at an example of what these figures might mean to Sears. Say that a Sears store does $15 million in sales. A .05 percent improvement in sales is $75,000. That turns into $15,000 in profit. It seems highly unlikely that a store would be able to get a 5 percent improvement in employee morale for less than $15,000.00. Just doing the survey to collect the employee morale data probably costs more than $15,000.

Tip: Look at correlations like a businessperson, not a scientist—you might find two measures to be statistically correlated, *but that there is no* practical correlation.

Defining the correlations between measures of employee morale, customer satisfaction, and revenue was a good experience for Sears. It clearly illustrated how much employee morale needed to improve in order to have any noticeable impact on the other measures. However, this exercise also convinced them that it probably didn't make sense to spend a lot of money trying to improve employee morale or customer satisfaction, because the payoff was extremely slim. The *HBR* article was published in January 1998, when things were looking up for Sears. Recent financial results are not so positive, and it remains unclear whether their strategy of investing in employees and customers is really working.

PROCESS FOR DEFINING LINKS BETWEEN SCORECARD METRICS

Step 1: *Identify two metrics that might be linked.*

The first step is to identify two important metrics that you think might be correlated, and do some research. Usually, it is not necessary to identify links between *all* the possible combination of metrics on your scorecard. Select only those that you think are most critical. These might be either strategic metrics linked to KSFs, or key leading and lagging indicators from the business fundamentals section of your scorecard. Those selected by Sears were fundamental versus strategic metrics. Every retail store needs to measure employee morale, customer satisfaction, and revenue. A strategic metric for Sears might be growth in merchandise sales of soft goods, consistent with their strategy of promoting the "softer side of Sears."

Typically, one selects a leading and lagging indicator to test whether movement in the leading indicator predicts corresponding movement in the lagging indicator. You could evaluate the potential links between two lagging indicators, but this information tends to be less useful for managers. It is OK to select two measures from different boxes on your scorecard for this study—for example, you might want to measure if there is a link between human capital performance (leading) and asset productivity (lagging).

Step 2: *Establish baseline data on the two metrics until stable.*

The next step is to either gather historical data on the two metrics from the past year or two, or begin collecting data on new metrics. The length of time for which you need to collect data will vary depending upon the type of measure and the frequency of measurement. In general, you should look for at least three datapoints and at least six months' worth of data to study for any kind of trend. If performance is extremely variable you'll need to collect baseline data for a longer period of time, until the data is more stable.

Step 3: *Develop and implement a plan designed to improve performance on the leading indicator.*

Your next task is to conduct an experiment of kinds and introduce a change in the work environment designed to cause the performance of the leading indicator to improve. For example, let's assume that the leading indicator you have chosen is customer satisfaction measured via telephone surveys, and the lagging indicator is growth in repeat orders from existing customers. An area that has huge impact on customer satisfaction is on-time and accurate delivery of orders.

The company introduces a new, automated delivery-tracking system, which results in an improvement in on-time and accurate order processing from a previous baseline of 77 percent up to 86 percent over a six-month period. During this same time period, customer satisfaction with company performance rises from 81 percent to 88 percent.

Step 4: *Track performance of leading and lagging indicators, showing both baseline and performance after introduction of the improvement action.*

The first type of analysis to conduct is a visual one to determine if a change in the leading indicator seems to result in a concurrent change in the lagging indicator. In other words, does it look like the two lines of data follow similar trends on a graph? One might need to track both metrics for a period of time, because a change in customer satisfaction levels might not immediately result in customers spending more money.

Step 5: *Determine the practical significance of the correlations.*

There is a big difference between a correlation that is statistically significant and one that is practically significant. Sears may have found, for example, a statistically significant correlation between customer satisfaction and revenue. However, from the looks of these links, the correlation is of not much practical use to Sears' managers, except to tell them that there is a slight relationship between improving customer satisfaction and increasing revenue. In assessing the practicality of the data, you must look at the cost of the innovation or change that was introduced to improve performance and the value or benefit of the resulting improvement in the lagging indicator(s). In our example, let's say that we spent $300,000 for the new order-tracking system, which resulted in a 7 percent improvement in customer satisfaction. Your study revealed that a 7 percent improvement in customer satisfaction led to a 5 percent improvement in revenue in one year. Since your revenue last year was $20 million, this translates into $1 million in increased revenue the first year alone. Hence, the new order-tracking system was a great investment, since it produced a three-to-one return the first year!

Calculating the statistical significance of a correlation might be helpful if your management team is of an analytical or technical bent. This sort of analysis might be used to supplement your final practical correlation analysis. Whether or not the correlation is statistically significant is usually not of great interest to management, however.

Step 6: *Replicate your study in another unit or area of the organization.*

In order to have confidence in your findings regarding the correlation between leading and lagging indicators, it is important to repeat your study in at least one other part of the organization to see if the same performance occurs. When IBM discovered the link between their overall index of customer satisfaction and growth in profits, they replicated the study in other parts of the business, looking at different products, services, and customer markets. This made them confident that a strong enough link existed between satisfied customers and profits to link compensation to the measure of customer satisfaction—they knew it would pay off. The degree to which you replicate your correlation research is up to you. In most organizations, it is necessary to conduct research in at least two or three units or segments of the organization in order before management trusts the credibility of the research. Performance might vary with different products/services, different market segments, and in different parts of the world.

Step 7: *Program the correlation into your scorecard software.*

Most organizations put their performance data into a proprietary system or use a packaged software program, such as those reviewed in Chapter 12. Once you determine that a strong and practical correlation exists between a leading and lagging metric on your scorecard, it is important to input this information in your scorecard software. Some the packages I review in Chapter 12 will allow you to forecast future performance based on this correlation, and analyze the data at a deeper level than simply looking at one metric at a time. The software allows you to do "what-if" scenarios to show what would happen to, say, profitability if customer loyalty could be increased by 5 percent over current levels. Such analyses can be extremely useful in strategic planning. After you have analyzed possible links between many pairs of metrics on your scorecard, all of your information can be programmed into the software, allowing very sophisticated analyses to be done before making business decisions or setting improvement targets.

Below is a checklist that will help you assure that proper linkages are built into your scorecard metrics.

CHECKLIST FOR EVALUATING LINKAGES

In designing your scorecards, make sure that you:

☐ Begin at a level high enough that appropriate linkages exist.

☐ Require that each level look at the scorecard of the next level up in developing their performance metrics.

☐ Establish the scorecard metrics as those by which the organization evaluates and manages performance—don't keep two sets of books.

☐ Use scorecard metrics for individual and team performance objectives and appraisal.

☐ Link employee recognition programs to key scorecard metrics.

☐ Integrate the balanced scorecard metrics into strategic and annual operational plans.

☐ Review scorecards for different levels and functions to identify inconsistencies or disconnects, and correct them.

☐ Link performance-based compensation to key performance metrics from the scorecard.

☐ Fine-tune the metrics to make sure that they drive appropriate behavior and cannot be cheated on before linking pay and recognition to performance.

☐ Conduct research to identify potential correlation between leading and lagging indicators.

☐ Replicate correlation studies in different parts of the business.

☐ Use the information on correlation to analyze performance and make business decisions.

☐ Input correlation data into balanced scorecard software so that you can perform "what-if" analyses and improve your planning.

Planning: Developing a Project Plan for a Balanced Scorecard Initiative

The purpose of this final chapter is to provide you with a step-by-step guide to designing and implementing a balanced scorecard in your own organization. Even if you choose to use an outside consultant to help in this effort, it is important to understand how such a project is completed. As I've discussed in other chapters, plenty can go wrong when designing and implementing a scorecard. Working as a consultant with many different organizations over the years, I've seen a number of successful and not so successful scorecard initiatives. In this chapter, I'll review some good, and some misguided, approaches that I've witnessed.

The project planning approach I present in this chapter assumes that a consultant (either internal or external) works with a unit in the organization to design and implement the scorecard. It is not necessary to use an outside consultant on a project like this; however, most projects that have succeeded without the benefit of an external consultant have been led by a team of internal consultants. The approach works equally well with internal or external consultants. If yours is a small organization that cannot afford either outside or inside consultants, you should form a team to work on the scorecard project part-time and present their work to others in the organization.

All of the steps outlined in a scorecard project have been discussed elsewhere in this book, with a focus on the *what* and *why* of each element of a good strategic plan and balanced scorecard. This chapter focuses on the *how* of building and implementing a balanced scorecard in your organization.

Step 1: *Select a starting point.*

An important and difficult decision that needs to be made right off the bat is where to begin the scorecard project. One simple answer is to begin at the top. Several organizations I've worked with started with the CEO or president, and designing the scorecard for this person first. Conceptually, this makes a lot of sense because it is easier to develop lower-level scorecards that link together if the metrics for the CEO have been defined first. At Lutheran Brotherhood, we began the scorecard project by designing measures for the president first, and then proceeded to design scorecards for each of his direct reports. At the start of each session for the vice presidents and their staffs, we handed out the scorecard for the entire company for reference, to ensure that the metrics would align with those on the president's scorecard.

At Discover Financial Services, we started at the business unit level. We selected as the pioneer for the scorecard initiative one of the largest business units in the company in terms of personnel and budget, whose work was fairly easy to measure. Once the project for this one unit was underway, another major unit in Discover Financial Services began its own balanced scorecard project.

At Cargill, the approach was a little different in that the corporation let business units volunteer to participate in the balanced scorecard training and then provided those volunteering units with help in designing their own metrics. Business units from all over the world ended up being interested in the approach, and we conducted balanced scorecard training in Europe, South America, Australia, Asia, and India. Enough of the units and facilities in Cargill began developing and using the balanced scorecard approach to make other units take notice of their results, and this generated greater interest in the approach.

At a securities company, we began the project in the half of the company called the Private Client Group (the other half of the company did institutional investing). Within the Private Client Group, we selected the Marketing Group as the pioneer for the scorecard effort. Because the nature of the work in marketing is creative, intellectual, and difficult to measure, we felt that if we did the Marketing Group first, the other functions would be easier. We also selected the Marketing Group as our starting point because of the increased importance of this group in achieving the company's vision. The Marketing Group was actually quite large (400-plus people) and diverse. It included functions such as professional development, marketing communications, advertising, event marketing, market research, segment marketing, and electronic marketing.

I've helped groups in the Navy, Air Force, and Coast Guard develop balanced scorecards. In these military organizations, we designed scorecards for the commanding officer of a facility, base, or unit. For example, the Coast Guard is divided into geographical districts, each of which is headed by an admiral. The largest and busiest Coast Guard district is in Miami, where I helped them design a balanced scorecard for the entire organization. District 14 in Honolulu did the same thing. The scorecards differed slightly because the nature of the work varied somewhat, but there were some shared metrics since they were both within the Coast Guard and had very similar missions.

The point of these examples is that it is OK to start the scorecard initiative at any level in an organization. Starting at the very top is probably the easiest in some ways, but politically this is often just not possible. Often, the best way to sell the chief executive on the concept is to show it working well in key parts of the business or organization. I've also found that CEO scorecards tend to be better if they are designed after those at the next level down, because some of the metrics on the business unit or functional scorecards are often applicable to others in the organization. CEOs get ideas for metrics on their scorecards by reviewing those of their direct subordinates.

If you can't start with the chief executive, the next best person is the head of an intact business unit. This works especially well if the business units are somewhat autonomous, and it is probably the most common approach to scorecard projects. One unit volunteers to be the pioneer and works the bugs out of the approach before scorecards are designed for the remaining units. This approach is also smart from an advocacy standpoint, because the success of the initial business unit can be used to convince others that this is a worthwhile endeavor. If you can't get the head of one of the units in your organization to agree to be the first to design a balanced scorecard, your third choice should be a large, visible department in the company. For example, you might select the marketing function, like we did at the securities company, or the information technology function, like we did at Los Alamos National Laboratory.

In fact, the only place that's not a good starting point is a very small unit or a very small department.

> *Tip:* Start your scorecard at the top and work down, or in the middle and work up, before you work down.

Step 2: *Conduct kick-off workshop.*

Your next step in the project is to prepare and conduct a kick-off workshop to introduce the participants to the balanced scorecard concepts, sell them on the value of the approach, and provide them with some skills in evaluating performance metrics and scorecards for different types of organizations. Usually, this is a one-day session that is attended by the unit leader, his or her direct reports, and as many staff members as is feasible.

> *Tip:* The initial workshop is designed to convince people of the importance of the project and allow them to intelligently critique the scorecards. Make sure all important decision-makers attend.

I have conducted these workshops for as few as a dozen people, and as many as 80. The ideal group's size is about 30 to 40 individuals. It's OK to have people from several different units or departments attend the same workshop—in fact, this is usually a good idea because people get to work with others with whom they might not typically interact. The agenda for the workshop shown in Figure 14-1.

This workshop is very interactive, with participants spending most of their time on either individual or group exercises rather than listening. At the end of a day's training like this, I find that 90

AGENDA

Scorecard Workshop

8:00–8:15	Introductions and Overview
8:15–9:30	Presentation on Scorecard Concepts
9:30–9:45	Break
9:45–10:15	Presentation on Evaluating Scorecards and Linking Them to Strategic Plans
10:15–10:35	Individual Exercise—Case Study 1: R & D

Department, Manufacturing Company

10:35–11:00	Team Consensus Exercise—Case Study 1
11:00–11:10	Case Study 1 Debriefing Discussion
11:10–11:30	Individual Exercise—Case Study 2: Service Company
11:30–11:50	Team Consensus Exercise—Case Study 2
11:50–12:00	Case Study 2 Debriefing Discussion
12:00–1:00	Lunch
1:00–1:20	Individual Exercise—Case Study 3:

Nonprofit Organization

1:20–2:00	Interview Simulation Exercise—Case Study 3
2:00–2:20	Team Consensus Exercise—Case Study 3
2:20–2:30	Case Study 3 Debriefing Discussion
2:30–2:45	Break
2:45–3:05	Individual Exercise—Case Study 4:

Support Department

3:05–3:25	Team Consensus Exercise—Case Study 4
3:25–3:35	Case Study 4 Debriefing Discussion
3:35–4:00	Presentation on Scorecard Project Plan and Roles of Participants

Figure 14-1. Keeping Score Workshop Agenda

percent or more of the participants become very good at critiquing performance metrics and scorecards. They also usually walk away convinced that the balanced scorecard is something worth doing, and that their present set of performance measures needs major surgery. The case studies I use for the workshop are similar to the ones you will find in the Appendix to this book. They consist of three- to five-page descriptions of an organization, its mission, vision, and performance metrics. The cases are written to include both strengths and weaknesses, and some are much better than others. Participants will see an example of a great scorecard, one that is really horrible, and a couple that are average. I also vary the case studies by focusing on different departments (i.e., manufacturing, service).

It is important, in some instances, to customize case studies to make them conform to an organization's own industry. For example, in the training we did for Lutheran Brotherhood we used a case study called Catholic Services, which was very similar to LB. Likewise, I developed a case study based on a university for several sessions I have done for University of California campuses. The advantage of using a case study that is similar to the organization for which the scorecard will be designed is that no one can use the excuse that they don't see how it applies to them.

I think it is often a good idea to use an outside consultant to conduct this training, simply because it runs much more smoothly in a workshop that has been tested and refined over many sessions with many organizations. The consultant also typically has heard all of the objections and questions that might be raised by the group, and has some good answers and examples from other companies. Another reason for using a consultant for the initial scorecard training is that the consultant may have more credibility than an insider simply because he or she has helped many different organizations design and implement balanced scorecards. Sometimes this is the only involvement I have with a client: I conduct the initial kick-off workshop, and the internal consultants continue the process of designing and implementing the scorecard. I've worked with several groups in the Navy this way, and they have done well on their projects.

Before deciding to use a consultant to do the training, check to make sure that they are willing to do *only* the training. Many of the larger consulting firms want you to contract for the full balanced-scorecard consulting project and are unwilling to help with the front-end alone.

Tip: *If you decide to develop and conduct your own workshop, run through it several times before using it with a high-level audience.*

If you can't afford a consultant, or simply do not want to use one for the training, you can pull together your own workshop using a variety of available materials. The articles on balanced scorecards by Kaplan and Norton from *Harvard Business Review* (see "References") are available as reprints for about $5.00 each. Harvard Business School Press offers a video on balanced scorecards called "Measuring Corporate Performance," which features Kaplan and Norton and a couple of their clients who have implemented the approach. If you do decide to conduct your own balanced scorecard training, I caution against making it a lecture-based course. Measurements and balanced scorecards can become dull topics, especially if you lecture about them for eight hours!

Step 3: *Gather background information on plans and existing metrics.*

In any organization, some time must be spent reviewing documents, conducting interviews, and generally assessing the current state of affairs before designing the scorecard. Every organization has some sort of a plan, even if it is only in the CEO's head, and every organization collects some data on some measures of performance. Some of the documents you might want to review in this phase of the project are:

- Annual reports to shareholders
- Strategic plan
- Operational plan

- Monthly performance reports reviewed by senior executives
- Finance data
- Marketing/customer service data
- Human resource data
- Competitor data
- Industry studies
- Consultant studies

It is not uncommon to have a couple of consultants spend a couple of days each reviewing documentation and preparing questions for background interviews.

After reviewing these documents, time must be spent interviewing various individuals to get background information for the project. Obviously, you need to interview the executives involved in the project, and probably some other executives who may not be directly involved. For example, if the scorecard project is focused on a single business unit, several of the corporate business executives might be interviewed.

Some of the questions you might ask when interviewing executives and managers are as appear in Figure 14-2.

In addition to interviewing the typical executives, several other people usually need to be consulted. Some of the staff I typically interview include those involved in:

- Information technology
- Intranet
- Marketing communications
- Market research
- Finance
- Human resources.

Tip: A number of people in your organization can help to make the scorecard project a success. Make sure to identify them, and enlist their support early on in the project.

GENERIC EXECUTIVE INTERVIEW QUESTIONS

1. What are your personal views about where this organization needs to be in the next three to five years?

2. What are some of the challenges that you will face in the near future?

3. What data do you currently collect and/or look at on a regular basis?

4. What do you think are the key success factors you need to focus on in order to achieve your vision?

5. How do you know that your organization is performing well?

6. What data or reports do you receive that are not very useful? Explain.

7. How do you set performance targets or objectives?

8. How do you decide on strategies to achieve your targets?

9. What are some of the barriers you will encounter when trying to implement this balanced scorecard project?

10. Are there any measures the organization tracks right now that sometimes drive the wrong behaviors? Explain

---

Figure 14-2. Generic Executive Interview Questions

Often, individuals from these functions are extremely helpful in designing data-collection instruments, maximizing use of existing data, and communicating performance data via the company's intranet site. On a typical scorecard project, it takes a week or two to finish this step. This does not mean five to ten days of solid interviewing and document review—it just usually takes this long to schedule everyone's interview.

Step 4: *Develop guiding documents.*

The next task is to develop guiding documents, if they don't already exist. It is important to define mission, vision, key success factors, and values or guiding principles as part of the scorecard process. Most organizations I work with already have a fairly well-defined set of values, so I often skip this step in the process and focus on the vision, mission, and KSFs. Values also tend to be common for all parts of the organization. As I discuss in earlier chapters, it is generally not a good idea to try and write these statements via a team or committee. This tends to lead to long, frustrating sessions where otherwise rational people argue over words, phrases, and sentence construction.

A successful approach that I have used with several clients is to interview executives, ask them about the organization's mission and vision, review their recent speeches, then draft a "straw man" version of the mission and vision statements and a starter list of 10 to 20 possible KSFs. This draft is then sent to the executive for review, and a follow-up meeting is held to revise the statements. This entire process usually requires less then an hour or so of work. After getting the top executive to agree to the mission and vision statement, the next step is to get the staff to agree to them and prioritize the KSFs. This can be done in a staff meeting or as a separate meeting. Before you present the draft mission and vision statements to the team, explain that the CEO has already reviewed them and that you are interested in hearing their feedback if they disagree with the content. You're not interested in "wordsmithing" here. Inevitably, you will receive some comments on the wording, but it is fairly easy to skirt around these by asking for more substantive feedback.

After discussing the mission and vision, lead the group in a discussion of key success factors. Present them with your starter list, and spend about a half-hour brainstorming additional ones (or keep going until the group runs out of ideas for possible KSFs). Several groups I've worked with were able to brainstorm 50 or more key success factors in 30 minutes. List them all on flip charts, and have each individual select the three he or she considers most important, without discussing it with the others. Discuss those that get the most votes until the group reaches consensus on the three or four key success factors most important for achieving their vision.

Once the staff buys into the basic mission, vision, and key success factors of the organization, you can continue this process with them to create departmental vision and mission statements and departmental KSFs. This is usually fairly easy; the mission and vision for the entire organization have already been created, so the subsidiary missions and visions should flow into them. While there tend to be similarities in vision statements across different levels of an organization, the mission and KSFs need to be unique to each function or department. Use the same approach: interview the executives, draft a mission and vision statement, and list the key success factors. Then review these with the staff, prioritize the KSFs, and prepare a second draft.

In an organization that consists of three or four levels of personnel, I recommend working on the guiding documents for the first two levels only at the outset. For example, if you are designing scorecards for a business unit, you would develop guiding documents for the entire unit and for the individuals who run departments or subunits that report directly to the unit's executive. Don't be concerned about getting the guiding documents perfect in the review meetings—gather people's input, then you and your team can refine the wording right after the meeting. Key success factors, for example, are often written vaguely and will need to be defined and polished. One company I worked with identified "leadership" as their most important key success factor. This could mean many things, and it needed to be further defined. After further probing, we learned that it meant that the company needed a clear, coherent vision, and that the entire executive team had to work as a group toward the achievement of that vision, rather than trying to build their own empires and fighting one another for resources.

This step is complete after you have gathered the staff's input on the mission, vision, and key success factors, rewritten these into a second draft, and gotten everyone's agreement on the statement.

Step 5: *Design scorecard framework and identify metrics.*

Now you will actually begin construction of the scorecard for the senior executive of the organization. In Chapter 3, I discussed different approaches for specifying the categories (or boxes) on an organization's scorecard. If you'll recall, I reviewed the Kaplan and Norton model with its four boxes: 1) Financial, 2) Customer, 3) Internal, and 4) Learning and Growth. I also discussed using the Baldrige criteria as a model, with its five categories of performance data:

1) Customer, 2) Financial and Market, 3) Human Resources, 4) Supplier/Partner, and 5) Organizational Excellence. Either model might work well for your organization, or you might be better off identifying your own categories.

In any case, this is not an emotional process like deciding on a corporate vision. Once you decide on your organization's scorecard categories, keep in mind that they must be consistent across your entire organization. In other words, you don't want each business unit or facility to have their own unique scorecard categories. Thus, you might want to solicit the input of executives outside of the unit for whom you're designing the scorecard.

One approach that has worked well for me in the past is to present the executive and his or her staff with three choices for the scorecard categories in a staff meeting, and let them vote on the one they like best. Because there is no one right answer—there are several good ways to sort data into balanced scorecard categories—don't spend too much time on this.

The next assignment is to identify metrics to go into each box on the new scorecard. This involves three steps, in the following order:

- Insert existing metrics into the appropriate boxes that you believe are important to continue to measure.
- Identify strategic metrics linked to the high-priority key success factors
- Identify fundamental business or mission-related metrics to complete the scorecard
- Code each metric as to whether it is strategic or fundamental, and as to whether it looks at the past, present, or future.

All of this information should be summarized on a single page that includes the mission, vision, key success factors and metrics. Figure 14-3 shows an example.

Figure 14-3 represents the level of detail you need to present in order to get feedback from the staff. The types of questions you need to ask when requesting feedback on the initial draft of the scorecard are:

- Do these measures make sense?
- Will data on these metrics help you plan and manage better?
- Will it be feasible to collect data on these metrics?
- Can you foresee any problems with any of the metrics?

EXAMPLE SCORECARD—SHARED SERVICES ORGANIZATION

Mission: To provide our internal and external customers with the most cost-effective procurement, human resources, legal, and facilities management services that they can get from any source. We act as both consultants, helping our customers with their shared-services strategies, and as service providers.

Vision: To become a partner at the table in helping the organization manage its performance in the areas where we provide service and advice, and to provide service levels and value that are better than any other inside or outside resource.

Key Success Factors

- Increase our credibility by learning more about our customer's business
- Eliminate non-value-added services and work processes
- Manage Shared Services like a business versus a collection of cost centers

Customer/Partner

- Customer Value Index (present)
- Market Share * (past)
- Customer Relationship Level (future) (past)
- Supplier/Vendor Report Card (present)

Business Excellence

- Cost vs. Outside Services * (present)
- Cash Saved in Process Improvement *
- Recovery Cash/Profit *(past)

Human Resources

- Skill Development Index* (future)
- Employee Satisfaction Index (present)

Learning and Growth

- Percent Strategic vs. Mission Work* (future)
- Percent Budget on New Products/ Services (future)

* = strategic metrics linked to key success factor(s)

Figure 14-3. Example Scorecard

- Do some of the metrics link back to the vision and key success factors?
- Do we have a good mix of business fundamental metrics that look at past, present, and future time perspectives?

Once you've designed the overall scorecard for the entire organization, repeat this process with the next level down. In our Shared Services example, you would design a scorecard for the managers of procurement, human resources, legal, and facilities management, and review the drafts with the staffs of these four departments.

Step 6: *Design data-collection plans.*

Your next step in the project begins the hard work of thinking through all the details for each metric and figuring out how to collect the relevant data. I often find that companies will buy into metrics as ideas, but remain skeptical about how data will be collected and its integrity ensured.

In preparing a data-collection plan, you will need to prepare answers to all or most of the following questions:

- Exactly how will this metric be calculated?
- If the metric is an index, what are the individual submetrics, and how are they weighted?
- What is the purpose of this metric—what will it tell us?
- What behavior is this metric designed to drive?
- Is this a past, present, or future metric?
- Is this metric linked to one or more key success factors? If so, which ones?
- Is this metric based upon counting or judgment, or a combination of both?
- If counting will be used, will a sample be used, and how will it be determined?
- How often will data be collected on this metric?
- How often will performance be tabulated and reported?
- What method(s) will be used to collect data on this metric?
- Who will design the data-collection instrument(s) and procedures?
- Will we need to use any outside sources for collecting these data or designing instruments?
- If the metric is based on judgment, who will do the evaluations?

- How will we ensure reliability and consistency in the judgments?
- How would it be possible for people to cheat on this metric?
- Will it be possible to get historical data on this metric?
- Will it be possible to get comparative/competitor data on this metric?
- Does this metric link to any others on the scorecard? If so, which ones?
- How much will it cost (in terms of inside and outside resources) to collect and report this data?
- What roadblocks are we likely to encounter in collecting data on this metric?

Obtaining answers to all of these questions often demands frequent phone calls, interviews, and review of documents. The idea is to think through all of the issues and questions that may arise. Another reason for preparing answers to all these questions is that it enables you to figure out how much time, money, and trouble will be involved in collecting data in the way you envision. I've often seen organizations remove metrics from their scorecards once they figured out how much trouble and cost would be involved in regularly collecting the necessary data. Cost factors are always important, but they needn't necessarily cause you to eliminate a metric. Sometimes it is possible to collect the data less often or by using a different approach.

This phase in the project tends to require several days of work because all of the questions need to be answered for each metric on the scorecard. It's easier, though, if data on some of the metrics already exists. In our earlier example of a Shared Services organization, one of their metrics is an Employee Satisfaction Index, which probably already exists and is measured by the Human Resource function for the entire company. Other metrics on the example scorecard probably don't exist, except perhaps for profit/recovery.

Let's take one of the more difficult metrics and prepare answers to some of the data-collection plan questions so you can see the required level of detail (see Figure 14-4).

DATA-COLLECTION QUESTIONS AND ANSWERS
EXAMPLE: SHARED SERVICES ORGANIZATION—CUSTOMER VALUE INDEX

Q. What is the purpose of this metric? What will it tell us?

A. The purpose of this metric is to tell us how satisfied our various customers are with our services and products, and how they perceive the value they get from us. This metric focuses on all three groups of internal customers: Corporate, Field, and Consumers

Q. What behavior is this metric designed to drive?

A. This measure is designed to encourage Shared Services managers and staff to balance the needs of all three of their customers in delivering products or services, and to allocate their priorities appropriately. We currently place too much emphasis on satisfying the corporate customers, and too little emphasis on the Consumer and Field customer. This metric helps us measure our ability to better balance this.

Q. Exactly how will this metric be calculated?

A. Each service area within Shared Services will be assigned a percentage weight to each of their three customers, depending on the importance of the product/service to each of the three customer groups. For example, for the Procurement Card service area, the customer might be weighted as follows: Corporate: 20 percent, Field: 20 percent, Consumer: 60 percent. The Product Liability group in the Legal Department might have very different weights, since their major mission is to protect the corporation: Corporate: 65 percent, Field: 10 percent, Consumer: 25 percent.

Q. What methods will be used to collect data on this metric?

A. Customers will rate our service on a 1–5 scale twice a year during focus groups and individual interviews wherein they are asked a series of 4–6 standard questions, supplemented by 3–4 questions unique to the function or service area. Overall scores will be tabulated and multiplied by the percentage weight assigned to each customer group, to come up with a total level of customer satisfaction. If all customers provided 5 ratings on all questions, a score of 100 points would be achieved. Each department and each function or service area in Shared Services will have their own Customer Value Index score. Surveys will be administered by the Market Research function in the Marketing group.

Figure 14-4. Data-Collection Questions and Answers

While it is important for you and your scorecard design team to figure out fairly detailed answers to these questions, not everyone in the organization may need this level of detail. I often present data-collection plans using a series of overhead transparencies that summarize the answers to the questions. A good way to get feedback on the data-collection plan is to prepare a brief report that outlines your recommendations for each of the metrics. Distribute this report and allocate at least two to three hours for a meeting to review the data-collection plan it describes. Most projects I've worked on involve two review meetings for the data-collection plan. The first meeting usually generates significant changes to the plan. A second draft needs to be prepared and reviewed with the group at a later date. The time spent reviewing and revising the data-collection plan for the entire organization will pay off in shorter meetings on and less revision of departmental data-collection plans.

Step 7-A: *Develop data-collection instruments, procedures, and systems.*

The previous step is akin to drawing up blueprints and getting clients to approve them. During this next step, the actual construction begins. This part of the project can take a few weeks or many months, depending on the complexity of your data-collection plan. It's sometimes tempting to try and do all of this work yourself rather than engage professionals, either within or from outside the company. How much skill is needed to write a 10-question survey, for example? Actually, constructing a good survey requires quite a bit of skill, as does the creation of most measurement instruments used by organizations.

Using your data-collection plans for reference, decide how you will develop or purchase the instruments needed for your new scorecard. Instruments might consist of paper surveys or focus group questions, or a piece of equipment that measures an aspect of your products or services. Before going outside, think about your potential internal resources. In large organizations, market research people are often a great source for developing instruments. Human resource, finance, and procurement specialists are also great resources. It might be a good idea to get a bid or proposal from both an inside and outside group. Regardless of whether you are asking for assistance from an internal or external group, you need to:

- Send them the data-collection plan and ask them to review it.
- Attend a meeting with the instrument designers to get their ideas and ask them for a proposal to develop the instrument and data-collection processes.
- Review the proposals and decide which one best fits your needs.
- Pilot test the instruments and data-collection processes and correct any bugs.

In organizations that have a lot of existing data, this step in the process can usually be completed in less than a month. If almost no data exists, this phase in the project usually requires two to three months. It takes time to find sources for developing the instruments, testing them out, and getting client feedback on both the instruments and data-collection procedures. This portion of the project is complete when the data-collection instruments and procedures have all been created and approved.

Step 7-B: *Design implementation and communication strategy.*

This is considered part of the seventh step because it typically is concurrent with the design of instruments and data-collection procedures. This phase of the balanced scorecard project is often forgotten—and that's one of the reasons why some projects fail. The balanced scorecard must be marketed and communicated throughout the organization so that all understand it and how it changes the way performance is measured. Part of the communication strategy is deciding how to present the new scorecard. ITT Sheraton Hotels used graphics based on a car dashboard to communicate performance data. Another client used a "Company Scoreboard," featuring graphics that resembled the scoreboard from a baseball game. The baseball theme was used for other aspects of the program as well.

The marketing communications and information technology groups are usually consulted for this portion of the project. The marketing communications folks can help you devise effective graphics and select the media and materials best suited to communicate the scorecard to managers, employees, and outsiders such as suppliers or customers. The IT department needs to be consulted to determine how performance data will be reported on company computers. If you are considering purchasing one of the balanced scorecard software packages reviewed in Chapter 12, the IT folks definitely need to be involved in choosing a vendor. If you are not going to buy packaged software, but instead develop your own, the IT department will undoubtedly work with you on the project.

The approach I described in Step 7-A for specifying your data-collection and measurement strategies applies here as well. Before going to see the IT or marketing communication professionals, it is important for you to prepare an RFP or conceptual design document that outlines your objectives or what you want to accomplish with the scorecard. Based upon your ideas and specifications, the professionals in these functions can help you prepare a plan that suits your needs. If you don't have internal resources to help in these areas, many good marketing and IT consulting firms are available to assist you. The outputs for this step are a plan for marketing the scorecard inside the organization and a communication plan that spells out how data will be displayed and communicated to employees and managers.

Step 8: *Collect baseline data, set targets, and develop strategies.*

Sometimes it is possible to gather baseline data by extracting historical data for the last couple of years from the company's databases. When this is the case, targets can be set almost immediately. Recall the guidelines in Chapter 4 about setting targets, and the importance of having competitor data, benchmarks, and information on your own resource constraints. If historical data do not exist, it could take three to six months of collecting data on all the measures on your new scorecard to gather enough for a stable baseline. During this time period, it is important to get managers and staff members used to the idea of reviewing scorecard performance in their staff meetings and on their own. Without targets, the data will not provide any information on level of performance, but can be still be used to evaluate trends.

When enough time has passed that stable baseline data exist for all of the new scorecard metrics, it is time to work with the group to set targets for all metrics. As you'll recall from Chapter 4, targets might be set as absolute numbers or as ranges of performance. The next step is to work with the group to identify strategies for achieving the targets. This process has been described in Chapter 4. Once targets and strategies have been defined for the entire organization or unit, the same process needs to be followed for the next level down in the organization.

Step 9: *Scorecard maintenance.*

It's important to let people know that the scorecard will never be final. Some existing metrics may turn out to be unnecessary several years from now, and new challenges will crop up that necessitate new gauges on your company dashboard. While strategic or vision-related metrics are the most subject to change, I find many organizations also change their mission or business fundamental metrics from time to time. If your scorecard is not changing a little each year, this is a danger sign. All industries and fields are subject to rapid change today. Technology, regulations, customer needs, and so forth are never stable. Today's successful organization must change and adapt to survive, and so should its scorecard.

Typically, organizations with successful scorecard efforts thoroughly evaluate their scorecards at least annually, and discuss the need for changes during monthly management meetings. Some companies appoint a metrics steering committee that is responsible for evaluating and improving the scorecard. Others simply rely on the senior management team to do this, with the aid of an internal consultant or two who were involved in the design of the measurement systems. In any case, you should plan on spending 10–20 percent of the resources needed to design and implement the scorecards on maintenance each year. As your organization improves its performance or ventures into new areas, the performance measures on your dashboard should continue to provide feedback on your progress.

---

*Tip: Plan and budget for evaluating and improving
your metrics at least once a year.*

DESIGNING LOWER-LEVEL SCORECARDS

One school of thought holds that the balanced scorecard is a tool for executives and managers only and need address only the first three levels in a typical organization with five or six levels. Employees and supervisors can look at the managers' scorecards and thus do not need their own. Individual performance metrics already are covered by other systems, like the performance management/ appraisal system.

Another school of thought on this issue argues that every employee needs his or her own scorecard. Looking at a boss's scorecard is not as interesting or informative as looking at your own. The issue is one of control or influence. An individual employee may not be able to see how her day-to-day performance makes the needles on her boss's scorecard move. Consequently, looking at the scorecard does not control many behaviors. Since the vast percentage of employees in an organization work at the lower levels, this means that most employees don't have their own scorecards.

As you've probably guessed, I believe that every employee should have his or her own scorecard; however, I don't think that most of them need 10 or 12 metrics. I've often seen employee scorecards with three to four metrics, and that is sufficient. (Some broader metrics, like customer or employee satisfaction, fit better on a manager's scorecard.) Failing to design scorecards for lower-level employees is one of the most common reasons for failed balanced scorecard projects. This is not an approach that applies to managers exclusively—*every* employee needs feedback on performance in order to drive improvement and aid in decision making.

Tip: *Many scorecard projects fail to drive performance improvement because scorecards have not been designed for lower-level managers and employees. Make sure to design scorecards for all levels of employees.*

EVALUATING THE SCORECARD PROJECT

Your initial scorecard project should be viewed as a trial or preflight test of the approach, which is used to determine if the remainder of the organization will benefit from this approach. In some companies I've worked with, however, this has not been an option: every unit of the company develops its own balanced scorecard that feeds into the one for the CEO or president. In organizations that aren't completely sold on this approach, it is important to evaluate thoroughly the scorecard project to present evidence for or against expanding it to other parts of the organization. In essence, what you need is a score-card for the scorecard project. Some of the measures that ought to go on the evaluation scorecard include:

- Project costs—estimated and actual
- Customer feedback
- Schedule performance and total cycle time
- Cost savings realized by eliminating metrics and reports
- Examples of how the scorecard improved analysis and decision making
- Feedback from support groups that helped with the scorecard project (marketing, information technology, finance, etc.)
- Links to other organizational systems and how this might benefit the company

SCHEDULING THE SCORECARD PROJECT

The length of time needed from initial design through implementation of the scorecard can vary from four months to several years. The length of the project depends upon the size of the organization, its number of levels, the units for which scorecards are to be designed, the amount of difference between the units, and the resources the organization is willing to assign to the effort.

If you want to hire one of the big consulting firms to do the project for you, they will assign a team of consultants to work at your office, and probably complete the scorecard designs for the top three levels in the company in roughly 12 weeks. Of course, they will also charge you $200,000-400,000 to do so, but the work will be done quickly and well. An advantage of using a consulting firm to help you design scorecards is that they have experience in doing so at other companies and may have some great ideas about including metrics successfully employed by their other clients. Aside from the cost, other downsides to using a big consulting firm are that you have to pay them to gather quantities of background information on your organization, and their approaches tend to be more packaged. A consultant-designed scorecard also may not be supported fully by your management team, since they did not develop it.

Most of my clients see me as a teacher and coach—they themselves do most of the work in designing and implementing their scorecards. This makes sense if your company has internal consultants who can devote a significant chunk of time to the project, or if the management team is willing and can spend up to a few days per month on it. At Discover Financial Services, for example, I worked very closely with internal consultants whose full-time job was the scorecard project. I might spend a few days a month coaching and guiding them, but they did the lion's share of the work. The key to the success of this approach is assigning top-notch people to the project who possess both expertise and credibility with senior management.

Regardless of how you decide to do the project or who does the work, the effort will probably require about a year before you have scorecards on the computers of most managers and are using scorecard metrics to run your operation. It can be done faster, but usually is not.

WHAT TO EXPECT FROM THE SCORECARD

A balanced scorecard will not automatically transform your organization. The best performance data in the world will not improve your performance one bit unless that information is used to develop better plans, implement better initiatives, and make smarter business decisions. Awareness of performance data, though, is not enough to cause behavior to change. Similarly, excellent measures of employee satisfaction and morale will not make your company a great place to work. The data only tell you how good or bad things are today. The real work comes in making needles move into the green zone for all your performance gauges. Many organizations don't seem to understand this aspect of the approach. Claiming "employer of choice" as your vision and producing solid data on employee satisfaction is the easy part.

In short, a balanced scorecard in and of itself will not solve all of your problems or make your organization healthier. However, it *will* enable you to:

- Look beyond financial results to evaluate your organization's performance
- Identify leading indicators that help predict future performance
- Consistently communicate performance data to managers and employees
- Eliminate misguided metrics that were driving the wrong behavior
- Cut back on reports and meetings wherein meaningless data are reviewed
- Link performance metrics with strategic and operational plans
- Improve decision making and planning
- Evaluate process metrics based on their ability to predict output performance
- Measure factors everyone knows are important but no one knows how to track (customer satisfaction, human capital, etc.)
- Reduce the number of metrics managers must regularly review to evaluate organizational performance

In essence, the scorecard allows you to run your organization more "scientifically," by using relevant data to make informed business decisions and develop realistic plans.

Our final checklist will assist you in evaluating your company's overall scorecard project plan.

CHECKLIST FOR EVALUATING YOUR SCORECARD PROJECT PLAN

When evaluating your scorecard project plan, make sure that you:

☐ Thoroughly screen any outside resources or consultants you are considering using for the project.

☐ Begin at the highest level possible in the organization.

☐ Conduct a one- to two-day workshop for all project stakeholders to teach them about the balanced scorecard concepts.

☐ Include time to review existing plans, metrics, and databases that exist in the organization.

☐ Interview key professionals and managers from finance, information technology, human resources, and marketing functions.

☐ Interview key executives to find out about their personal vision and mission.

☐ Draft mission and vision statements and key success factors for executives to review, rather than have a group create these from scratch.

☐ Get the executives to agree on a single framework for all organization scorecards.

☐ Clearly identify roles and responsibilities for all individuals involved in the scorecard project.

☐ Plan time for fairly extensive revisions to the first draft of the data-collection plans.

☐ Use internal and external resources to develop data-collection instruments and procedures.

☐ Schedule the project so that it is completed in a time frame that corresponds to the company planning cycle.

☐ Include a phase for packaging and marketing the scorecard to employees.

☐ Include time for implementation of balanced scorecard software if it will be used.

☐ Include resources for scorecard maintenance after initial implementation.

Appendices:
Balanced
Scorecard
Case Studies

This final section of the book includes several case studies that depict how certain types of organizations have designed scorecards. Use this material to test your understanding of scorecard concepts by comparing your analysis of the strengths and weaknesses of each case to my own critiques. Our analyses may differ, but we should reach some of the same conclusions. For your convenience, a checklist is provided that may prove useful when evaluating an organization's performance metrics.

Four case studies are provided, covering a manufacturer, a service provider, a government organization, and a support department. Each is a fictitious enterprise based upon my actual experiences as a consultant. Study all of them to ensure that you master the ability to critique performance metrics in any organization.

CHECKLIST FOR CRITERIA FOR EVALUATING SCORECARDS

☐ Reasonable number of metrics (less than 20; 12–16 better).

☐ Measures focus on past, present, and future time perspectives.

☐ All key success factors or business strategies covered by at least one metric.

☐ Important metrics (i.e., those linked to scorecard factors) given higher priority or weight in overall scorecard.

☐ Absence of short-term operational/financial metrics that might cause future problems.

☐ Absence of metrics that can easily be cheated on.

☐ Use of indices where possible to simplify data and aid in analysis.

☐ Establishment of mathematical correlations between key metrics such as customer or employee satisfaction and financial performance.

☐ Performance is measured often enough to detect trends so action can be taken before things get too bad.

☐ Measures are consistent with research on the needs and priorities of customers, employees, shareholders, and other important stakeholders.

☐ Process measures can be clearly correlated with important outcome measures.

☐ Scorecard includes measures relating to busines fundamentals, even though these may not be key success factors.

☐ Scorecard shows history of evolution, with metrics changing as company needs and circumstances change.

☐ Users of performance data are asked about metrics, methods of data collection, and frequency and format of reporting.

☐ Data are collected on the frequency with which data are reviewed and used by management for decision making and planning.

Manufacturing Case Study:

Great Northwest Paper Company– Three Rivers Plant

OVERVIEW

The Great Northwest Paper Company (GNPC) is an 82-year old company owned by the McGregor Corporation, a $13 billion corporation. GNPC contributes $2.5 billion in annual sales. The Three Rivers plant, one of the corporation's seven paper mills/plants, produces a number of different types and grades of paper. The Three Rivers plant produces two products: carbonless paper and specialty-coated, high-grade stock used by publishers of books and magazines. These paper stocks are very expensive, but they are known in the industry as being of the best quality. Their carbonless products are known for being competitively priced and for printing more smoothly than their competitors' products.

Three Rivers has just a few competitors for their high-end, specialty-coated papers. These companies produce similar products that are slightly lower in both price and quality. They are also known to be less reliable than Three Rivers in service. Consequently, Three Rivers usually gets the best, most demanding high-end customers, who are willing to pay a little more for both product quality and service. They compete against several companies in the carbonless market, some of which are the major paper companies in the United States and more than 10 times the size of Three Rivers. Compared to the competition, their carbonless paper is only slightly better in quality, and their service levels are on par or slightly better. Their edge in the carbonless business is the tight relationship they maintain with key customers. Since most of their carbonless business comes from 20 or so major accounts, they spend a lot of time continually strengthening their relationships with these customers.

The plant is the low-cost producer of carbonless paper due to the company's highly skilled workforce. Three Rivers has established a family culture in the plant, and has morale and safety levels that are at benchmark level. Their financial results and customer satisfaction results are also quite impressive. They've built strong relationships with most of their major customers and have become the sole-source supplier for a number of them.

Three Rivers actually manufactures base stock paper in the plant, but mostly the work consists of applying coatings to existing paper stock. They have two paper machines and seven coaters. Two of the coaters are fairly new and represent state-of-the-art technology. They ship some stock directly to customer sites, using outside carriers. The rest gets delivered to one of the company's regional distribution centers. Orders are generated by their corporate customer-service center and processed in the facility.

They buy a great deal of paper stock and pulp from another of GNPC's mills, Three Rivers' biggest supplier. Three Rivers buys about 20 percent of their paper stock and pulp from outside suppliers with whom they have also established partnerships. They have narrowed down their pulp and paper suppliers from 17 six years ago to 4 companies today. Some of their other suppliers are chemical companies, utilities (electricity, water, gas, telephone), and equipment manufacturers. Three Rivers has a very elaborate process of evaluating suppliers on a regular basis and certifying them at three different levels.

Their customers consist of printers, such as form printers and book printers, paper merchants, and converters. Merchants buy Three Rivers' paper and sell it to their customers. Three Rivers has two types of merchants: those that stock their paper, and those who do not stock it but expect Three Rivers to maintain inventory. The third type of customer is a converter, who takes the paper and converts it into a final product. For example, a converter may buy a huge roll of carbonless paper that it will turn into small rolls to be used in cash registers or ATMs.

In the area of environmental performance, Three Rivers is the benchmark within GNPC. They have converted some of their chemicals to more environmentally friendly substances, and currently meet or exceed all EPA guidelines for control of hazardous materials. All other GNPC mills and plants have studied Three Rivers' approach to environmental performance and learned from it. Their approach is to set specific measures and goals in this area based on benchmark-level paper companies, and to monitor performance on a regular basis. Their internal goals and objectives always exceed those mandated by the EPA, and they've never received any kind of fine or citation from the EPA since the plant has been in business.

One of Three Rivers' greatest assets is their employees. The average employee has 12 years of service. They literally have no turnover. They run three shifts and have 580 full-time employees, as follows:

- Management   74
- Administrative/support   111
- Production/technical (unionized)   395

Three Rivers spends several thousand dollars per year training each employee, so they also have a well-trained workforce. Employees are empowered to make many decisions previously made by managers, and they have a suggestion program that receives an average of 40 suggestions per week, with a 60 percent implementation rate.

SCORECARD DESCRIPTION

GNPC began to develop and implement the balanced scorecard approach to measurement several years ago. The Three Rivers Plant was selected as the first plant in which to pilot the approach. A consulting firm worked with the management team to develop the scorecard for the plant manager, and then proceeded to develop scorecards for his direct reports and their organizations. What follows is a description of the scorecard for the plant manager. Other metrics in the plant contribute toward making the plant manager's metrics look healthy.

The Three Rivers Plant does not have a separate vision statement, because they are a unit of GNPC. Their role is not strategic, but rather to assist the parent company in achieving its strategic and operational goals. While they do not have a vision statement, they have identified the following three-year goals for the plant that contribute to the company's vision:

- Reduce manufacturing cost of carbonless paper by 12 percent over current levels.
- Improve the safety index from a score of 74 today to 85 over the next three years.
- Achieve 90 percent productivity from the two new coating machines that were installed last year.

The measures on the scorecard for the plant are divided into the following four categories of data: financial, operational, people, and customer/partner.

Financial Measures

The first category of data looks at financial metrics. Three Rivers is not responsible for pricing the paper or selling it, but they do have a great deal of control over the cost of the paper. The three metrics in this section of the scorecard are described next.

- **Cost per ton vs. industry average.** This measure is a combination of both specialty-coated and carbonless stocks. It is presented as a percentage difference from industry averages that are collected on a monthly basis. Their target is to be an average of 1.5 percent lower than average for carbonless paper, and no more than 2 percent higher than average for specialty-coated stock. This measure focuses on the past.
- **Inventory costs.** This is a present-focused measure that looks at the cost of carrying inventory. Three Rivers attempts to schedule production so as to minimize inventory, which improves company cash flow. This metric, which is tracked every day, measures the total

dollar value of inventory (in wholesale prices) on hand in the plant.

- **Cost reductions.** This future-focused metric looks at total dollars saved each month due to process improvements. Three Rivers has a number of process-improvement initiatives underway in the plant, including Lean Manufacturing and Activity-Based Costing (ABC). Many of their process improvement ideas also come from employee suggestions. This gauge keeps the plant manager informed about the success of these efforts.

Operational Measures

This section of the scorecard includes measures of productivity and schedule performance. Many managers in the plant monitor the metrics in this section of the scorecard every day.

- **Tons/day.** This is simply a measure of how many tons of paper Three Rivers produces each day in relation to production goals. Volume varies quite a bit, depending upon factors such as orders over which they have little control. Consequently, this measure is only meaningful by showing actual production versus targets. The plant manager looks at the overall gauge, but may examine the data by shift, product, line, etc., depending on what he needs to look at.
- **On-time delivery.** This is a key measure linked to end-user customer satisfaction. About 40 percent of Three Rivers' paper is shipped to distributors who also care about timely delivery, but not to the same degree as their end users. This measure is calculated by tracking the number of late deliveries as well as the dollar value of the order and the number of days late. This timeliness index gives them a better measure of the severity of a late delivery than simply tracking percentage of deliveries late or on time. The graph is presented as percent on-time, so an ascending trend is positive.

- **Productivity.** This is a measure of the productivity of
  labor, equipment, and energy, all rolled into one index.
  The index is a number ranging from 0–100; Three Rivers
  currently has a target of 88. The three different factors are
  weighted depending on their contribution to the overall
  manufacturing cost. Overhead and administrative costs
  are not included in the figure.

People Measures

This section of the scorecard includes important measures of
employee well-being and satisfaction. Three Rivers prides itself on
the plant on being both safe and a pleasant place to work. They realize that a paper mill can be an unpleasant work environment, so they
make an extra effort to help their employees feel good about the
company and their workplace.

- **Safety index.** This metric is tracked once a month and it
  provides the plant manager and others with an assessment
  of the safety level of the entire plant. One-half of the index
  is based on actual accidents that have occurred and their
  relative severity. The cost of each accident in lost time and
  medical expenses is also figured in. The remaining 50 percent of the index is a preventive measure that includes
  safety audit scores, safety training, safety improvement
  actions, and "near misses." If everything were perfect,
  Three Rivers would receive a score of 100 on this index.
  Their current goal is to achieve a score of 88, which would
  make them the best plant in the company.
- **Employee training.** Employee training is a priority at
  Three Rivers. Once per quarter, they calculate the
  Employee Training Index, which is comprised of two statistics: number of hours of training received (must pass
  test to get counted) and dollars spent on training per
  employee. Their current goal is to have each employee
  spend 16 hours per year in training (4 hours per quarter)
  and to spend an average of $2,100.00 per employee each
  year on training.

- **Average seniority.** The Three Rivers Plant prides itself on having one of the most experienced workforces in the paper industry. The average employee has 12 years of experience at their company and can perform an average of 3.2 jobs. This measure, which looks at average seniority, is related to both our productivity and morale.

Customer/Partner Measures

This section of the scorecard includes data on how well Three Rivers satisfies their customers, and how well their suppliers and partners perform.

- **Customer satisfaction index.** This measure is based on a quarterly, one-page survey Three Rivers does for all its customers. Different surveys are used for distributors and for end users, but all scores are translated into average ratings on a scale of one to five. Also included in this index are complaints and returns. This measure looks at both the past and present, since it is largely based on customers' current perceptions of Three Rivers' performance based on their past experience.
- **Partner performance.** This is a measure of how well Three Rivers' suppliers perform to their standards. Suppliers include pulp mills that are part of GNPC, and a number of outside companies from whom they purchase goods and services. The score on this metric is based upon quarterly ratings that Three Rivers gives suppliers, using the same one-to-five scale that they use for their customer surveys. Similarly, they also include in this metric returns and complaints that they make.

AUTHOR'S ANALYSIS—MANUFACTURING CASE STUDY

Analysis of Strengths

- There are a reasonable number of metrics that cut across the categories of financial, operational, people, and customer/suppliers. This indicates a good start towards a balanced scorecard.

- The scorecard for the plant manager was developed first, which should help ensure that lower-level metrics contribute to the overall performance of the plant.

- All of the metrics identified seem to be ones that the plant can influence.

- A number of indices are used, which combine the performance of several discrete measures into one summary gauge for the plant manager

- Qualitative factors are incorporated into indices to make the measures more meaningful. For example, on-time delivery includes factors relating to the size of the order and the number of days it is late.

- Attempts have been made to include some future-focused metrics on the scorecard, such as the dollars saved due to process improvements.

- Operational and financial measures are both good and appear to include the sorts of factors the plant manager ought to be tracking.

- The plant's safety index sounds like a great way of measuring both preventive factors and accidents, and should provide the plant manager with a good picture of the level of safety in the facility.

Areas for Improvement

- Almost all of the metrics focus on the past and the present. Even though the plant may not be responsible for R & D or new product development, there should be a few more future-oriented metrics on the scorecard.

- Some measures do not appear to provide the manager with much information that would help improve performance. For example, the average seniority of employees, or the employee training metrics, would not vary much, and what information do they provide?

- The cost-reduction metric in the financial portion of the scorecard is a good idea, but would be easy to fake or falsify. This metric sounds like a measure known as price of non-conformance (PONC), which a number of companies tracked in the 1990s as part of their quality programs. Many showed millions of dollars saved on their PONC charts, but somehow that money never showed up in any bank account.

- Overall, the scorecard lacks strategic metrics. All of the measures sound like mission-related metrics that a plant manager would always want to track. Even though the plant's role is to be more operational than strategic, they still need to have some sort of vision, key success factors, and a few strategic measures.

- One of their goals is to improve productivity of the two new coating machines they have installed. There is no measure of the productivity of these two machines on the scorecard. There is a measure of productivity, but it combines labor, equipment, and energy into one index. If the productivity of the new coaters is important enough to be one of their three goals, it should be measured separately and appear on the plant manager's dashboard until the goal is achieved.

Overall Recommendations

This scorecard is off to an excellent start. A number of creative indices have been developed, thereby keeping the total number of measures down. I would not recommend eliminating or changing any of the existing measures. The scorecard achieves a good balance between customers, shareholders, and employees, and includes important high-level measures that the plant manager ought to be tracking. I would recommend establishing some sort of vision for the plant, or at least some longer-term goals that are broader than the three that have been specified. Next, I would develop a list of three to five key success factors and the metrics associated with them. Most of these metrics would probably be future-focused, so this would serve to round out the scorecard.

Service Case Study:

Customer Pro

OVERVIEW

Customer Pro provides a unique service to its clients. Do you have a question about the television you just bought? Your gas barbecue is not lighting properly; how do you replace the spark plug? You bought a new sewing machine; who do you call about how poorly you were treated? More than likely the 800 number you dialed was Customer Pro, and the quality service you received was provided by a Customer Pro representative.

You may never have read their literature, or even have any idea that they exist, but they are often your connection to products you buy.

Customer Pro, a telephone-based customer service company founded in 1990, specializes in consumer information. Both small and large companies know their slogan, "When the phone rings, Customer Pro answers it." They serve the customers of small manufacturers with sales of $1 million a year as well as customers of large retail chains of over $5 billion a year. Their customer base is over 300 companies, and they provide after-sale product information and resolve complaints. They also provide customers with monthly customer satisfaction reports to improve their sales and service.

Customer Pro's marketing strategy is designed to attract and retain new customers. They are located in four zones in the United States, each of which covers a geographic area—Northeast, South,

Midwest, and Pacific Coast. This strategy allows them to "talk the language" of their customers' customers. They believe that people are more willing to state their needs if they hear a voice that makes them feel comfortable.

The system has three tiers. At the regional level there are two tiers: the customer service representative, and a technical expert who is capable of answering 90 percent of the questions. The third tier is located in a national Technical Information Research Center. This Center also has communications experts who provide interpersonal skills, training, coaching, and on-the-spot assistance with difficult consumers. The Technical Information Research Center is housed at Customer Pro's corporate headquarters. A critical but important task is keeping their massive product database current. This is done at both the regional offices and the Tech Center.

Nationwide, 85 percent of the 3,000 employees engage in answering the phones, 10 percent provide technical expertise, 3 percent provide professional support functions (such as information systems), and 2 percent manage the business and operations.

Customer service representatives are provided with a pleasant, ergonomically sound work environment. They have efficient access to product information through automated workstations, a call-management system, extensive customer service training, and a reward and recognition program that reinforces the communication of accurate information and positive customer treatment.

Customer Pro is a highly competitive business. It owns a 10 percent market share (the industry leader has a 15 percent market share). Since Customer Pro began operating, it has pursued quality service. While it is nearly impossible to pull customer representatives off the phones, Customer Pro uses "floaters" to permit employees to participate on teams, primarily for planning and problem solving. Planning teams identify new systems, new training and reference materials, and approaches to addressing special customer requirements, such as promotions. Problem-solving teams use quality assurance data to solve problems in level and quality of service. One critical result is that costs for contract employees for special promotions have been reduced to nil.

Customer Pro has identified three KSFs critical to their business—analogous to the speedometer, gas gauge, and tachometer on a car dashboard. Additional metrics address other critical performance factors that can be monitored less frequently

Each metric relates to one of three key success factors, or to business fundamentals such as profit, growth or internal quality. In order to be included on the dashboard, a metric must meet all of the following criteria:

- **Measurable.** The performance metric must be one that can be tracked consistently.
- **Linked to requirements.** Measures must relate to the needs/priorities of the owners, customers, employees, or key stakeholders.
- **Predictive.** Measures must be linked to and help predict the company's success.

Their key success factors are:

- **Cost.** The expertise to perform the customer service function better than their clients' internal functions, for less cost.
- **Image.** The ability to promote positive word of mouth for their customers' products/services.
- **Service levels.** The commitment to provide consumers who purchase their customers' products with better, more efficient service than they have received in the past.

SCORECARD DESCRIPTION

As noted, Customer Pro has identified a few key gauges that are critical to the success of their business and the achievement of their vision of becoming the number one call-based customer service business in the next three years. They are currently number one in profitability, number three in sales, and number two in market share. They plan to be number one in all three areas. The strategic gauges on their dashboard are monitored very closely and continually by management. Other, smaller gauges tell the company how it's doing in running the business day to day.

By focusing on three key success factors, Customer Pro differentiates itself from other call center companies. Their scorecard is a combination of metrics that link to the three KSFs and focus on business fundamentals. The graphics that they use to communicate performance data resemble a car's dashboard and include color-coded gauges. Every employee in our company has his or her own dashboard available on the company's intranet site.

Below is a description of the different metrics on the CEO's dashboard. Some of the metrics require a fairly lengthy explanation, and others require almost no explanation because they are obvious.

Customer Satisfaction Index

This index is made up of three separate variables: value, satisfaction, and loyalty. Value is the *relative* value of the client to Customer Pro—some clients are obviously more valuable than others. Each one is given a rating of 1 to 10, depending on how valuable the account is considered to be. Satisfaction is a measure of how Customer Pro's clients grade their performance. Satisfaction data is gathered once a month by account executives during an existing meeting wherein call report data are reviewed. Loyalty, the third variable in the index, is a measure of the strength of the relationship Customer Pro has with the account. The highest rating of 10 would signify a long-term partnership and that Customer Pro handles 100 percent of their products/services.

Consumer Satisfaction Index

This metric looks at how well Customer Pro handles consumers who call their 800 numbers. Over 85 percent of Customer Pro's staff spend their time handling phone calls from consumers, so this is a critical metric. Based on extensive market research, Customer Pro has learned that when customers call an 800 number about a product, they are concerned with three things, in this order of priority:

- Accurate, complete advice
- Timely, efficient answers
- Courteous, understanding technicians

Therefore, the Consumer Satisfaction Index is based upon these three factors, weighted as follows:

- Accuracy/Completeness   50 percent
- Efficiency   30 percent
- Courtesy   20 percent

Data are gathered via telephone surveys to customers, which are conducted within one hour of a call made to Customer Pro, and by having supervisors listen in on phone calls and evaluate technicians for their accuracy, efficiency, and courteousness. This metric is tracked every day, and most employee bonuses are linked to it.

Market Share

This is a measure of Customer Pro's relative slice of the call center customer service market. They currently have 10 percent market share, but the largest company only has a 15 percent share and has yet to become profitable. Customer Pro has been profitable from day one. Their industry is going through consolidation right now, with larger companies aggressively acquiring smaller ones. The fact that the size of the market is rapidly expanding further complicates matters. Customer Pro obtains data on market share once a month from an outside company, the Gartner Group, which does an outstanding job of gathering industry statistics.

Profit and Cash Flow

These are two standard financial metrics that provide a past and present view of the company's financial health. They calculate both statistics once a month, and can break down the data into a number of different configurations such as by region, industry, customer, and so on.

Money in Outstanding Proposals

This is an interesting future financial metric that allows them to predict future sales. Based on their history, Customer Pro wins 40 percent of the proposals they submit, and averages nine months between the time a proposal is submitted and an account becomes active (meaning that $8 million in outstanding proposals will turn into $3.2 million in sales within nine months).

Cost versus Competition

This metric is directly linked to Customer Pro's first key success factor—demonstrating that they are less expensive than internal customer service and also less expensive than any competitor. This metric looks at the percentage difference between their fees and those charged by others. This data is gathered versus competitive mystery shopper techniques once a month.

Calls per Day

Phone banks are the "factories" of Customer Pro, so it is important to monitor call volume each day. This operational metric is helpful for planning, staffing, and equipment acquisition.

System Downtime

In the old days, this metric was percent downtime; then Customer Pro went to minutes of downtime. They now track it in seconds of downtime during critical and noncritical time periods. Because downtime has been near zero for almost two years, they will be making this gauge an "idiot light" on their dashboard next year.

Service Quality Index

This key operational metric is linked to the key success factor of demonstrating that the company provides consumers with outstanding service. Included in this index are the following individual measures, each of which is weighted:

- Call waiting hold time
- Blocked calls (busy signal)
- Abandoned calls (hang ups)
- Second, third calls for same problem

This metric is computed each day and is on the dashboard of all technicians and managers in the company.

Employee Satisfaction Index

This important measure monitors how employees feel about working for Customer Pro. It is made up of several different measures and is calculated once a quarter. The ESI includes the following measures:

- Turnover $\times$ seniority $\times$ level
- Quarterly morale survey with sample of employees
- Absenteeism
- Monthly focus group data from all four centers
- Employee complaints

Suggestions/Empowerment Index

This future-focused metric is a 50/50 combination of the number of suggestions per employee and the percent that are implemented, along with employee attitudes about empowerment/authority levels and the number of decisions pushed down to lower levels in the organization.

Sales from New Accounts

This final metric appears in the innovation and growth box of the scorecard because it looks at Customer Pro's ability to generate new business. Expanding sales to existing customers is important, but their drive to become the biggest and most successful call center company will require them to sign many new accounts annually. This metric looks at the number of new accounts, their dollar value, and the strategic value of the account to the company. For example, they are targeting the hotel industry, so a dollar in sales to a major airline might get more points than landing another small appliance manufacturer.

Customer Pro evaluates their measurement approach by looking at the following factors:

- **Reliability:** Can the measure be tracked reliably and consistently?
- **Predictability:** The extent to which good performance on this measure is linked to other success metrics.
- **Use:** How often do managers and employees call up reports/data on the system, or request hard copies?
- **User feedback:** Manager and employee feedback on the format, timeliness, frequency, and overall usefulness of the data in helping them manage performance.

The dashboard and reporting system are formally evaluated once a year, but changes are often made as opportunities or problems arise. Since Customer Pro started the business in 1990, they have made the following changes to their measurement system:

- Their number of metrics has gone from 6 in 1990 to 37 in 1992 to 14 in 1997.
- In 1990, most of the data was financial; they now have a balanced scorecard.
- They've improved their customer and customer satisfaction indices.
- In 1992, they began providing daily feedback to employees and teams on key statistics such as call productivity.
- They developed key success factors in 1993 and linked performance measures and goals to these success factors.
- Their customer and consumer satisfaction indices have improved each year since 1990, based on item analyses and other evaluations.
- They have identified links between most major measures on their dashboard, so they can improve their ability to make good business decisions.
- They have linked all team process improvement efforts to one or more of their 14 key metrics.

Information on performance is deployed to employees in the company through a variety of methods:

- Weekly staff meetings held at all levels to review performance
- Bulletin boards show team and department performance
- Online individual performance measures are available on everyone's computer
- Monthly employee newsletter
- Quarterly company performance review meetings
- Monthly performance reports
- Online database that can be used for diagnosing problems in performance

- Linkage of performance metrics to individual and team performance metrics and goals
- Quarterly bonus tied to performance on key measures for each employee.

A scorecard implementation team interviewed a number of individuals to identify user requirements for performance data reporting and analysis. The team benchmarked some of the best companies in the world to come up with ideas on the best ways of designing and implementing a performance measurement and management system. For example, they decided upon the dashboard graphic by benchmarking IIT Sheraton Hotels.

Changes in the needs of the users of this performance data are identified via weekly staff meetings, employee suggestions, and informal comments and complaints. Customer Pro makes use of automation whenever possible to ensure that they are collecting reliable data.

AUTHOR'S ANALYSIS—SERVICE CASE STUDY

Analysis of Strengths

- The company scorecard contains a reasonable number of metrics, with a good mix of those that look at the past, present, and future.

- The scorecard has gone through several major revisions and continues to be fine tuned as company strategy changes.

- Customer Pro has identified correlations between leading and lagging indicators.

- The scorecard contains a number of creative indices that include both leading and lagging indicators.

- The approach to measuring customer satisfaction is a big improvement over the traditional survey measures used by many companies. Looking at the value of each account and account loyalty are two important dimensions of performance.

- The consumer satisfaction index is also a great way of driving the right behavior from employees who answer the phones.

- The use of the intranet and dashboard graphics to communicate performance data are sound ideas. In addition, the company communicates data using a variety of other media and methods to ensure that it gets through to everyone.

- Compensation is tied to key performance measures for most employees.

- The Employee Satisfaction Index is a creative and thorough way of measuring employee morale.

- There is a good mix of strategic and business fundamental metrics, and the strategic metrics generally link well to the vision and key success factors.

- Scorecards have been designed for all levels of employees in a hierarchical fashion so that lower level measures link to higher level ones.

Areas for Improvement

- It's not clear which gauges on the dashboard are the most important, or if they are all accorded the same importance.

- There is no metric for the key success factor of image. There are direct measures for the other two KSFs (cost and service), but no measure of how Customer Pro's service helps improve the image of their clients' products and services. This might be tough—measuring image is fairly straightforward; the difficult part is showing that Customer Pro's proficiency in answering the 800-number calls caused the image to change. If something is a key success factor, it should have its own discrete metric on the dashboard.

- It would be interesting to know what metrics are correlated with what other metrics, and how these linkages help improve business decisions and plans.

- There is no measure of technology. Because this company is so dependent upon technology to provide information to consumers, there should be some metric on this in the climate/innovation section of the scorecard. This might be more important than the suggestion/ empowerment index, or take the place of the downtime metric that they are already planning to eliminate.

Overall Recommendations

This organization needs only to continue fine-tuning the scorecard in the future—it is fairly close to perfect. Actually, it is better than any I've ever seen in a real corporation—it being a conglomeration of some interesting metrics I have seen in real organizations, but not all in a single company. You may have found other faults with the scorecard than the few I have listed, but there are far more existing strengths in this case than improvements needed.

*Support Department
Case Study:*

Pamco
Commercial
Credit

OVERVIEW

Pamco Commercial Credit (PCC) is a wholly-owned subsidiary of the PMC Engineering corporation, a manufacturer of the highest quality machine tools, used by a variety of manufacturing companies all over the world. PCC's mission is to offer leasing, financing, and other related services to PMC's customers and dealers. The company was launched with a $3 million dollar investment in 1978. Since that time their assets have grown to $1.8 billion, making PCC the ninth largest leasing company among 2,000 such firms in the United States. Their $230 million in revenue last year accounted for about 10 percent of the entire corporation's profits, making it clearly the most profitable division. The corporate finance department consists of 108 professionals and administrative personnel.

VISION AND KEY SUCCESS FACTORS

PCC's vision is that corporate finance will become a value-added partner with internal customers and help them manage the financial performance of the company, using state-of-the-art technology and the most cost-effective internal and external resources available. Corporate finance currently is often seen as expensive, unresponsive, and unwilling to make use of outside resources when appropriate.

Therefore, achieving their vision will be quite a challenge. A new CFO was appointed about a year and a half ago, and she has worked with the corporate finance team to develop metrics and a strategic plan.

Some of the KSFs for achieving the vision are as follows:

- Increase use of outside resources to provide customers with the best quality at the lowest price.
- Eliminate non-value-adding finance activities through customer requirements research and process reengineering.
- Establish greater levels of credibility with the PCC senior management team.
- Empower corporate finance employees to make decisions and challenge processes and procedures that don't make sense.
- Increase levels of knowledge of internal customers' businesses, technologies, and needs.

Customers and Their Requirements

Corporate finance has three types of customers, all of whom are employees of the company:

- PCC senior management team
- PCC managers and employees who use corporate finance's services and products
- Field finance people who work in branch offices

The senior management of the company is concerned about managing risk, keeping administrative/finance costs as low as possible, and being provided with accurate, timely financial information to use in running the company. PCC managers and employees that use corporate finance's services and products are concerned with responsiveness, products/services tailored to their needs, and use of the best technology available. The field finance people report to corporate finance on a dotted-line basis, but actually work for the branch management. They want a voice in designing new products/services, timely delivery of products and services (mostly data), and flexibility, plus a certain degree of autonomy where appropriate—they don't like to be controlled or told to follow rules/procedures that don't make sense.

Key Processes

Although corporate finance performs a variety of tasks, most of their work can be grouped under three major categories of activities or processes:

- Data collection and reporting
- Auditing
- Financial management

Corporate finance currently spends about 60 percent of their time on data-collection and reporting activities, with 20 percent on each of the two remaining processes. Their vision is to spend about a third of their time on each process.

Corporate Finance Scorecard

The company began implementing the balanced scorecard approach to measurement several years ago. It began by establishing a balanced set of measures for the president, which looked at the entire company's performance. Each of the president's direct reports then developed his or her own scorecard, showing links back to the president's. Following is a list of performance metrics used by the CEO and the entire finance department. These same five categories of data appear on the company scorecard:

- Customer satisfaction
- Growth
- People
- Efficiency
- Profitability

Following is a description of the metrics PCC tracks on a regular basis and uses to manage corporate finance's performance. Metrics listed in bold type in the tables are the ones PCC considers to be their vital few.

Customer Satisfaction Measures

As mentioned earlier, corporate finance has three distinct customer groups (PCC senior management team, PCC managers and employees who use corporate finance's services and products, and field finance people who work in branch offices) whose needs and priorities vary.

Metric	Description
Senior management satisfaction	Biannual meetings between the CFO and each of the nine other senior executives to gather feedback
Staff satisfaction surveys	1-page staff survey done biannually that looks at all aspects of performance
Project report cards	Report cards given to PCC by customers at the end of a project such as an audit
Web site hits	Number of times customers look at the corporate finance web site

Growth Measures

This category of data applies more to the company overall than to a support function like corporate finance. PCC has established some growth measures, but they look more at growth and development of new products/services and innovation, as opposed to expanding staff and budget.

Metric	Description
Number of new products/services	Focuses on continuous improvement of products and services
Suggestion index	Number of employee suggestions and percent implemented
Market share	Amount of work done by others (internal or external) that should be done by corporate finance
Technology index	Dollars invested in new technology/total operating expenses
Financial management	Percent of time spent doing financial management vs. data collection or auditing

People Measures

Metric	Description
Employee satisfaction	Biannual survey by Mayflower done by entire company
Development index	Measures training hours, dollars, and achievement of developmental objectives
Turnover	Voluntary turnover and transfers not due to promotions
Leadership effectiveness	Measure of senior management effectiveness as seen by finance employees

Efficiency Measures

These measures look at our quality, productivity, and ability to meet deadlines.

Metric	Description
Dollars saved in process improvements	Encourages innovations and process reengineering
Rework	Hours spent repeating work that was not done right the first time
Product quality	Internal measure of accuracy and completeness transaction time for key tasks
Cycle time	Transaction time for key tasks
Percent work done by suppliers	Focuses on outsourcing work that can be done better and cheaper by outside firms

Profitability Measures

Because PCC is not a profit center, they don't have a separate P&L, nor can they generate income for the company. Therefore, their financial metrics look at cost control.

Metric	Description
Performance to budget	Standard financial measure
Cost vs. best-in-class	Cost for key transactions compared with best outside firms
PCC profit	Expressed in dollars and percent of sales
PCC return on equity	Since corporate finance helps manage financial performance, this is also a good measure

IMPROVEMENTS TO THE SCORECARD

Corporate finance's overall approach to performance measurement has changed over the last few years. Previously, they did not have measures of customer satisfaction, and they looked at the PCC staff as their only customer. Nor had they any measures that looked at the future. Given their accounting and finance backgrounds, they believed that all measures should look at past performance; now, they believe, their metrics are a good mix of past, present and future, and they've incorporated a number of creative measures. Comparing their internal costs to best-in-class outside firms, and measuring new product/service development, are two important measures.

They have developed subsidiary scorecards for each of the three managers that report to the CFO, each of whom has worked with their own staff to develop related metrics. Plans for the future involve continually fine tuning measures and doing a formal evaluation and improvement once a year by a metrics steering committee.

AUTHOR'S ANALYSIS—SUPPORT DEPARTMENT CASE STUDY

Analysis of Strengths

- The corporate finance department has a very clear vision and some very specific key success factors that can help them achieve it.

- Finance has adopted the five categories that the company uses for their scorecards, and has found a creative way of defining growth metrics for an internal support function that is not supposed to grow.

- Specific metrics have been identified for most of the KSFs. One of the better ones is the percent of time doing financial management versus other types of work. This measure directly relates to the vision of spending less time on data collection and auditing and more time helping the organization manage its financial performance.

- Measures exist for all three groups of customers that are served by corporate finance.

- The project report card sounds like an excellent way of obtaining customer feedback at the end of an audit or similar project. It should provide much more useful feedback than a periodic survey on all of corporate finance's services.

- The market share metric is an interesting way of looking at a hard measure of customer satisfaction with the services provided.

- They have a good mix of metrics that look at the past, present, and future; and the scorecard is well balanced across the needs of customers, employees, and the shareholders of the corporation.

- Transaction cost versus best-in-class companies sounds like a great way of measuring the cost effectiveness of corporate finance.

Areas for Improvement

- Although the vision of corporate finance is conceptually a good one, it relies too much on buzzwords and could be stated much more concisely.

- There are far too many metrics on this scorecard. The number of employees in the department is not mentioned, but it is unlikely that they exceed 50. For an organization of this size, the scorecard appears unnecessarily complicated.

- The criteria were for selecting the metrics that appear in bold type are not clear. Some of them are strategic measures linked to the key success factors, and some of them are not. I would imagine that the CFO probably looks at performance on all the measures as well, not just those marked in bold.

- A few metrics don't seem to add much value. For example, what does counting the number of hits to the corporate finance web site tell you?

- The technology index is conceptually a good idea, but the metric that has been defined would simply drive the behavior of spending more money on the latest technology. This is not what most organizations want from their support functions.

- Overall company profit and ROE may not be good measures for the CFO dashboard because too many other factors influence these metrics.

- Some of the metrics might easily be manipulated. For example, the cash saved in process improvements usually consists of hypothetical dollars that are easily inflated. Or the percent of work done by suppliers could be embellished by farming out work that actually would be done better and less expensively inside.

Overall Recommendations

Corporate finance appears to understand the concepts of the balanced scorecard and has incorporated the appropriate balance into their design. They have a good mix of metrics that take into account all of their stakeholders, and their measures cut across the past, present, and future time perspectives. Although most of the measures are good ones, they probably have too many metrics on the CEO's dashboard.

I recommend editing the vision statement to make it concise and free of jargon. The department's plan might be better focused if they reduced the number of KSFs to three rather than five. I also recommend removing some metrics that might drive the wrong behavior, are easily cheated on, or would be hard to influence/control. This should reduce the number by at least a third.

Overall, this is a fine start on a scorecard for a support function like finance. It simply needs some thoughtful pruning. It might be better to start with eight to ten metrics in total and gradually increase the number of measures as the department becomes more sophisticated and accustomed to reviewing performance data and using it for planning and decision making. There is a danger of turning everyone off to the balanced scorecard concept by making the initial version far too complicated.

Government Case Study:

Midstate Department of Transportation

OVERVIEW

The Midstate Department of Transportation (MDOT) operates in the executive branch of the Midstate government. The department employs 6,480 individuals at locations across the state, in a total of 188 facilities. The organization is divided into the following departments:

- Streets and Highways
- Aviation
- Department of Motor Vehicles
- Public Transportation
- Traffic Safety
- Intermodal Planning

MDOT provides the following products and services to Midstate residents and visitors:

- Road/highway construction and maintenance
- Engineering design
- Transportation planning
- Aviation planning
- Public transportation
- Licensing and tax collection
- Research and product development
- Liaison with Federal Government DOT and others

Customers and Requirements

MDOT provides products and services for a wide variety of customers, including:

- Midstate residents
- Other branches of Midstate government
- Federal government
- Transportation and construction companies
- Visitors to Midstate

Most of their resources are expended providing goods and services to the 8.9 million residents of Midstate who use its roads, public transportation, and Department of Motor Vehicles. Most of MDOT's funding comes from tax dollars, so residents are their most important customers. They also provide services for other government organizations. MDOT collects taxes and tolls for the State Department of Treasury, keeps records on traffic violations for the State Police, and completes construction projects and does research for the Federal Highway Administration. Theirs is a very diverse mission, and it is a constant challenge to balance the needs of all of their customers.

Vision and Key Success Factors

The Midstate Department of Transportation's vision is to be recognized as one of the top five states in the America for:

- Taxpayer satisfaction with road conditions and ease of driving
- Efficient use of tax dollars
- Research and development of new products and services relating to MDOT products and services

They are currently not recognized in any of these three areas, so this vision will challenge them. The key success factors they've chosen to focus on for achieving that vision are as follows:

- Increased funding for road/highway construction and maintenance. Road conditions have seriously deteriorated in the state over the last eight years, given the previous administration's focus on tax cuts and spending in other areas. Roads and bridges are currently in need of major repairs. The state is experiencing population growth in mid-size cities in its northern counties, so additional roads and highways will be needed to deal with the increased traffic.

- Eliminating waste and managing contractors better. Over 60 percent of MDOT's budget is spent on outside contractors and vendors who do most of their construction, maintenance, and engineering projects. In the past, MDOT's contractors have managed them—they need to regain the upper hand, and implement more specific project plans and incentive contracts. They also need to critically evaluate their own work to assess tasks and processes that add value and eliminate those that do not.

- Increased emphasis on research and development so as to generate a constant stream of new products and services that will improve customer satisfaction and save taxpayer dollars. MDOT's role in the past was to focus mostly on projects; innovations primarily came from the federal DOT research facility or from other states. MDOT needs to turn that around and focus on developing new products and services in its own state. In order to become known as a center of innovation, they must focus on building core competencies in this area and creating a culture that rewards risk taking and creativity.

SCORECARD

MDOT has divided its scorecard into the following four categories of data:

- Operational
- Safety and employee development
- Customer
- Innovation

Descriptions of each metric on MDOT's scorecard for the Secretary of Transportation are in the following tables. Many of these metrics also appear on the scorecards of other managers in the organization.

Operational Measures

This section of the scorecard looks at MDOT's performance on their mission-related work of ensuring smooth transportation for all customers. (Many of these metrics had been tracked long before MDOT developed its balanced scorecard, two years ago.)

Metric	Description
Project management index	Measure of performance on cost, quality, and schedule for all project work
Cost effectiveness	MDOT unit costs for key products and services versus best states and outside companies
Budget performance	Actual expenditures versus budget, and total budget versus outputs
Contractor report card	Ratings of supplier/contractor performance, done quarterly

Customer Measures

This section of MDOT's scorecard provides information on how well they are meeting the needs of their most important customers.

Metric	Description
Road quality index	This is a measure of ride quality of state roads and highways—it is 50 percent based on hard data collected using automated equipment, and 50 percent based on driver surveys done by phone.
Taxpayer satisfaction—DMV	Just about every citizen of Midstate must deal with the DMV for various licenses; this metric is based on surveys handed out at DMV offices statewide.
Government satisfaction	This measure is based on annual surveys of government officials in other state and federal agencies for whom we provide services and products.

Safety and Employee Development Measures

This section of the scorecard for MDOT includes data on how MDOT is doing in providing employees with a safe and pleasant work environment.

Metric	Description
Safety index	Index includes number of lost-time accidents, severity rating, and associated costs; number of hours of safety training per employee is also in the index
Employee satisfaction	Index includes turnover, annual morale survey, absenteeism, and complaints to HR hotline
Employee competency	Measure of the average number of skills per employee and skill level
Environmental index	Measures performance on key environmental strategies; includes both process and output metrics

Innovation Measures

This section of the scorecard includes measures that focus on developing new products and services, and continually learning from shared experiences.

Metric	Description
Best practices index	A measure of the number of new products, services, and processes that are developed by MDOT and implemented in other state and federal DOT offices
Process engineering index	A measure of the percentage of MDOT work processes that have been documented, analyzed, and improved
External recognition	Awards and press citations relating to MDOT products, services, and accomplishments; the caliber of the award/citation is considered, as well as the number of awards received

This scorecard was designed for the Secretary of the MDOT two years ago; scorecards for each director who runs a functional unit have also been designed, and for their corresponding direct reports as well. Performance data on scorecard measures is communicated through internal websites that are updated daily, bulletin boards, newsletters, and quarterly meetings that are held via video conference.

AUTHOR'S ANALYSIS—GOVERNMENT CASE STUDY

Analysis of Strengths

- The MDOT scorecard shows good balance, with measures that look at the past, present and future, and their various stakeholders.

- The operational section of the scorecard includes some excellent metrics for a government organization. The project management index fits the nature of DOT work, much of which involves major projects. The measure of cost effectiveness is also a good one and should help show taxpayers that they are getting good value from the MDOT.

- In general, there is good linkage between the scorecard metrics, the vision, and MDOT's key success factors.

- The road quality index is a good overall measure of customer satisfaction that is half based on an objective measure using automated equipment, and half based on customer opinions of road quality.

- The measure of government satisfaction provides data on how other government agencies view the service they receive from the MDOT.

- The safety and employee development section of the scorecard includes some good measures of safety, employee morale, and environmental performance. Because of the nature of MDOT's work, it makes sense to include a measure relating to the environment.

- The best practices index is a great way of tracking MDOT's ability to come up with innovative, useful products and services. This metric links directly back to their vision of being recognized as one of the top states for the development of new DOT products and services.

- Measuring the awards and recognition received by MDOT for its accomplishments is a good external measure of their work.

Areas for Improvement

- There is no measure of MDOT's success in obtaining additional funding for road repair and construction, which is one of their key success factors.

- Measuring customer satisfaction in the DMV via surveys does not reflect most of the functions of the MDOT, and hence would not be a good metric for the Secretary's scorecard.

- Measuring actual performance versus budget is of questionable value as a metric, because most government organizations manage to spend all of their budget so as prevent the budget's being reduced next year.

- The safety index includes only lagging indicators. It could be improved by including preventive factors such as audits or safety inspections.

- The process engineering index could end up driving a lot of activity (e.g., drawing process models/flowcharts and arbitrarily changing them) that may not add value or save money for MDOT.

- The measure of external recognition is a good idea, but it may end up encouraging employees to spend time applying for awards and preparing press releases to tout their strengths when that time could be better spent on improving service to taxpayers.

Overall Recommendations

MDOT has an excellent scorecard for a state government organization. It includes both operational and strategic measures, and addresses the needs of taxpayers and other stakeholders. There are several creative indices included in the scorecard, such as the best practices index and the cost effectiveness measure.

I would add a metric that looks at MDOT's progress in obtaining additional funding for road construction, if this is one of their key success factors. I would also drop the measure of customer satisfaction with the DMV from the Secretary's scorecard and put it on the scorecard for the individual who runs the DMV. I might also work on the contractor report card metric to make it more sophisticated. Because most of MDOT's budget is spent on outside companies, this measure might look at more than simply how suppliers performed against contract requirements.

In summary, this is an excellent scorecard for this type of organization. The strengths far outweigh any areas of weakness, and the improvements identified should be easy to make.

References

Aitken, Sandi and Morgan, John. "How Motorola Promotes Good Health." *Journal for Quality and Participation* (January/February 1999): 54–57.

Barrett, Richard. "Why the Future Belongs to Values Added Companies." *Journal for Quality and Participation* (January/February 1999): 30–35.

Berglas, Steven. "Know When to Fold." *Inc. Magazine* (May 1998): 31–32.

Bontis, Nick. "How to Measure Dot-Com Stocks." *Toronto Globe and Mail*, 11 April 2000, sec. B, p.15.

Brown, Mark Graham. *Keeping Score*. New York: Quality Resources/AMACOM, 1996.

Burkan, Wayne. "Giving New Meaning to the Competitive Edge." *Journal for Quality and Participation* (March/April 1998): 14–19.

Campbell, Andrew. "Tailored, Not Benchmarked: A Fresh Look at Corporate Planning." *Harvard Business Review* (March/April 1999): 41–51.

Collins, Jim "Fear Not." *Inc. Magazine* (May 1998): 39–40.
———. "What Comes NeXt?" *Inc. Magazine* (October 1997): 41–50.
———. "Turning Goals Into Results: The Power of Catalytic Mechanisms." *Harvard Business Review* (July/August 1999): 71–82.

Correll, Dean, Villa-Garcia, Sombrita, and O'Brien, Paul. "Creating Organizational Alignment and Linking Performance Measures." Presentation at Association for Quality & Participation National Conference, Las Vegas, Nevada, March 1999.

Guyon, Janet. "Next Up for Cell Phones: Weaving a Wireless Web." *Fortune* (October 25, 1999): 225–232.

Quenten Hardy, "Motorola Broadsided by the Digital Era, Struggles for Foothold," *Wall Street Journal,* 22 April 1998.

Iverson, Kenneth F. and Varian, Tom. "Plain Talk." *Inc. Magazine* (October, 1997): 81–83.

Kaplan, Robert S. and Norton, David P. *The Balanced Scorecard: Translating Strategy into Action.* Harvard Business School Press, 1996.

Kaplan, Robert S. and Norton, David P. *The Balanced Scorecard: Managing Future Performance Video,* Harvard Business School Publishing, 1994.

Kanter, Rosabeth Moss. "From Spare Change to Real Change." *Harvard Business Review* (May/June 1999): 54–57.

Levering, Robert and Moskowitz, Milton. "The 100 Best Companies to Work For." *Fortune* (January 10, 2000): 82–110.

Loomis, Carol. "Citicorp's Far-Out Quest for a Billion Customers." *Fortune* (February 2, 1998): p. 36.

Mescon, Michael H. and Mescon, Timothy S. "Management with a Mission." *Sky Magazine* (June 1995): 24–29.

Meyers, Bill. "What Do PC, Razor, Car Share? A Sense of Style." *USA Today,* 19 October 1998, sec. B.

O'Brien, Tina. "Mission Impertinent." *West San Jose Mercury News Magazine,* 16 November 1997.

Peterman, John. "The Rise and Fall of the J. Peterman Company." *Harvard Business Review* (September/October 1999): 58–66.

Pfeffer, Jeffrey and Sutton, Robert I. "The Smart Talk Trap." *Harvard Business Review* (May/June 1999): 134–144.

Porter, Michael E. *On Competition.* Harvard Business School Publishing, 1998.

Rucci, Anthony J., Kirn, Steven P., and Quinn, Richard T. "The Employee-Service-Profit Chain at Sears." *Harvard Business Review* (January/February 1998): 83–97.

U.S. Department of Energy Strategic Plan. U.S. Government Printing Office, September 1997, DOE/PO 0053.

Index

Productivity, Inc. Consulting, Training, Workshops, and Conferences

EDUCATION...IMPLEMENTATION...RESULTS

Productivity, Inc. is the leading American consulting, training, and publishing company focusing on delivering improvement technology to the global manufacturing industry.

Productivity, Inc. prides itself on delivering today's leading performance improvement tools and methodologies to enhance rapid, ongoing, measurable results. Whether you need assistance with long-term planning or focused, results-driven training, Productivity, Inc.'s world-class consultants can enhance your pursuit of competitive advantage. In concert with your management team, Productivity, Inc. will focus on implementing the principles of Value-Adding Management, Total Quality Management, Just-in-Time, and Total Productive Maintenance. Each approach is supported by Productivity's wide array of team-based tools: Standardization, One-Piece Flow, Hoshin Planning, Quick Changeover, Mistake-Proofing, Kanban, Problem Solving with CEDAC, Visual Workplace, Visual Office, Autonomous Maintenance, Overall Equipment Effectiveness, Design of Experiments, Quality Function Deployment, Ergonomics, and more! And, based on continuing research, Productivity, Inc. expands its offering every year.

Productivity, Inc.'s conferences provide an excellent opportunity to interact with the best of the best. Each year our national conferences bring together the leading practitioners of world-class, high-performance strategies. Our workshops, forums, plant tours, and master series are scheduled throughout the U.S. to provide the opportunity for continuous improvement in key areas of lean management and production.

Productivity, Inc. is known for significant improvement on the shop floor and the bottom line. Through years of repeat business, an expanding and loyal client base continues to recommend Productivity, Inc. to their colleagues. Contact Productivity, Inc. at 1-800-394-6868 to learn how we can tailor our services to fit your needs.